100 YEARS OF ARMY-NAVY

FOOTBALL

Gene Schoor

Introduction by Pete Dawkins

A Donald Hutter Book

Henry Holt and Company ★ New York

To Fran Schoor,
my personal triple-threat quarterback star,
a tried and true Army-Navy fan.

And to the late Bob Farrell, columnist,
editor, and publisher . . . and dear friend who
loved the Army-Navy competition.

Published by Henry Holt and Company, Inc.,
115 West 18th Street, New York, New York 10011.
Published in Canada by Fitzhenry & Whiteside Limited,
195 Allstate Parkway, Markham, Ontario L3R 4T8.

Library of Congress Cataloging-in-Publication Data
Schoor, Gene.
100 years of Army-Navy football / Gene Schoor.—1st ed.
   p.   cm.
"A Donald Hutter book."
ISBN 0-8050-0831-4
1. United States Military Academy—Football—History.   2. United
States Naval Academy—Football—History.   I. Title.   II. Title:
Hundred years of Army-Navy football.
GV958.U5S36 1989
796.332′63—dc20   89-2119
                                                     CIP

Henry Holt books are available at special discounts
for bulk purchases for sales promotions, premiums,
fund-raising, or educational use. Special editions
or book excerpts can also be created to specification.

For details contact:
Special Sales Director
Henry Holt and Company, Inc.
115 West 18th Street
New York, New York 10011

First Edition

DESIGNED BY LUCY ALBANESE

Printed in the United States of America
10 9 8 7 6 5 4 3 2 1

Contents

Acknowledgments

I want to thank all the people who have helped make this record of what I believe is the most thrilling competition in college football. I am grateful to all the Army-Navy players, coaches, sportswriters, and friends who took the time to answer hundreds of questions and to respond with their precious scrapbooks, stories, and photographs of the thrilling competition between these two service schools.

A very special debt of gratitude to one of Army's immortal stars, on the gridiron, in the classroom, and in the service to his country, General Pete Dawkins, for his vivid and memorable introduction to this book; to Colonel Earl Blaik, former Army coach, for his dramatic word picture of a few of his coaching seasons; a special salute to Army's great "accidental coach," Tom Cahill, for his dramatic story; Colonel Red Reeder, former Army player and coach; Colonel Ed Garbisch, Army's great kicking star and Hall of Famer; Dale Hall, former Army player and coach; General Monk Meyer, for some unusual stories of his playing career and for his V.I.P. invitation to a "special" cocktail party in Vietnam; General Harvey Jablonsky, former All-American and Army coach; General Bill Shuler; General Gar Davidson, former Army star, coach, and supe at West Point; General Georgey Smythe; President

Dwight D. Eisenhower, for those five pages of his personal trials and tribulations on the gridiron; General Vern Prichard; General Omar Bradley; General John Heavey; Colonel Harry "Lighthorse" Wilson; General Norm Edwards; Reverend John Markoe; to Captain Tom Hamilton, Navy's All-American coach and director of athletics, for his hours and hours of taped material, detailing some of the thrilling moments in his memorable career; to the "Kids from Kankakee," Colonel Harry Stella and Captain Alan Bergner; Captain Buzz Borries; Captain Oscar Hagberg, Navy star and former coach; Admiral Lou Kirn; Captain George Dalton; Captain Percy Northcroft; Admiral Emory Land; Leon Bramlett; Coach Bill Elias of Navy; Captain Bill Busik, Navy's great halfback, currently director of the alumni association of the Naval Academy; and the late great sportswriter Tim Cohane. Also Mrs. Kenneth Rapp at the U.S. Military Academy Library; and for her gracious help on any number of occasions, Ms. Andrea Hamberger, Special Affairs Department, U.S. Military Academy, West Point; Wide World Photos; *Brooklyn Eagle* Photo Department; *New York Daily News* Photo Department. And a very special tribute to the best editor in town, Don Hutter, and to the best damned literary agent anywhere—Julian Bach.

Introduction by Pete Dawkins

As for all of us who have stood on the field of an Army-Navy game, my remembrances are sharp and clear, even today, thirty-one years later.

I recall in precise detail Coach Earl "Red" Blaik taking me aside after we had won the toss and telling me he had a feeling Navy would kick off to me. Further, Blaik said, "Don't try to run for a touchdown. Just make sure you don't fumble the ball!"

With those words ringing in my ears, I went out onto the field at Municipal Stadium in Philadelphia for my final game of college football, aware that I was entering the arena where much of the great tradition and lore of Army-Navy football had been written, aware that the eyes of the entire Corps of Cadets, of almost 100,000 frenzied and shivering fans, of millions watching on TV were focused on me.

And I fumbled the ball!

It wasn't your ordinary fumble. In fact it was a quite spectacular fumble.

Starting up the field with Blaik's admonition

Pete Dawkins (left) smiles happily as he holds his diploma at graduation ceremonies at West Point June 3, 1959. An All-American halfback, Heisman winner, and team captain in 1958, Dawkins earned numerous other awards at West Point.

foremost in my mind, I cradled the ball with both arms. Then, suddenly, a huge opening appeared, and for one brief moment all caution went to the wind, all counsel was forgotten.

Sensing daylight (and the chance for an opening kickoff touchdown), I cut sharply to my left and ran smack into my own teammate, the great Army center Bill Rowe. The ball squirted into the air, Navy recovered, and several plays later Navy scored.

So much for my observance of military discipline. And so much for the august beginning of my final Army-Navy game!

Fortunately, the 1958 Army team was a team marked by good fortune, and at least a pinch of magic. Pluckily we pulled out of the hole I'd put us in and beat Navy to complete a proud and undefeated season.

That is my most indelible recollection of Army-Navy football. Yet it is only a tiny fragment of the whole. What Gene Schoor has chronicled here is so much more. He has culled the drama, the excitement, the record, the names, faces, and events—the whole story—of the Army-Navy game.

This is a book about competition. A hundred years of competition, this human trait that stretches back into our deepest history, hundreds of thousands of years. For as the centuries swept forward we learned to compete for power and attention and pride. And we came to pit Army against Navy in an annual football classic that has brought competition to a level which, if not supreme, is at least a stout example of what competition can be, and what it's really all about.

This is a book about rivalry. Rivalries aren't new, either. From the Spartans and Athenians of ancient Greece to the Hatfields and McCoys, rivalries have brought out the best, and sometimes the worst, in us. But they have always called forth enormous effort and sacrifice, and many have left their permanent mark on us. If ever there was a rivalry whose mark remains bright and positive, it is this one, which has been played out for the past one hundred years—over one hundred yards of possibly the toughest turf in America.

Still, why the Army-Navy game has become a true American classic is something I don't fully understand. What I do understand is that it *is* an American classic, with a rightful place in what Grantland Rice so aptly termed the "wonderful world" of sport. One sure index is the fact that in recent years, even when the teams were not ranked in the top twenty, and the games may not have been technically of top quality, the TV ratings have remained as strong as ever.

Americans, young and old, are drawn to the game. Why? Perhaps the reason is simply that this particular rivalry represents a purity, an appealing innocence—a standard we as a nation all respect: hard, tough, determined, fair.

History also contributes to the aura of the game. Army versus Navy began in 1890, when American football bore a much closer resemblance to rugby than to today's game. Football, at the end of the nineteenth century, was essentially an irreverent modification of British rugby, played with the same pudgy (and often soggy) leather ball, only slightly oblong. It was played with raw abandon—and no helmets—and from that very first Army-Navy game every annual renewal has embodied the spirit that has come to characterize this great rivalry.

Through the years the game grew steadily in stature. What built that stature? Partly the excitement of the games themselves, like Navy's 1954 win that took them to the Sugar Bowl, or the 1922 game, won by Army 17–14 in a dramatic come-from-behind finish highlighted by Smythe's 48-yard punt return. And then, of course, the great players, who through the years have brought to the game their special individual talents: Slade Cutter, Red Cagle, Johnny Dalton, Ed Garbisch, Paul Bunker, Doc Blanchard and Glenn Davis, Ron Beagle, Don Holleder, Joe Bellino, Roger Staubach, and many, many others.

It's also fair to say that this stature is partly due to the careers and exploits of former players, those who excelled in their nation's service *after* their football days: Dwight D. Eisenhower, Vice Admiral John "Babe" Brown, and even Douglas MacArthur—who is tied to the Army-Navy tradition not as a player but as a team manager, and yet is clearly linked, and remembered, as being part of the Army team.

I first met General Douglas MacArthur in September 1956, on the sidelines of Michie Stadium, but I first listened to him in the locker room earlier that day, before going to the stadium for a preseason scrimmage.

I remember with unusual clarity the words MacArthur spoke with such telling emotion, about what the Army team means to the men and women of the Army all around the world. By extension, he was speaking of what the Navy team means to the men and women of the Navy, and what, together, the two teams mean to this country:

> *Since our earliest gridiron victories, the story has been the talk and the boast of every campfire gathering—every barracks mess hall—every garrison assemblage of the American Army.*
>
> *In my twenty campaigns, covering more than twenty-five years of foreign service, from the Rhine to the Yalu, from Vera Cruz to Tokyo, through the muddy sludges of Europe to the blistering jungle trails of Asia, in all that welter of breathless struggle between life and death, always a central topic*

of discussion and of paramount interest was—will the Army team win this year?

Army-Navy. It's a great rivalry, a great spectacle, a great tradition. And it's all here, in this fascinating account by Gene Schoor.

Even if you've never seen an Army-Navy game, you'll enjoy this book. Even if you're not addicted to football, you'll be drawn to the drama and pageantry of this special rivalry.

If you are attracted to sports and competition, you'll find Gene Schoor's narrative bright and memorable and fun, and the fabulous illustrations a treat in themselves. And if you have an interest in this country of ours, and what makes us tick, I think you'll find this book provides an insight into one proud facet of American life.

1

The Birth of a Tradition: 1890

It was the spirit and challenge of competition that brought about the first Army-Navy football game, perhaps beyond the origin of any other collegiate sports rivalry. For at no other schools is the competition so intense as at the Military and Naval academies. It has always been so, as men trained for the life-and-death struggles of a nation face the ultimate challenge—survival. All of the training, discipline, and regimentation of military life are geared to this end and are easily transferable from the blackboard to the athletic arena.

When America's first Corps of Midshipmen was established in 1794 by presidential order, they came into existence fifty-one years before the founding of the Naval Academy.

For that first group of forty-eight Middies, there was no defined course of academic instruction; thus they were free of any distractions from becoming satisfactory sailors. At the time of their appointment, education was considered rather a liability, for the service felt strongly suspicious of educated young men interested in the sea. A sailor needed no education.

When George Bancroft became secretary of the Navy in 1845, he determined to do something about the Midshipmen's lack of education. He took over the abandoned Army post at Fort Severn, Annapolis, and it was here that the Naval Academy was formally opened, October 10, 1845.

In the mid-1860s, Admiral David Porter, superintendent of the Naval Academy, was greatly disturbed by reports of drinking and carousing. He decided the naval Midshipmen needed an entirely new kind of leisuretime activity, a system of intramural sports activities and competition in track and field events, swimming, and wrestling. By 1867 these activities were well established, keeping the Midshipmen out of the taverns and on campus.

Commander Hawley Rittenhouse, who attended the Academy from 1866 to 1870, described what is believed to be the earliest development of football at Annapolis:

"In 1869, a Midshipman returning from leave appeared on the drill field with a round ball. As he tried to toss it to another Middie, the ball fell to the ground, and there was an immediate scramble. A dozen eager sailors bore down on the ball, then kicked and passed it from one group to another. Before long, sides were chosen and the two teams faced each other and battled up and down the field for the ball. Finally, one of the Middies kicked the ball into the river, and the first football match at Annapolis had ended."

West Point today is hardly a country club, but it is not the grim, dreary place of 1890. The Academy was founded March 16, 1802. A Cadet of that day, returning in 1890, would have discovered life was just as severe. Much of the iron militarism, popularized by the Prussian Army of Frederick the Great, hung about the somber buildings. Drill, study, and discipline all but strangled the Cadets. There was scarcely any relief from the grinding routine. Sports had made only minute, tortuous progress through the nineteenth century and were thoroughly informal.

Physical training through bodily exercise had begun at West Point as early as 1817, before any other college in the nation, but not until 1885 had it become systematized on a scientific and beneficial basis under Mr. Herman Koehler.

From 1830 the Cadets were instructed in riding and fencing; in 1839 dancing lessons began. That same year the Cadets played a little town ball, an early form of baseball. Cadet Abner Doubleday, Class of 1842, had drawn up a diamond and a set of rules like today's baseball while on leave at his home in Cooperstown, New York. He is usually given credit for inventing baseball.

In the spring of 1863 the Cadets obtained permission to play baseball, and in 1867 they began a series of interclass games.

But some form of football was played at West Point even then.

In his memoirs, General Jim Longstreet, a classmate of General Doubleday, wrote that he "enjoyed playing football as a Cadet, even though we had no organized matches." And a "gig sheet" at West Point during the 1840s records "Cadet Phillip Sheridan was disciplined for kicking a football in the vicinity of the barracks." Then, too, Cadet Jérôme Napoleon Bonaparte, grandnephew of Emperor Napoleon, wrote his father: "The Officers have presented the Cadets with a football and you may depend that they will take exercise even after the very laborious drills. Even though they are so tired they can hardly sit astride a horse, when they see the football they dash about, kicking and scuffing, running up and down field like little children."

At the Naval Academy, Bill Maxwell, a Middie from Washington, D.C., organized the first Navy football team in 1879. He was coach, manager, and trainer. Maxwell arranged the first game against a group of ex-collegians representing the Baltimore Athletic Club.

Upon learning that his Naval Cadets would be outweighed by as much as ten pounds per man, Maxwell decided to compensate for his team's lack of weight with help from the Academy's tailor.

"Our men went to Bellis [the tailor]," said Maxwell, "and he made us heavy sleeveless jackets of double-lined canvas, laced down the front, drawn tightly to fit each player's body.

"Walter Camp [the Father of American Football] said that I invented the first uniforms used in football. But I did not know at the time there was anything unusual or original about the idea. All I knew was that the padded, laced jackets made our boys look heavier and that when the canvas jackets became wet, from sweat or rain, they were very slippery and an opponent couldn't hold on to a player. This was specially true in the cold weather."

That first Naval Academy football game, played on December 11, 1879, ended in a 0–0 tie. But according to a news report in the *Baltimore News American*, it was "a battle royal from the beginning to end, a regular knock-'em-down-drag-'em-out affair."

Kicking, scratching, fighting masses of Naval Cadets chased and fought for the ball up and down the drill field. After the match all the players descended on the taverns at Annapolis to discuss their tactics and to salute each other with a brew.

Between 1886 and 1890 the Naval Cadets played a total of 21 football matches, winning 12 while losing 9. But it was not until Army was challenged to play in the autumn of 1890, and accepted the challenge, that the awesome football rivalry between Army and Navy began.

Despite its increasing popularity at such eastern colleges as Yale, Harvard, Princeton, and Rutgers, football had been slow to develop at West Point. In 1890 only three Cadets had ever played an organized football game: Leonard Prince, Butler Ames, and Dennis Michie.

Michie was born at West Point, the son of Lieutenant Colonel Peter Michie, who had served with great distinction during the Civil War and had been stationed at West Point to teach philosophy. Professor Michie was a member of the powerful Academic Board and one of the most respected officers at the Point, but Dennis always seemed able to get his way with his stern father.

It was Dennis who arranged for an Annapolis Midshipman to send a formal written challenge to West Point for a football match, and who then promptly took the challenge to his father, arguing that a formal challenge from Navy could not be ignored. Young Dennis was so persuasive that Professor Michie readily agreed to the idea and even secured final approval for the match from Colonel John Wilson, superintendent of the Academy.

Though he had gained permission to accept Navy's challenge, Dennis Michie's problems had just begun. He was the head coach of a football team, but he had no team. He had to search the Academy for suitable players, organize them into a team, teach the fundamentals, and get the team ready to play Navy in eight weeks.

General John Palmer, a classmate of Michie's, recalled those hectic eight weeks in *The Assembly*, a U.S. Army magazine.

"Dennis now had his hands full. He was captain, coach, trainer and business manager of a non-existent team. He had little time to teach the simplest of fundamentals to his raw recruits. They had no practices except for a few riotous scrimmages against an even more inexperienced second eleven. There was no time for any coaching except in the brief intervals between military duties.

"Only on Saturday afternoons when the weather was too bad for military drills and dress parade could Denny count on time for a continuous practice with all his team members. On rainy afternoons he had almost two hours in the drill hall, but that rarely happened.

"Dennis was able to rouse his teammates at

The staid New York Times *report of the first Army-Navy football game, November 29, 1890.*

rk Times.

1890.----TWENTY PAGES.   PRICE FIVE CENTS.

REPUBLICAN BAD TEMPER

A VERY IRRITABLE CROWD GATHERED IN WASHINGTON.

VERY LITTLE, APPARENTLY, LEARNED FROM THEIR LATE DEFEAT—THEIR TALK ABOUT CANDIDATES—BLAINE'S BUREAU AT WORK.

WASHINGTON, Nov. 29.—Speaker Reed will call to order at noon on Monday the second session of the Fifty-first Congress. At last, only a day before the event, the possibility of the attendance of something like a quorum begins to impress itself upon the observer. The streets are dotted to-day with newly-arrived members, most of whom have come, post haste, from their Thanksgiving Day dinners. As might be

HILL'S EDITOR THRASHED.

EX-ASSEMBLYMAN O'CONNOR SETTLES A FEW OLD SCORES.

ELMIRA, N. Y., Nov. 29.—A disgraceful scene occurred in front of the *Gazette* office this morning. Royal R. Soper, manager of the *Gazette*, Gov. Hill's local organ, and ex-Assemblyman J. J. O'Connor were the participants. The parties mentioned had a war of words, ending in the complete discomfiture of Mr. Soper. During the mêlée O'Connor made remarks that have been a subject of discussion since. He said, addressing Soper: " —— you! You and Gov. Hill ought to be in State prison, and if you had your just deserts you both would have been there long ago." These remarks were followed by a stinging blow in Soper's face, sending him sprawling into the gutter. The newsman seemed bewildered and again faced the scrap, but a

THE NAVY WHIPS THE ARMY

ANNAPOLIS'S FOOTBALL MEN CONQUER WEST POINT'S BEST.

THE YOUNG ADMIRALS SWEEP ALL BEFORE THEM, SMITING THE ENEMY HIP AND THIGH, AND FORCING COMPLETE CAPITULATION.

WEST POINT, N. Y., Nov. 29.—West Point was the scene of a mighty battle to-day. The flower of the United States Navy invaded the classic precincts of the National Military Academy and captured the flower of the army.

This internecine struggle was not with bayonets nor with cutlasses, but only with canvass-covered arms and legs, and bared heads. For the first time in

Above: *The Navy team forms a solid flying wedge of interference as they advance with the ball in the first Army-Navy game ever played; Army players rush forth eagerly to halt the Navy.* Right: *The Army team (in black caps) is defending the goal; the Navy team (striped caps) is on offense.*

5:30 A.M., half an hour before reveille, for a run around the Plains, down and back Flirtation Walk, over past Thayer Hall, around the Supe's quarters, and then back to the barracks in time for reveille."

The day of the great game finally arrived. Saturday, November 29, 1890, was a cold autumn day, and the clouds hovered over the Plains as a special ferryboat chugged to the shore to stop at the Point. A happy, spirited group of Naval Cadets stepped briskly ashore and began the uphill walk to the playing field. Near the top of a hill, they passed the home of a noncommissioned officer, where a goat blinked at the antics of the happy players, kicked up his heels, and started to walk away.

"Hey, that goat would make a good mascot," said a Naval Cadet.

"Let's take him. He ought to bring us good luck," said another. Quickly, two of the Midshipmen captured the goat and led him away. The football team of the Naval Academy has never been without a goat as a mascot since that day in 1890.

The setting for that first game was old, but something new had been added. A gridiron had been laid out on the southeast corner of the parade grounds. Along its sides stood a crowd of perhaps 1,000—Cadets, the Army band, West Point officers and their wives, some enlisted men, and a group of Naval officers from a ship anchored in the harbor, as well as about 150 other visitors from outside the Post. The ladies occupied the only seats along the field, borrowed from nearby classrooms.

There was a stir and then a roar from Navy's side as the Navy team ran onto the field. They were wearing white canvas jackets and breeches, maroon and white stocking caps, and maroon stockings. The Navy visitors greeted their players with an organized cheer just before the ball was put into play:

Rah, rah, rah!
Hi, ho, ha!
U.S.N.A.!
Boom, siss bah!
Navy! Navy! Navy!

Two "officials," William Hyndman of Yale and Reggie Belknapp, an undergraduate Naval Cadet, called the two captains, Dennis Michie of West Point and Charles "Red" Emerich of Annapolis, to the center of the field.

Mr. Hyndman then took a coin from his pocket, tossed it into the air, and watched as it tumbled into the palm of his hand.

He pointed to Red Emerich, the Navy captain, indicating that Navy had won the toss. Emerich told the referee his team would defend the south goal. Then he turned and ran to his team.

The Navy team gathered around Emerich and Army around Michie. As the Cadets prepared to take their positions on the field, Colonel Hamilton Hawkins, the commandant of cadets, shouted:

"I shall slug the first Army player who leaves the field in an upright position."

The term "slug" at the Point meant then, as it does today, a demerit given a Cadet, and an accumulation of slugs meant that the Cadet would spend a certain amount of his leisure time parading about the barracks area.

The Army team was composed of Jim Moore and Len Prince at ends; Joe Crabbs and Fran Schoeffel, tackles; Truman Murphy and John Heavy, guards; Sterling "Bud" Adams, center; Kirby Walker, quarterback; and Ed Timberlake, Butler Ames, and Dennis Michie also in the backfield.

The Naval Cadets lineup included John Beuret and George Laws at ends; Charlie Macklin and Heber Ward at the tackle positions; Rufe Lane and Marty Trench as guards; Noble Irwin at center; Moulton Johnson at quarterback; Renwick Hartung and Emerich, halfbacks; and Al Althouse at fullback.

The ball was put into play, and from a V-wedge formation Red Emerich ran for 20 yards before he was smothered by a host of Army players led by Michie.

On the next play, quarterback Johnson called his first signal. "Reef the topsail," he barked, and the ball went back to Emerich, who drove for another gain, smashing through a mass of tangled bodies. Again and again

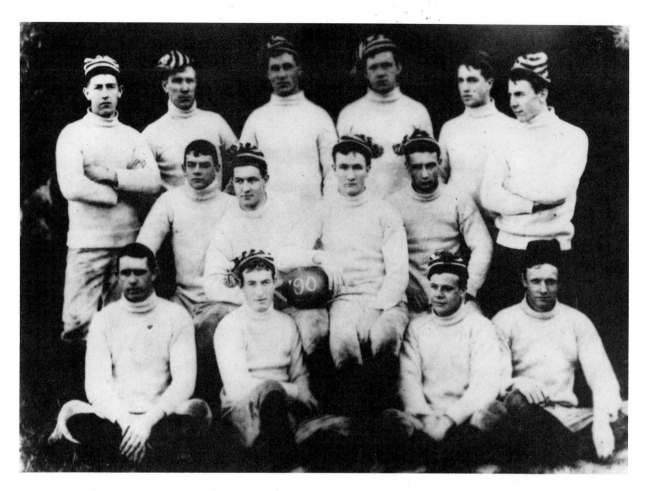

Above: *The victorious Navy team that defeated Army in 1890. Final Score: Navy 24, Army 0. Captain Charles Emerich holds the ball.* Right: *Captain Dennis Michie (with ball) and the first West Point team.*

Emerich carried the ball, and Navy plowed ahead. Emerich often displayed a quick change of pace in his running that had the Army tacklers sprawled on the ground as he drove around them for yardage.

The first Army-Navy game was not more than two minutes old before the most eager West Point partisan realized that Navy was too well drilled for the Army team, and with its new mascot and its organized cheering, Navy had Army completely frustrated.

One particular Navy play was very effective.

Al Althouse, the fullback, dropped back as if to kick the ball, but instead he ran for a sizable gain. The Army players were indignant,

protesting that this was an illegal play. But the officials let the play stand.

Navy then scored the first touchdown in the history of its football series with Army. Head down, knees churning and driving, Charlie Emerich plunged the last 3 yards for the touchdown. Emerich's kick after the score was good.

In 1890, and for a number of years thereafter, a field goal was worth 5 points, a touchdown accounted for 4 points, and the kick after a TD was good for 2 points. So Navy led 6–0.

A few minutes later, Navy once again had possession of the ball. Moulton Johnson, only plebe on the Navy squad, tucked the ball under his arm behind a mass of interference, skirted

Army's left end, and scored Navy's second touchdown. Once again Emerich's kick was good and the score stood, Navy 12 Army 0, at the end of the first half.

Navy had clearly outplayed Army in every possible manner, but Army had fought back courageously with everything they had.

In the second half the Navy backs continued to gain ground each time they carried the ball, until the teams were lined up in the shadow of the Army goalposts.

Navy's quarterback, young Kirby Walker—an eighteen-year-old speedster weighing all of 145 pounds and half-hidden by Army's husky center, Bud Adams—shouted a string of nauti-cal terms in which the word "mainmast" was emphasized. Then twenty-two players heaved and slammed each other until time was called, at which point one of the officials noticed that Navy's ball carrier, Charles Emerich, lay stretched across the goal line, the battered foot-ball in his hands.

General Harvey Jablonsky, a former Army All-American tackle in the 1930s, later the military adviser to the Shah of Iran, described the action in the second half of the game as recon-structed by witnesses and participants:

"West Point had learned a bit more about the game as the second half began. In conse-quence, Annapolis scored but twice more.

=== ★ ★ ★ ===

Letter from William F. Heavey*

John W. Heavey, class of '91, played in that very first Army-Navy game in 1890. His son, also a West Point graduate, relates a rare story about how his father made the team and an amusing incident concerning his father's retirement. Brigadier General John W. Heavey, who died in 1941 just before Pearl Harbor, saw service in the Spanish-American War, under Pershing in the Philippines in 1902, and in World War 1.

Thought you might like to hear how my father (USMA, 1891) made the first Army team, as he told me:

At noon the cadet adjutant read in the mess hall that Annapolis had challenged West Point to a game of football, to be played at West Point. An order followed that all cadets weighing over 180 would report to try out for the team. My father had come from Illinois, had never even seen a football, but weighed 198. He reported and was told the idea of the game was to stop the man with the ball. No instruction was given that first day in tackling. The coach lined up two scrub teams. All who had played *any* football were on the first team; all others on the second team. My father was assigned right guard. At the very first scrimmage, the man with the ball charged right at right guard Heavey. Remembering he must stop that man, Father grabbed him around the waist, threw him up in the air several feet. Still clutching the ball, he fell on his head unconscious. The coach rushed in and said, "Who did that?" Father kept quiet but several on the first team shouted, "Heavey did it," and pointed him out.

The coach shouted to him, "Get over on the first team at right guard." That is how Heavey made the team.

Incidentally, someone in the bottom of the pile at the second or third scrimmage of the game sunk his teeth into one of Father's ears. Years later he proudly showed the scar to his sons, all of whom went on to West Point.

I suppose you know the Army team wore hockey stocking caps that first game. Father said he lost his in the first scrimmage and played all the game without ever seeing it again.

Another episode that may be of interest. When Teddy Roosevelt was President, all "obese" officers were ordered before a Retiring Board. Father weighed 201 so was ordered to appear. President of the board asked my father if he wanted a counsel to assist him. My father replied No, that he merely wanted to present one paper. Told to proceed, he handed the board a copy of the program of the first A-N football game, which showed the weights of the players. The president of the board read: RIGHT GUARD HEAVEY 198, whereupon Father looked along the line of the nine members of the board and said, "Gentlemen, how many of you have added only three pounds since you entered the Army?" The nine members slouched down behind the long table, all of them. Father was NOT retired for obesity—he retired for AGE at 64.

Best regards,
W. F. Heavey

*Early in the 1960s, well before plans for this book took shape, I initiated a correspondence with over a hundred of the outstanding participants (or in this case, son of a participant) in the first half century of Army-Navy football. This letter is the first of ten selected for this book from those responses. —G. S.

"The signals by which the Annapolis captain directs his team are something appalling. 'Clear ship for action,' he yells. But the ladies who looked on and feared that blood was going to be spilled only saw the ball sent far down the field by a well directed punt. Even the Military Cadets, brave though they were, looked uncertain when, 'Fire to the front, change front to the rear for the left piece,' was signalled by Navy. All this meant that Navy's right guard was to try to run around Army's left end.

"Young Walker, the West Point quarterback, had the wind knocked out of him. He recovered, however, and a few minutes into the second half was knocked out again when several Navy players smacked into him. Still he played on. Once again he was knocked out and a pail of water was dumped on him and he again recovered and remained on the field. Five minutes before the game ended Walker was knocked cold again and this time was carried off the field.

"One thing that was shown very clearly during the game was that both elevens did have splendid material. Every man on the two teams played hard during the two 45 minute halves, and was in pretty good condition at the end of the game.

"By the time the second half of the game got under way the Army players seemed to understand the rules better than their supporters rooting on the sidelines. When Emerich faked a kick and ran the length of the field for a touchdown [for Navy's fourth and final score], the Cadet rooters became indignant at the officials, some even shouted their displeasure because they did not call the ball back. But Dennis Michie, captain and coach of the Army team, laughed and clapped Emerich on the back.

"Another time Emerich was knocked to the turf by Truman Murphy of Army, who spun him around and held him. But Emerich broke away and sped on for another touchdown. [In those early days of football, a runner had not only to be tackled but to be held firmly to the ground until an official called the play dead.] When Murphy was asked why in the world he allowed Emerich to get away, he said:

" 'When I stopped him, I heard a lot of yelling from the sidelines. I thought I had done something wrong, so I let him go.'

"All during the game, a rather dignified, well-dressed officer's wife kept shouting at the Cadets in a distinctly foreign guttural:

'Ghhuard yourr man! Ghhhard yourr man!'

"But this was Navy's day. Final score: Navy 24, Army 0. To climax the victory and to pay respects to their rivals, the Cadets threw a dance for the visitors, and a wonderful relationship was established."

The New York newspapers accorded the first Army-Navy game front page coverage the next day. The staid *New York Times* said:

THE NAVY WHIPS THE ARMY

ANNAPOLIS FOOTBALL MEN CONQUER
WEST POINT'S BEST
YOUNG ADMIRALS SWEEP ALL BEFORE THEM,
SMITING THE ENEMY HIP AND THIGH AND
FORCING COMPLETE CAPITULATION

The *Times* reporter called the game "the greatest victory the Navy has achieved since Decatur and John Paul Jones."

From Michie's Miracle to the Duel: 1891-93

In 1891, Japan was shaken by the worst earthquake in history as hundreds were swept to their death by huge tidal waves that inundated the nation. . . . Ignace Jan Paderewski, pianist and patriot, made his musical debut in the United States, with Walter Damrosch assisting. . . . It was a very good year on Wall Street, and as reported in business magazines, the Astor family, "who had a stock or two, served dinner on solid gold plates." . . . Gentlemen members of the New York Athletic Club shunned the prizefights conducted there. . . . As an indoor substitute for baseball and football, Dr. James A. Naismith, a physical ed instructor at the YMCA Training College (now Springfield College), invented a game he called basketball. "The game," said Naismith, "retains the speed and competitiveness, while eliminating the violence of football." . . . The famous actor, Edwin Booth, played Hamlet in a Brooklyn, New York, theater, his last performance before retiring. . . . Bob Fitzimmons became the first American prizefighter to hold three international championships; he held the middleweight, light-heavyweight, and heavyweight crowns. . . . And on November 27, 1891, the Army football team traveled to Annapolis, Maryland, to engage the Naval Academy in the second match between the two schools.

This was the first time since West Point was founded in 1802 that Cadets had left the Academy grounds to engage in an athletic contest. The mist that enveloped the Plains at the West Point Military Academy that Thursday morning seemed to indicate a portent of things to come.

There was an ominous quiet that was most unusual in the dining hall as the 273 Cadets sat down for breakfast on this great day. The constant hum of conversation was missing. Instead there was a strange feeling, an uneasy feeling that suddenly erupted into a roar as Cadet Captain Dennis Michie left his detail to gather his teammates.

"Mr. Moore," called Michie.

"Here, sir," saluted left end Moore.

"Mr. Haule."

"Here, sir."

"Gleason, Adams, Clark, Smith, Prince, Walker, Dawson, Timberlake—are you ready?"

"Yes, sir. Ready and able to go."

One by one, as the members of Army's 1891 football eleven rose to their feet smartly, then saluted, the Cadets roared with anticipation,

Play along the line of scrimmage in the second Army-Navy game, 1891. There were plenty of bloodied noses.

for this was a historic hour in the early epoch of football at West Point.

To avenge the 24–0 defeat by Navy in 1890, seventeen Cadets, led by Lieutenant Daniel Tate, Coach Harry Williams, and Captain Dennis Michie, were leaving West Point for their second encounter with the Navy football team. Army had lost the first game ever played between the two service schools a year earlier, but Michie, Leonard Prince, Butler Ames, and Ed Timberlake, as well as the other players, had vowed vengeance. To back up their vow, officers at the Academy and at Army installations all over the nation had sent contributions to defray the cost of the 1891 season.

Michie, who had devoted countless hours to organizing, then coaching the Army team, realized his own knowledge of football was quite limited, and so, early in the fall of 1891, he had approached Lieutenant Dan Tate, the officer in charge of football.

"If we're going to have a try at beating the Navy, we need somebody to help coach the team—somebody who knows more football than I do," he said.

"There's no one here at the post to fill that role," said Tate.

"I think we can get Harry Williams. He was a marvelous player at Yale. He's teaching here at Newburgh. Perhaps, if you talk to him, he might be able to spare some time, help us out. And I think we can get him without pay, 'cause we really don't have any money for him."

Lieutenant Tate contacted Williams, and Harry agreed to spend two afternoons a week with the Army team. Williams, a football and track star at Yale, later became famous at Minnesota, where he created the famous Minnesota shift. Under Williams's more expert tutelage, Army slowly emerged as a team. They now moved as a unit, on set signals, with previously arranged plays that had been thoroughly and

Cadet Dennis Mahon Michie, who organized, coached, and managed Army's first football team. Michie Stadium is named in his honor.

painstakingly practiced. As a further test for the big Navy game, Williams set up several preliminary games, and Army scored its first football victory ever, by a 10–6 score against St. John's College, eventually to become known as Fordham University. The Princeton reserves battled Army to a hard-fought 12–12 tie, but then Army defeated St. Stephens 14–12, lost to a more experienced Rutgers eleven by 27–6, and scored an upset win over Schuylkill Navy College by a 6–0 margin.

Meanwhile, Navy's season was being noted for a succession of startling wins. The Midshipmen easily defeated St. John's 28–6, then went on to defeat Rutgers 21–12, then beat Gallaudet College 6–0. Georgetown was beaten 16–4, and just three days after the Georgetown victory, Navy romped over Dickinson, 34–4.

In the Dickinson victory, Worth Bagley, a lithe, 156-pound speedster, caught a punt and dodged and twisted his way some 60 yards through the entire Dickinson team for a touchdown. Navy then took on their third opponent

in seven days and lost to a heavily favored Lafayette eleven 4–0.

Informed that Army had hired a professional coach in Williams of Yale, Navy called on the great Princeton star Edgar Allan Poe to handle the team and prepare Navy for the Army game. Poe, a descendant of the immortal author, had at one time been a West Point Cadet, then had transferred to Princeton, where he quickly developed into one of the great Tiger stars. In 1889 Poe was named to the All-American team. He came to the training field at Annapolis several days before the Army game and barely had time to supervise a Navy practice before the big game was at hand.

The Army team stayed in Baltimore on Friday, then on Saturday morning traveled to Annapolis, arriving there at 10:15 A.M. The Naval Cadets who met the Army team proved to be most gracious hosts. They took the Cadets on a sight-seeing tour of the Naval Academy grounds and then sat down to a pleasant lunch with their adversaries.

Meanwhile, spectators by the hundreds, including many of the highest military and naval officers, began arriving from Washington and Baltimore on special "football trains."

The day was cool but overcast, and there was a brisk wind that blew off the Severn River. But there was an air of excitement and gaiety as the 3,000 spectators, including several hundred ladies, added to the air of expectancy as the big moment for the start of the game approached.

As the Army players, clad in gray suits with black stockings and black-and-gray caps, trotted onto the field led by Captain Dennis Michie, the Army band broke out into a rousing song.

A few moments later, Captain Charlie Macklin led the Naval Cadets onto the field. The Navy players wore red-and-white caps, white shirts and pants, and red stockings.

The crowd roared with cheers for both teams as the referee, Mr. Robert Vail, called the two team captains, Michie of Army and Macklin of Navy, to the center of the field. Army won the toss of the coin and chose to receive the opening kickoff.

Army put the ball in play with a well-organized drive, with Michie, Timberlake, and Elmer Clark crashing through the heavy Navy line for substantial gains. Then, with Army on Navy's 7-yard line, Captain Michie called a surprise play, a "guards back play." For just a moment, the Navy defense was caught off balance before Elmer Clark, a burly 200-pound Army guard, who had dropped back to receive the ball, cracked through the Navy wall for a touchdown.

The staid sports department of *The New York Times* reported the game in its most graphic prose: "Captain Michie's goal after the touchdown put the score at 6–0 and the Army began to gather in a compact line about General Flager, Chief of Ordnance, and Lt. Al Perry, Ninth Cavalry, and some few of the subalterns from the Washington Arsenal. 'Rah, ray, ray, Rah, rah, ray, West Point, West Point, A-Army' was making the welkin ring, and all of the four Army substitutes sprang into the air and sent out solitary and collective shouts; they also stood on their heads and waved their heels, and slapped each other on

the back until the drummer of the Navy Band thought his instrument had got adrift."

But now the Navy team came alive and started to move the ball slowly up the field. Worth Bagley, the Navy quarterback, carried the ball on several quick thrusts into the Army line, eventually smashing through to Army's 10-yard line. And it was Army's Dennis Michie who tackled Bagley time after time. Then it was Bagley once again, carrying the ball to the Army 5-yard line, and once again it was Michie, this time assisted by Timberlake, who stopped Bagley's drive. But on the next play Navy would not be denied, and Martin Trench, a guard dropped back to halfback for this one play, pounded through for a score. Now it was 6–6.

Army took over the ball and again moved surely up the field. Michie and Timberlake took turns advancing the ball on well-developed plays that had the Navy line reeling. Finally, Michie was stopped on the 10-yard line by Bagley.

The game had developed into a personal duel between the two great stars, Bagley of

Michie's "miracle" 1891 team, which easily defeated the Navy in the second encounter, 32–16.

Navy and Army's Michie, battling each other yard for yard.

Navy took over the ball on the 10-yard line and on the first play attempted to punt. But Army blocked the kick and Bill Smith of Army fell on the ball in the end zone for a touchdown. It was now Army 12, Navy 6.

Navy failed to move the ball past midfield and Army took over on the Navy 45-yard line. A few plays later Elmer Clark took a shovel pass from Michie and dashed 25 yards for another Army touchdown. Now Army led 18–6.

The field was by now a complete wreck; piles of turf had been torn up as the players battled each other furiously up and down its length. Stockings were torn off many of the players and the noses of five Navy players were bleeding. One player had a split ear (it had been bitten by an opponent), and two Navy players were knocked out and were carried off the field, though they were quickly revived.

The second half began as Navy received the ball and Macklin quickly scored a touchdown. Then Henry Pearson brought Navy even closer with a fine run through the entire Army team for a touchdown, and now it was beginning to be a close game. Army still led but only by a 24–16 score.

Then Timberlake scored on a long run for Army, Clark converted, and it was 32–16. That was the final score of the game. The great match was over.

When the score came over the telegraphic wires at West Point, the Cadet postmaster, Jim Jervey, dashed down to where the Cadets had assembled for evening formation and blurted out the news to the captain of the First Corps. The captain never wavered. He executed a snappy about-face, then announced: "The final score of the game: Army 32, Navy 16. Dismiss your companies."

The Cadets went wild with joy. They called the band and paraded about the Academy grounds, halting at the home of each officer where they serenaded, sang, and danced wild jigs.

At Annapolis, the Army players attended a dance as guests of the Navy team. Players from both squads reviewed the game while comparing their various injuries, and before the evening had ended, virtually every Army and Navy player had personally congratulated each other. When the final waltz played out its rhythmical beat across the Severn River, Captain Dennis Michie, Army's great star, and Navy's marvelous captain, Worth Bagley, shook hands. "Till we meet again."

The Army Cadets were down at the railroad station at West Point the next afternoon, singing and cheering as the train chugged in with the returning Army team. They lifted the players to their shoulders and bore them triumphantly up the hill. The tradition of hauling a victorious team up the hill in an old stagecoach would not appear until the turn of the century.

When the team reached the Plain, the Cadets called on Dennis Michie for a speech. What Denny said is lost in the years, but it is safe to say that he was grinning as he spoke.

The Honor Roll of participants in the great Army-Navy football rivalry who gave their lives for their country begins with perhaps the most outstanding players on each team over those first four games: Army's Dennis Michie and Navy's Worth Bagley.

When war with Spain broke out in 1898, Captain Dennis Michie was stationed at Forth Leavenworth, Kansas, as aide-de-camp to his old friend General Hamilton Hawkins, and shortly found himself in the middle of the Battle of Santiago in Cuba. Just before noon of July 1, 1898, he returned from reconnaissance at the front during the action at Bloody Bend of the San Juan River.

"I could see the Spanish up there on the hill," Denny informed Lieutenant Harry Pattison, his old teammate. Then he added: "We will give them hell in a few minutes."

Then he went to the aid of the Sixteenth Infantry unit preparatory to an assault on the hill. Just as suddenly as he was leading the assault, a bullet from a Spanish gun killed him.

He was just twenty-eight years of age. And like so many of the "long gray line," he died very young. But his name will live forever in the annals of Army-Navy football.

The Navy football team victorious over Army in 1892 by a 12–4 margin. Team Captain Martin Trench is at center with ball (note that it resembles a basketball more than it does today's football).

Ensign Worth Bagley, star quarterback of the Navy team in 1891, was the executive officer of the USS Winslow, on duty in the waters off Cuba in 1898. Suddenly, and without warning, hidden Spanish guns opened up with a thunderous barrage of fire. The *Winslow* was hit and a boiler exploded, spraying fire and shell fragments all through the ship. Another shell hit the steering engine, leaving the big ship helpless.

Acting without hesitation, Ensign Bagley immediately took over the exposed position on deck of the engine room. Desperately he attempted to direct the steering of the stricken ship by its propeller—again the quarterback, this time in defense of his fellow seamen and ship. Once more the hidden Spanish guns poured forth their deadly fire. This time a shell crashed directly on the exposed deck, and Bagley and the five seamen assisting him were killed.

Worth Bagley was the only United States naval officer killed in the Spanish-American War. The date was May 11, 1898.

After the devastating upset loss to Army in 1891, Navy hired a full-time football coach for the 1892 season. The Naval Cadets wanted revenge for the 32–16 debacle and selected a former Yale star, Ben Crosby, as the Academy's first head coach.

Crosby had played under the immortal Walter Camp at Yale and was considered one of Yale's outstanding ends until forced to the sidelines in 1891 because of an injury.

Crosby was a stern taskmaster who believed that the team in the better physical condition would win most games. The Crosby method of conditioning consisted of having his teams practice by playing two double (ninety-minute) halves of football every day against a scrub team of twenty-two players. Then, to cap off the workout on the gridiron, Crosby would have his players swim in an ice-cold pool just before dinner.

Captain Chester Wells, a smashing tackle on the 1892 squad, remembered those practice sessions. "It got so bad," said Wells, "that a regular game on Saturday against a major team was considered a holiday by the players."

But the Crosby method paid dividends. The Navy football team was so well conditioned and so tough, it played the entire game against Army without a single substitution—and on a raw, turfless, pebble-filled, frozen drill field.

Navy had opened the 1892 season against the nationally ranked University of Pennsylvania and was fortunate to hold mighty Penn to a 16–0 score.

Three days after the loss to Penn, Navy took on another nationally ranked eleven, the Princeton Tigers. Outweighed some 28 pounds per man, Navy lost 28–0.

The following Saturday, Navy scored its first win of the season against Lafayette, 22–3, thereby reversing a 4–0 Lafayette victory in 1891. Then, on successive Saturdays, the Middies trounced Franklin & Marshall 24–0; bewildered Rutgers with an offense led by Worth Bagley and Moulton Johnson, running wild to pile up a 48–12 Navy win; then shellacked Georgetown 40–0, for their fourth straight victory.

While Navy was amassing this impressive record under its first full-time coach, Army was doing at least as well under its original student-coach, Dennis Michie. Having graduated in June, Michie took over the team when Harry

Williams left West Point to enter the University of Pennsylvania Medical School and to coach football and track at the nearby William Penn Charter School.

Army opened its 1892 season with a 6–6 tie with Wesleyan in a game marred by frequent slugging. The following week Army defeated Stevens Institute by a 42–0 score, then romped over Trinity, 24–0. The Princeton Reserves were beaten by Army by a 14–0 score on November 19 in a fitting workout a week before the Navy game, to take place at West Point.

Worth Bagley was just nineteen years old and weighed all of 156 pounds, yet this speedy Navy fullback played the greatest game of his three-year Navy career as he led the Middies to a startling 12–4 victory over Army in the best-played game of the series to date.

Bagley and his sidekick, the 145-pound halfback Walt Izard, were outstanding as the Middies scored 12 points in the second half to defeat a highly favored West Point team.

Bagley advanced the ball 50 yards in eighteen carries, kicked two goals after touchdowns, and punted the ball eight times to keep Army's offense back in its own territory for much of the game.

After a scoreless first half, Bagley and Izard alternated in carrying the ball and gained great yardage every time. Finally, with the ball on Army's 10-yard line, Izard, behind some fine blocking, pounded through for a touchdown. Bagley kicked the goal and it was Navy 6, Army 0.

But Tommy Carson quickly scored for Army and it was a 6–4 battle.

Halfback Moulton Johnson dashed 15 yards to score Navy's second touchdown, and after Bagley converted the goal the score was Navy 12, Army 4.

But Army fought back gallantly, and as the game wound down, the Cadets were pounding the lighter Navy eleven. They had the ball on the Navy 5-yard line as the battle ended.

Navy's eleven "Iron Men" had dominated play from the start, however, and had remained in command for most of the game.

After changing into their student uniforms, the Middies gathered on a hill at the Point and began a rhythmic chant en route to their train:

Twelve to Four
Twelve to Four
Wasn't it a dandy score?

By 1893, the fourth year of the rivalry, the Army-Navy game had become the leading sports attraction in military circles in both Washington and New York. High officials in the two areas vied with each other for the opportunity to purchase the limited supply of tickets, and a crowd estimated at more than 10,000 attended the 1893 contest in Baltimore.

It was a bitter, frenzied battle, one that roused service tempers to such a pitch that the series had to be broken off the next year, not to resume until 1899.

International tempers were raging, too, with several nations on the verge of breaking off diplomatic relations. England and France seemed poised on the edge of war with Germany. The Belgian people, at the point of revolution, demanded and received universal suffrage. And there was much unrest in Germany until Kaiser Wilhelm and Bismarck were reconciled.

That fall of 1893, the Army football squad—despite a rugged schedule that saw the Cadets lose 4 games while winning 3—was confident they would defeat the Middies. Backers of the Cadets were so sure of victory that they arrived in Baltimore with money in their hands, giving eager Navy betters odds of 3–1.

Navy's 1893 season was a successful one as the Middies, despite losses to Penn, Lehigh, and Virginia, emerged with wins over Virginia, Georgetown, Franklin & Marshall, then Kendall in a tune-up game just prior to the Army contest.

Early in the game, Army's forward line battered the smaller, lighter Middies while the Army backs led by Captain Tom Carson and Lucian Stacy tore the Navy's line apart for long gains. But each time Army threatened, Navy's

Navy's first great football hero, 155-pound Worth Bagley, guided Navy's team in 1891, 1892, and 1893 as a swift, hard-running back.

stout defense held, and whenever Navy had the ball the Middies' star fullback, Worth Bagley, would drive the Army back on fourth down with long, booming punts. The Cadets fumbled the ball frequently, but Navy could not take advantage until midway into the second period.

At that point Navy recovered an Army fumble and drove to the Cadets' 10-yard line. Then with Henry Kimball and Bill Davidson carrying the ball, Navy advanced to the 1-yard line. On the next play, Kimball smashed through Army's right tackle for the precious last yard and Navy had scored the game's first touchdown. Worth Bagley then kicked a most difficult angle goal, and Navy had a 6–0 lead.

In what then became a tremendous defensive struggle, there was no further scoring until

Joe Reeves (center, with ball) was a fine tackle on the Navy teams of 1893 and 1894. In on virtually every line play, he suffered a number of head injuries until he devised the odd-shaped headguard he is wearing—the first helmet ever to be worn by a football player.

the final minutes of the game, when Army stormed down the field and, by the use of a "revolving wedge play," smashed over for an Army touchdown, fullback Tommy Carson carrying. Evidently the extreme pressure was too much for Captain Carson, for he hurried the kick that would have tied the score. The ball slipped off his foot and went wide. The missed kick was the difference between victory and defeat as Navy took the hard-fought battle, 6–4.

Midshipman Joe Reeves was an outstanding tackle for Navy in the game, as he had been throughout the season. A reckless, hell-for-leather player, Reeves plunged into every play without regard for his own safety. Consequently, Reeves was frequently battered about the head, and through the season he'd been knocked out in several games. So before the Army game he decided to do something about this. He went to a local shoemaker in Annapolis and had the man fashion a crude protective device, sort of a helmet, to protect his battered head from the impact of flying feet.

Reeves's first football headgear was a crude affair, shaped like a beehive, but it served the purpose. Reeves finished the season in a blaze of glory when his headfirst dives stopped numerous West Point runners before they got to the line of scrimmage.

With its hard-won victory, Navy had taken three of the first four Army-Navy games, but each contest was bitterly fought. Each of the games featured a good deal of hard, tough play, including a few instances where an Army and Navy player squared off and engaged in a few well-thrown punches.

But in the 1893 battle between the teams, there were more fistfights in the stands than on the field of play. In fact, two of the fans—a rear admiral and a retired general—found fists inadequate to settle their differences of opinion.

The two officers carried their feud into each other's camp long after the battling on the field had ended. In the elite Army & Navy Club in Washington, it was reported, the two men renewed their argument several days later . . . with firearms.

Both the Army & Navy Club and the War and Navy departments declared the affair "out of bounds" to the eager and curious press. No official record has ever been found of the fracas, and even the identities of the two belligerents remain unclear. Some accounts said a duel with pistols actually was fought, others said a duel was threatened. The only thing we can definitely establish is that as a result of this affair the great autumn classic between the two schools was banned and remained banned for six years! It was renewed only because Admiral Fred McNair, superintendent of the Naval Academy, had a son playing on the Navy team and because the admiral had a personal friend who just happened to be the secretary of the Navy.

Junior McNair constantly discussed the resumption of play with Army with his father and stressed the growing popularity of football throughout the college world and that it would be important for the service schools to compete once again, for the public relations value to both services. Finally, one day Admiral McNair went to Washington and consulted with the secretary of the Navy, the secretary of war, and the superintendent of the Military Academy. Their report to President William McKinley finally brought about resumption of this great annual sports classic in 1899.

There was a curious lack of sparkle and enthusiasm in the Navy football practices and games in the fall of 1894, and at West Point, too, the Cadets went about their dummy practice sessions and games without the anticipation and burning desire to beat Navy in the final game of the season, for there would be no game with Navy.

Everyone connected with the two schools knew what the reason was, but no one could do anything about it. Events in Washington had shaped a course frustrating to every true lover of Army-Navy football.

Following the tumultuous 1893 game, zealous reformers in the capital had taken advantage of the reported duel between an admiral and general to yell bloody murder and call for the abolition of the Army-Navy game. Some had even called for the abolition of service football altogether.

With an ear cocked to the electorate, President Grover Cleveland agreed to hear and discuss the situation and promptly convened a special cabinet meeting late in February 1894. When the meeting was adjourned after hours of stormy discussion, Navy Secretary Hilary A. Herbert issued a general order to his service academy:

"The game of football will be permitted at the United States Naval Academy under such regulations as may now or hereafter be promulgated by the Superintendent. He may permit various teams to visit Annapolis to play there with the Academy's team, but the team of Naval Cadets is prohibited from engaging in football matches elsewhere."

Daniel S. Lamont, secretary of war, thereupon issued a similar general order to the West Point team. The joint effect of the two orders was to cancel the big interservice rivalry.

And so the situation stood—both service schools continuing their intercollegiate games against schools in their immediate areas, but not playing each other—until 1899. In the fall of 1897 a new secretary of war, Russell A. Alger, suggested to West Point Superintendent Oswald Ernst that the Army-Navy game be resumed. Colonel Ernst refused the bid, but then, in August of 1898, Ernst was succeeded by Colonel Albert Mills, who agreed in principle with Alger's suggestion. Slowly, plans for the resumption of the game took shape.

There were two main points of difference that had to be settled before the game was set. Army wanted the game played on November 25, Navy insisted on December 2. There was also a question of player eligibility. The Naval Academy followed a six-year course of study and felt that a Naval Cadet should be allowed to play for six years. Army, with its normal four-year schedule, stoutly protested.

A mediator was called in. Dr. William White was a member of the West Point Board of Visitors, and through his offices the two questions were resolved, with Army agreeing to both Navy points.

The University of Pennsylvania offered its new athletic facility, Franklin Field, as a neutral site for the resumption of the game, and in 1899 both academies accepted the proposal.

The Big Game Resumes: 1899-1901

More than 27,000 invited guests attended the first Army-Navy game in six years. The tickets, free of charge, were divided between the two schools.

Navy, under new head coach Garry Cochran, a Princeton All-American in 1897, fielded one of its strongest teams yet. The Middies had dropped the season's opening game to a strong Princeton eleven by a 5–0 score, but then went on to defeat Georgetown, Penn State, North Carolina, Trinity, and Lehigh.

The Cadets, meanwhile, had defeated Dartmouth by a 6–2 margin and, the following week, squeezed out a win over Syracuse. In the third quarter of that game, Charlie Wesson took a kickoff, cut sharply to his right, scooted along the sideline, and was out in the clear for a fantastic 105-yard run for an Army touchdown. (That was the length of the playing field in 1899.) Wesson's miracle sprint was enough to give Army a 12–6 victory. But then the Cadets became mired in a slump and dropped games to Yale, Harvard, Princeton, Penn, and Columbia. Army thus found itself facing a heavily favored Navy team, winner of its last five games.

Herman Koehler, the Army coach, had never played football, but he had studied the game and had coached a number of enlisted men's teams. But a week before the Navy game, Harry Williams and Harmon Graves, both former Army head coaches, came up to West Point to assist Koehler for the Navy game. Williams devised a new set of "tackle-back plays" that worked so well in practice sessions, the Cadets' spirits soared.

These new plays that Army would use for the first time consisted of dropping the left tackle into the backfield and then running the play with five backs, perfectly legal in 1899. Army further planned to cross up the Navy defense by running a number of plays without the use of a huddle to call signals for the next play.

As the game began both teams played cautiously, and for most of the first half it was strictly a defensive game. Both Army and Navy fullbacks punted the ball frequently, each time forcing the other team back deep into its own territory.

Late in the second period, Army managed to advance the ball to midfield. Halfback Frank Clark picked up 13 yards, then continued to carry the ball on most of the following plays until he smashed to the Navy 5-yard line. From there Verne Rockwell ran through Navy's tackle for a touchdown. (By this time the rules had been changed. A touchdown now was worth 5 points.)

Army led 5–0 at the half.

The second half started with Army savagely pounding the Navy line for big gains. Clark was again Army's choice to carry the brunt of the attack, and he gained ground repeatedly. From the Navy 41, Clark circled his left end for 15 yards, bringing the ball to the Navy 26. Clark then smashed through for another 10 yards, then 5 more. With the ball on the 2-yard line, Rockwell, a substitute halfback, plunged over for his second Army touchdown, and Bill Bettison kicked the goal.

Now it was Army 12, Navy 0.

Army picked up steam once again and drove the Navy defenders back to their goal line as Clark, Rockwell, and Adam Casad easily pierced Navy's line for huge gains. Clark carried the ball to the 16-yard line and then Bob Jackson scored the third Army touchdown. Bettison missed the goal and it was Army 17, Navy 0.

Receiving the kick, Navy by sheer determination began to gain against the spirited Army defense; 10 to 15 yards at a time, they pounded the Army line and suddenly caught fire. They moved more quickly now, as Orie Fowler and Emory Land, the Navy halfbacks, quickly cut through Army's line for big gains. Then on a reverse play, fullback Charles Wade took the ball from Land and smashed over his own right guard for Navy's first and only score of the day. The kick was missed as the game ended with Army winning 17–5.

Army's stunning upset victory was coupled with the antics of an oversized white mule, a mascot of the First Army taken to the Navy game. Tradition says he answered the charge of Navy's goat by "hoisting him into the stands." From that day on Army's mascot has been a white mule. The game was further heightened by a military pageant that included a stirring parade of the colors and the marching of the Brigade of Naval Cadets and the Corps of Cadets, all with military music. The effect on the crowd was electric, and both Army and Navy officials vowed that this game must now be an annual affair.

Navy rehired coach Garry Cochran for the 1900 season, and with a number of experienced players back from the 1899 team it was hoped that the Middies would have one of their finest years. Such backfield stars as Emory Land, George Horning, and Captain Orie Fowler were back once again and the team was brimming with confidence as they opened the season against the unknown Baltimore Medical College squad. But Baltimore quickly showed the Middies they were a capable squad, and Navy had to go all out to manage a 6–0 victory.

Then came successive defeats by Princeton, Penn State, and Columbia. Navy's last hope for a successful season was a victory over Army.

Army's season was not much better as the Cadets dropped successive games to Trinity College, Penn State, Harvard, and Yale. In the final games before meeting Navy, Army responded with fine team play to defeat Hamilton and, a week before taking the field against Navy at Franklin Field, a very strong Bucknell team.

The game began with Navy kicking to the Cadets and halfback Frank Clark racing upfield for 15 yards before he was brought down by Navy tacklers. Clark and Casad advanced the ball to the Navy 45-yard line, but Navy's defense held and the Middies took over the ball. Charles Belknap raced 10 yards to the Army 40-yard line, and two plays later, Byron Long attempted the first of six field goals. The kick from the 45-yard line was short and Army took over.

Fullback Burt Phillips advanced the ball 15 yards on three carries, but Navy's strong line held and once more the Middies took over. Navy drove to the 40-yard line and again Long attempted a field goal, which this time went wide.

Army took over on the 20-yard line, and after two short gains, Ed Farnsworth kicked the ball to midfield. Belknap of Navy failed to gain on two running plays, then kicked the ball to the Army 20-yard line.

Clark circled right end for the game's biggest gain thus far, a run of 26 yards. Two line smashes gained 6 yards for Army, then Clark dropped back and booted the ball clearly through the goal posts and Army had its first score: Army 5, Navy 0.

Just before the half ended, Long again tried a field goal and failed.

The second half was strictly a punting contest between Farnsworth of Army and Navy's Charlie Belknap. Following one exchange, Long again tried a field goal. This time Farnsworth of Army blocked the kick, but Navy recovered the ball on the Army 25-yard line.

Long dropped back for yet another field goal attempt, and this time, his sixth effort, the kick was good and the score was tied, Army 5, Navy 5.

Now the Middies fought like a band of tigers. They charged in as an Army back received a punt and drove the player to his knees on the Army 10-yard line, causing him to fumble the ball, which was immediately pounced on by a Navy player.

The Middies' cheering section came to life with a roar that could be heard all over Philadelphia.

On a line smash, Semmes Read, the Navy

In 1899, after a six-year hiatus, Army and Navy resumed their football rivalry. The Cadets pounded out a 17–5 victory led by Captain Bill Smith (with ball).

fullback, was thrown for a loss by the hard-charging Army line. On the next play, halfback Emory Land took the ball on a handoff from his quarterback and crashed through a mass of would-be Army tacklers for a Navy touchdown. Fowler kicked the goal, which gave Navy an 11–5 lead. The Navy fans went completely berserk as they cheered and cheered until the stands shook under the roar of their efforts.

A few plays after the ensuing kickoff, Army was given the ball by the officials on a Navy holding penalty. Neil Nichols then punted to Navy and Charlie Belknap received the kick. But instead of running the ball back upfield, Belknap attempted to kick the ball right back. The ball slanted off his foot and slammed into the line, then bounced over Navy's goal, where Land recovered the ball for a safety. Now the score was Navy 11, Army 7.

And so it stood as the game ended.

When the victorious Navy squad returned to Annapolis the next afternoon they were met at the old Shortline Rail Station by the largest assemblage ever to gather in the streets of the old city. With the entire regiment of Naval Cadets augmented by about 2,500 townspeople, the welkin rang as the bruised and battered but delirious Navy gridiron warriors debarked from the train.

The joyous regiment unhooked the horses from several carriages sent to ferry the players back to the campus, and they themselves pulled the carriages by hand to the Academy grounds and Bancroft Hall.

There Captain Orie Fowler, in accordance with what had by now become a tradition, made a speech lauding the play of each of his teammates. Then he solemnly tapped out the score with eleven strokes on the huge Academy bell . . . a bell presented to the Naval Academy by Admiral Matthew Perry, who had obtained it on his historic visit to Japan.

Over three consecutive seasons, 1898–1900, Harvard had defeated Army, with the Cadets allowed only a single point over the three contests. In all three of the games Army had been unable to contain a shifty, speedy, clever 150-pound quarterback who ran like a deer and directed the Harvard football team like an Army general. His name was Charlie Daly. Nobody knew it at the time, but Charlie Daly's influence on West Point football would be as important as that of any single individual in Army's football history.

Daly would enter West Point after a star-studded career at Harvard, where Walter Camp had named him to his All-American teams in each of his three seasons. Daly was appointed to West Point by Congressman Honey Fitzgerald, who was to become the maternal grandfather of President John F. Kennedy.

Daly arrived at the Point in 1901 and, once settled into its routine, trotted onto the gridiron and into Army football immortality.

With Daly at quarterback, Army started its 1901 season with easy wins over Franklin & Marshall and Trinity, but then lost to the mighty Princeton Tigers by a close 6–0 margin. Princeton won in the final twenty seconds when halfback Bob Kerner, Princeton's great runner, sped 60 yards to a touchdown to give the Tigers the game, much to the chagrin of Daly and his mates after Army had completely outplayed the more experienced Princeton team through much of the game.

Army came back after that bitter loss to tie a strong Yale eleven, tied Princeton in a rematch, then defeated Penn and Williams in preparation for the big game against Navy, November 30.

The Naval Academy had a bright new athletic field within the confines of the Academy grounds, a new head coach, its ninth in eleven seasons—Bill Hillebrand, a Princeton All-American in 1899—and a group of football players that ranked among Navy's finest ever. Why shouldn't the Middies be confident that Army would be another of their victims at the end of a highly stressful season?

With such stars returning as Captain Neil Nichols, Emory Land, Roe Adams, Charlie Belknap, and Ralph Strassburger, the Middies had come through a difficult schedule in 1901, defeating such teams as St. John's, Lehigh, Pennsylvania, Dickinson, the great Carlisle Indians, and Washington and Jefferson. So naturally they were most anxious to defeat the Cadets, particularly since this year President Teddy Roosevelt had promised to be at the game.

Football in 1901 was just as rough and tough as it had been in 1890, when Army played its first game against Navy, but for the 1901 season the Cadets had added a few new safety features. They wore rubber nose guards, shin guards, shoulder and elbow pads, and their pants were well padded; players were personally responsible for their own equipment and were allowed to let their hair grow down to their ears for added head protection.

Lieutenant Leon Kromer, the Army coach,

=★ ★ ★=

Letter from Emory S. Land

Emory Land scored the only touchdown in the 1900 Army-Navy game, to win it for Navy, 11–7. During World War II, Admiral Land was director of the U.S. Maritime Commission. An ardent football fan, he holds a unique record for attending the classic rivalry, and is amused to recall how he overcame President Franklin D. Roosevelt's wartime travel restrictions and got an okay to attend the 1942 game from FDR himself.

Many times over the years some of my sportswriting friends here in Washington have written up the 1900 Army-Navy game frequently called "The Crap Game" as the score was Army 7 and Navy 11. As I made the only touchdown in that game, the scoring elements have been confusing. They consisted of a field goal (5 points) and a safety (2 points) for Army; a field goal (5 points) by Long of Navy, a touchdown (5 points) by Land of Navy, and 1 point for goal after touchdown. Navy 11, Army 7.

I have attended every Army-Navy game except two (when I was on the Asiatic Station) since 1898 and claim a record unequaled by anyone else in this regard. I even held the sticks at Annapolis and West Point in games played in WW II. I was a football official for twenty-seven years, 1905–32, and was once given the accolade of "All-American Linesman." In 1963 I was given an "Award for Distinguished Service" by "The Washington District Football Officials Association," which hangs in my office.

When the Navy–Marine Corps Memorial Stadium was built at Annapolis, I had the pleasure of furnishing the home team's dressing room. There is a large plaque at the entrance alley of this room indicating my gift. I also gave a trophy mountain goat (which I killed in British Columbia), which is on the wall of the dressing room, a symbol, of course, of the Navy's mascot.

During World War II, the President of the United States forbade any attendance for the games at West Point and Annapolis to those outside a ten-mile limit. This was done for travel restriction purposes. I got around this by getting the football officials concerned (all of them Army-Navy and game officials) to make me one holder of the linesman's sticks. Took it up with the President in a memo and he wrote on it, "Tell the damn fool if he wants to go that badly, to go ahead! FDR."

Emory S. Land
Vice Admiral, USN (Ret.)

was permitted to have the team in uniform only for two hours on Wednesday afternoon. The other four days the Cadets ran through signals in their Cadet uniforms, half an hour after supper. As the team left for Philadelphia in the early morning of the game, the entire Corps of Cadets cheered their departure.

Interest in the annual game had reached a new high. The 25,000 seats at Franklin Field had been gobbled up weeks in advance, leaving scalpers to sell their extra tickets for as much as $40.

The game now had taken on all of the color and brilliance of a national spectacle. As the Military Cadets and Middies made their stirring precision march onto the field, all of the

Two stars of the 1901 Army team. Below, left: Charlie Daly (top, left) transferred to West Point from Harvard that year and single-handedly defeated Navy by scoring all of Army's 11 points in an 11–5 victory; he scored one touchdown on a 105–yard dash through the entire Navy squad. Below, right: Paul Bunker (arms crossed) was a two-time All-American and a hero at Corregidor in World War II.

leading Washington officials were present, headed by President Teddy Roosevelt surrounded by several hundred Secret Service men. The President sat on the Navy side during the first half and went over to the Army side for the second.

Army started the game with an outstanding lineup: Charlie Daly at quarterback, Ed Farnsworth and Joe McAndrews at the ends; Tom Doe and the great Paul Bunker at tackle; Napoleon Riley and Nelson Goodspeed were the guards; Bob Boyers was center; and Captain Adam Casad and Horatio Hackett were the halfbacks, with the hard-hitting Pot Graves at fullback.

The Navy team consisted of Captain Neil Nichols and Lou Farley at the end posts; Roe Adams and Ross Schlabach at tackle; Charles Belknap and Reggie Carpenter, the guards; Paul Fritz at center; Fred McNair was the Navy quarterback; Frank Freyer and Emory Land were the halfbacks, and Ralph Strassburger was at fullback.

At the start of the game, Daly at quarterback ran his team like a Prussian field marshal, and the Cadets responded with the efficiency of a well-trained drill team. They worked in unison, blocked for their backs, and handled the Navy defenders easily as Daly and Pot Graves piled up big yardage. Yet the Navy team stiffened whenever Army passed midfield, and the long, booming punts by Navy's Charlie Belknap kept setting Army back into its own territory.

Finally, with less than a minute to play in the first half, Daly dropped back to the Navy 35-yard line and kicked a field goal to give Army a 5-0 lead. Navy then took over and slowly but surely battered the Army forward for 5-8-10 yards an attempt, until halfback Frank Freyer drove into the Army line for a touchdown to tie the score. But then Freyer missed the conversion and the score remained tied.

President Roosevelt became so excited when Navy tied the score, he forgot all about his Secret Service and police protection, leaped the rail separating the stands from the playing field, and with a wild Indian yell ran to the Navy bench and shook hands with the players.

But not even President Roosevelt could steal the spotlight that day from Charlie Daly, who played like a man possessed. He was all over the field, tackling the Navy runners, blocking for his teammates, carrying the ball for huge gains.

To open the second half, Daly caught the kickoff on his 5-yard line, avoided three Navy tacklers, veered past two more, then cut for the sidelines, his blockers opening huge holes ahead of him. Harry Nelly, a substitute halfback, threw the key block for Daly, knocking down Navy's last two would-be tacklers, and Daly was out in the clear, running for glory.

As Daly ended his run behind the Navy goal line, his Army teammates lifted him off the ground and hugged him while the huge crowd went berserk with excitement. Daly's touchdown run was the longest in Army-Navy history. It covered 105 yards, the full length of the field at that time.

That afternoon at Franklin Field, Philadelphia, Charlie Daly was at his dazzling best as Army defeated Navy 11-5. Not only was Daly's run the winning margin, together with his successful conversion, but Daly scored all 11 of Army's points.

At the end of the game, President Roosevelt shook hands with Army Colonel Albert L. Mills.

"Extend my congratulations to your team," he said, "and particularly to Daly. And please tell Daly I said this was a great day for the Irish."

"Anchors Aweigh": 1902-7

The outlook for Navy's football prospects in 1902 did not seem very promising, despite the fact that a number of experienced players from the 1901 season had returned.

Navy's coach, former Princetonian Doc Hillebrand, had installed the "Princeton System of football" at Annapolis, but it did not work nearly as well as expected, and as a result the Middies went through a horrible season, winning only three games before meeting Army.

Yet Hillebrand had drilled his team thoroughly, pointing them to beat Army, and he felt that he had the team in fine fettle for the big game.

A cheering crowd of more than 25,000 spectators jammed every inch of Franklin Field, despite a cold, soggy wet day. The field lay uncovered, with large mud puddles in midfield, but the crowd had come to see the great Charlie Daly perform and didn't seem to mind the weather.

So they were hardly prepared for a remarkable performance by Navy halfback Ralph Strassburger. Ralph completely captivated the crowd as he broke away for a brilliant 62-yard dash, slipping by Daly, the last Army player, with a beautiful display of broken-field running to score Navy's only touchdown. Strassburger also spilled Daly in the end zone for a safety to keep Navy in the game at halftime.

Navy did seem to have the upper hand over the heavier, more experienced Army team during the first half, even though Army took a 10-8 lead after Army's great star Paul Bunker, who shifted from tackle to fullback before the game, scored the first Army touchdown, and Daly scored the second.

Army's greater physical advantage took its toll in the second half. No less than seven Middies were injured and had to be carried from the field as Army pounded Navy for two more touchdowns. Horatio Hackett scored in the third period and then Paul Bunker, the only player to make Grantland Rice's All-American team in two successive years at different positions, scored his second touchdown of the day, and Army had a crushing 22-8 victory.

Years later, during World War II, Strassburger met Bunker in the Philippines.

"Bunker," he said, "I hate you. Let's have a drink."

Another member of that victorious Army team in 1902 also in the Philippines at the same time was the manager of the Army football eleven. He was also the top-ranked Cadet at West Point. His name: Douglas MacArthur.

— ★ —

Captain Charles Belknap of the 1902 Navy eleven was an outstanding guard for three years.

Early in the 1903 season, Navy officials suggested to Army that only those Cadets and Middies who had not played more than four years of football should be eligible for the service game. That would include any years they might have played at another college before being appointed to either of the academies.

Army replied by pointing out that Navy had twice the enrollment that Army had, but the Middies came right back by claiming that size of enrollment could in no way neutralize such experienced stars as Daly, who had played three years at Harvard; Pot Graves, with his three years at North Carolina; Ken Boyers, in his sixth year of football at West Point; and Captain Ed Farnsworth, who would be facing Navy for the fifth time.

Finally, realizing that he was the main cause of this furor over eligibility, Charlie Daly resigned from the football team and joined Army's coaching staff.

But Daly's retirement did not affect Army's play, for they ran roughshod over a poorly coached Navy team by the biggest score of the series, 40–5.

In the first half, Army jolted the Middies for two touchdowns and a safety, while Navy scored its only touchdown. Still, as the half ended with Army in front of a fighting Middie team by a 12–5 score, it was not yet a runaway.

In the second half, however, Fred Prince scored three times and Ray Hill scored two touchdowns as Army's superior manpower just ground down the Middies in a battle that saw two Navy players, Charley Soule and Hank Chambers, carried from the field unconscious.

Navy's best runner that day was fullback Billy Halsey, and a number of times during the game he was knocked down and jolted by Army's right guard, Charlie Thompson.

More than forty years later the two men crossed paths in the South Pacific. Admiral William "Bull" Halsey was now the commander of U.S. Forces in the South Pacific. Thompson was a major general in the Army.

"General," said Halsey, "last time I saw you, you were pounding my backside all over Franklin Field."

Thompson grinned: "Admiral, how did I know that you were going to be commander in the South Pacific?"

Navy had one of their greatest seasons in 1904 as they ran up a string of four consecutive victories, including a 10–9 triumph over a mighty Princeton team, before losing a game to Swarthmore by a 9–0 margin. The Middies then came back to defeat Penn State, Virginia, and Virginia Poly before getting set for the annual service classic.

So this year, at long last, the Middies felt they had the Cadets' number. Certainly they had a marvelously coached team, as directed by Paul Dashiel, a former math professor who had developed a system of play that consisted of putting two or three backs out in front of the ball carrier in order to break up the wedge defenses utilized by most of the teams of the era.

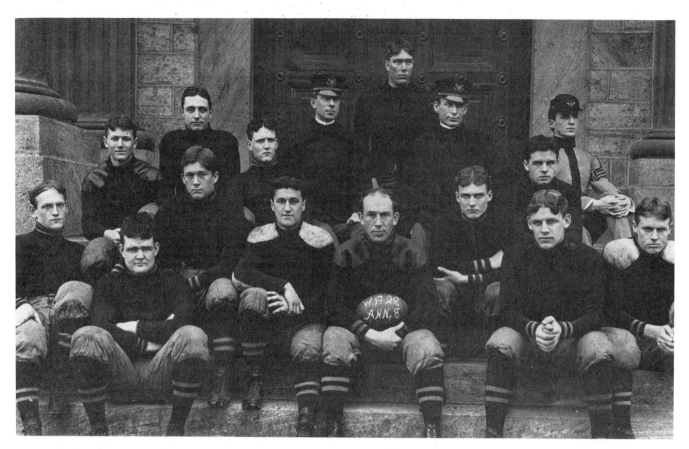

The 1903 U.S. Military Academy football team. Student manager Douglas MacArthur sits in Cadet uniform (upper right).

More than 26,000 spectators jammed old Franklin Field to witness the annual service classic, which saw an Army eleven jump out in front in the first five minutes of the game to take a hard-fought battle.

After the kickoff, Army failed to gain ground and they punted from the 35-yard line, and three Navy backs became confused over which one of them should take the ball. In the confusion, none of them caught the ball; instead it hit one of the players and Army's Art Tipton, tearing after the ball, kicked it toward the Navy goal. He kept on running, a step or two ahead of two Navy players, then he kicked the ball again, soccer style, until it was over the goal line. Then he fell on the ball for an Army touchdown.

Army scored again after a sustained drive, which Navy seemed incapable of halting. Then Jack Doherty, the Army halfback, broke loose

and sprinted 35 yards to the Navy 20-yard line. On the next play halfback Harry Torney hit the Navy line for a touchdown and it was 11–0.

There was no further scoring in the game, as both teams struggled through the second half without any team gaining an advantage, and Army had its fourth straight win over Navy, 11–0.

Navy's big end, Ken Whiting, starred in another "big game," in World War I. Whiting became the sixteenth Navy aviator following instructions from Orville Wright, and in 1917, Commander Whiting was awarded the Navy Cross for "exceptionally meritorious service commanding the first U.S. Air unit to reach France." In March 1942, Admiral John Wilcox, Navy's great quarterback on the 1904 team, was lost at sea in a naval battle in the Atlantic.

— ★ —

*Cadet Joseph W. Stilwell, a member of the 1904
Army team, who as Lieutenant General Vinegar Joe
Stilwell commanded the Chinese-British-U.S. forces
fighting in Burma in World War II.*

The New York Times reporter covering the 1905
Army-Navy classic called the game "one of the
most exciting ever played between these two
schools."

For some reason unknown today, the game
was shifted to Osborne Field in Princeton, New
Jersey.

President Theodore Roosevelt was the guest
of honor, sitting in a box next to the president
of Princeton University, Woodrow Wilson. Between halves, both dignitaries changed sides.

The game began in a drizzling rain as Army
got off quickly to roll up a series of first downs
on running plays. But every first down had to
be measured, as the Middies fought back and
battled every inch of the way. Halfback Harry
Torney finally broke through left tackle from
the Navy 7-yard line and scored for Army.
Verne Rockwell kicked the extra point, and it
was Army 6, Navy 0.

Navy scored in the second half as the result
of two successive penalties against Army, for
tripping and for holding. The penalties cost
Army 30 yards and brought Navy to the Army
25-yard line. Following a series of line smashes,
halfback Arch Douglas pounded in for the
touchdown, Homer Norton added the extra
point, and it was 6–6.

The game ended with that score. It also
ended on a sour note—ten minutes before
the official time was up. Poor handling by the
Princeton officials had delayed the start of the
game, and its last minutes had to be played in
semidarkness. Army not only charged the officials with incompetence for the delay and for
allowing the game to go on as long as they did,
but also for penalizing the Army team 100
yards, while Navy was penalized only 10 yards.

— ★ —

In 1906 President Theodore Roosevelt called in the football representatives of Army, Navy, Yale, Harvard, and Princeton and told them they had to remove such hazardous plays as "the wedge," which had led to serious injuries to more than 105 players during the 1903–6 seasons. In 1905, eighteen players died as a result of football injuries. From this meeting at the White House, a football rules committee was formed, called the Intercollegiate Athletic Association. Several years later the name was changed to the National Collegiate Athletic Association.

The IAA changed a number of rules in the game in 1906. These included the legalization of the forward pass, reducing the halves to thirty minutes, and increasing first-down yardage to 10 yards. The new rules established in 1906 saved the life of intercollegiate football and paved the way for a safer, more interesting, open style of play that added tremendous excitement to the game.

At the Naval Academy the new rules were especially welcomed, but Coach Paul Dashiel had lost half of his 1906 starting lineup, the team that had given Army such a stiff battle in 1905, and he faced the new season with much trepidation.

Captain Doug Howard, Navy's outstanding end for four years, had graduated; so had center Al Rees, quarterback Walt Decker, halfbacks Steve Doherty and Kirby Smith, and fullback Bob Ghormley.

Taking advantage of the new rules, the Middies adopted a "more open" style of play, including the use of the forward pass, and as a result had one of their best seasons, defeating some of the strongest teams in the East, including Penn State, Maryland, Lehigh, and winding up before the Army game with a record of 8 victories, 2 ties, and a 1-touchdown loss to a strong Princeton squad. But Army's record was almost as impressive; the Cadets had won 6 games, lost to Princeton, and tied Yale.

A crowd of more than 34,000 spectators welcomed the annual battle back to Franklin Field, Philadelphia, and roared as Navy's fullback Jonas Ingram took the opening kickoff and advanced the ball 10 yards before he was brought down.

Thereafter, both teams battled each other to a standoff, with neither gaining any clear advantage. The play during the entire first half was predominantly defensive, with both teams playing cautiously.

However, Navy came back in the second half like a ball of fire, and in a series of line smashes advanced to the Army 35-yard line. Two line plays failed to make any headway, and then Navy's great halfback, Percy Northcroft, dropped back to attempt a 44-yard field goal (worth four points at the time). Northcroft's kick was perfect—right through the crossbars—and Navy was out in front by a 4–0 score. Northcroft's kick was the longest in Army-Navy history.

Later in the game, after Navy had attempted three running plays without an appreciable gain, quarterback Homer Norton dropped back from midfield in kick formation as his fullback Ingram prepared to block for him. Norton took the pass from his center Frank Slingluff, and as he did so Ingram shot into the right flank completely out in the open, not an Army defender near him. Norton then tossed a beautiful arching pass to Ingram, who dashed 25 yards for the Navy touchdown to give the Middies a 10–0 victory. It was their first over the Cadets in six years.

Despite the fact that Navy had enjoyed three of its most successful football seasons from 1904 to 1906, including two straight victories over Army, Navy decided to release Paul Dashiel from his coaching duties. And for the 1907 season, Commander Joe Reeves, Navy's great tackle in 1893 (and inventor of the football headgear), was selected to be coach. Navy proceeded to win 10 games, including a stunning 6–0 victory over Army to close out the most victory-studded season in the Academy's football history.

Even though Navy had won more games than in any year in its history, Army was favored 3–1 to defeat the Tars. Army itself had won 6 games, tied a very strong Yale eleven, and lost but 1 game, to Cornell.

Admiral George Dewey, still a national hero for his amazing victory at the Battle of Manila Bay without the loss of a single sailor, was the honored guest, and both Navy and Army contingents honored the great Dewey.

Both teams played to a standstill for the greater part of the first half. Then Arch Douglas, the Navy captain, broke away on a fake kick and brought the ball from Navy's goal line to midfield, a gain of nearly 50 yards. Then Douglas kicked to the Army 25-yard line, where the Army defensive back fumbled the kick and Max Demott, Navy end, pounced on the ball. Ed Lange shot off tackle for 15 yards to the Army 10-yard line and the spectators screamed for a score. Ray Jones, the Navy halfback, picked up 2 yards; then Arch Douglas, on a delayed pass, cracked through the Army left tackle and scored the Navy touchdown. Ed Lange calmly kicked the extra point and it was 6–0 Navy. And that proved to be the final score after an evenly fought second half.

Between halves of the game the Naval Academy band serenaded President Roosevelt with a new, stirring song written for and adopted by the class of 1907 and first played at the June Week exercises some months before. The title: "Anchors Aweigh." There are many verses, but the one rendered most at Army-Navy games is this:

Left: *Herb Spencer was the fullback and captain of the 1906 Navy team that beat Army 10–0.* Center: *Tackle Percy Northcroft kicked an astonishing 48-yard field goal in that game.* Right: *Arch Douglas, an outstanding tackle on the 1906 team.*

Stand Navy down the field,
Sails set to the sky.
We'll never change our course, so
Army, you steer shy-y-y-y, and
Roll up the score, Navy,
Anchors aweigh,
Sail, Navy down the field and
Sink the Army, sink the Army gray.

Commander Robert Ghormley, fullback on the 1904 and 1905 teams, was awarded the Distinguished Service Medal for his efforts in helping transport two million men to France without the loss of a single man. In 1943, Vice Admiral Ghormley was awarded the Legion of Merit for his exceptional leadership in command of the naval forces in the South Pacific.

5

Changing the Rules: 1908-12

What follows is an eyewitness account of the 1908 game as recalled by Wally Philoon, captain and center of the Army team that year.

"In 1908, the 'experts' gave us no chance. Navy claimed the best team in its history. At West Point, 1908 graduation had almost cleaned us out. Red Pullen, a great tackle, handicapped by a bad knee, was about our only standout remaining. The squad was thin and light. We averaged 169 pounds against Navy. Our heaviest man, a guard, weighed 193, and our lightest, an end, 152. The pre-Navy season had been only fair with small scores by both West Point and its opponents.

"Our class had few good football players. Jake Devers, Robert Eichelberger, Harry Chamberlin, George Patton, Edwin Greble, and many others destined to play major parts in future wars were there, but only a few were varsity football material. However, 1909 did have something that usually brings results—fighting spirit, the will to win. And, of course, the corps followed such leadership.

"Head coach Harry 'Sheep' Nelly had the same fighting spirit. Capitalize on the breaks you get and avoid giving any to your opponents was the policy of the head field coach, Captain Joe Beacham. So, small scores were the result.

With no backfield stars, a light, green line—no wonder the experts passed us up.

"But in various games, although we messed things up, we did show a spirit that made us hard to beat. Yale, outweighing us twenty pounds per man, had been held to one touchdown made possible by a penalty. Princeton, sixteen pounds heavier per man, could not score even though they had had sixteen downs inside our 20-yard line. In another bumbling game our opponents finally scored in the closing minutes. This was the spark we needed. In six plays we had tied the score.

"We went to Philadelphia to battle Navy knowing we were the underdogs, but we knew also that we were not going to let the corps down. We were going to win. In the words of Sheep Nelly, every time we hit a Navy man we were going to give him something to put in his 'Lucky Bag,' the Navy yearbook. We were thoroughly keyed to Joe Beacham's slogan that we'd heard so often through his clenched teeth: 'Viciousness! Speed and fight will win! Viciousness!'

"The game in those days consisted of two thirty-five-minute halves—no quarters—and a player once taken out could not return. The forward pass was in its infancy—if incomplete,

Wallace Philoon, captain and center of the 1908 Army eleven, victor over Navy in a 6–4 thriller.

there was a 15-yard penalty. The *New York Sun* report of the game states 'The game was remarkable for the fact that the ball was punted almost incessantly.' Neither side could gain consistently by rushing. Scarcely three minutes after the kickoff our break came. Navy's star quarterback, Ed Lange, missed a punt, and Harry Chamberlain, our 156-pound fullback, taking the chance that our line and the other backs would give the kicker adequate protection, was on the spot to grab the ball and set

sail for the Navy goal. A desperate tackle stopped him on the 4-yard line. But in two plays halfback Bill Dean scored and then promptly kicked the goal. We had capitalized on a break. Now could we hold off powerful, confident Navy for another thirty minutes and then the long thirty-five-minute second half? Some fifteen minutes after our score Navy advanced to our 6-yard line. It was during those anxious minutes that 'Fight! Fight! Fight!' was born. As Navy forced us back, some Cadet began yelling: 'Fight! Fight! Fight!' Those around him at once took it up, and presently it swelled to a chant by the entire Corps.

"We on the playing field may not have been conscious of the words but we certainly knew the fighting spirit behind us. We knew that every cadet looked to us to make this 'Big Navy Day' an Army victory. We didn't let them down. The Middies were forced to try for a field goal. It was successful but we still led—6–4. The first half was scarcely half over. Could we hold them off until that final whistle?

"Well, we did. Navy never got a real break or again seriously threatened. Again quoting the *New York Sun:* 'The Army eleven showed a vast improvement over its previous games this fall and never lost a trick. The rush line was on tiptoe at all times, breaking through quickly and blocking with remarkable strength. The backfield worked like a piece of well-oiled machinery and during the second half did so much effective battering that the Annapolis eleven was literally cut to pieces, so that before the game ended Navy had six substitutes in the lineup.'

"We made three substitutions, one to strengthen a position and two near the close of the game due to the absolute exhaustion of a 179-pound tackle and a 152-pound end.

"A large part of the corps missed their train back to West Point because they insisted on escorting their team back to the hotel. But a new special was promptly arranged for them and a sympathetic supe forgave them their breach of discipline.

"A sore but happy squad was drawn up the hill on Sunday afternoon by a jubilant corps;

1908 had seen a victory over Navy. The corps and its team had certainly put a bitter pill in the Navy's 'Lucky Bag.' The Navy song, 'It Looks to Me Like a Big Navy Day,' had boomeranged. 'Fight! Fight! Fight!' had done the trick."

The number of serious injuries in college football continued to be high in 1907 and 1908, and authorities in a number of schools were talking about again altering the rules of the game.

Early in September 1909, Navy was playing a very rugged Villanova team and their fullback broke away and seemed headed for a touchdown. Earl Wilson, the Navy safetyman, was the only Navy player who could possibly stop the Villanova back. Wilson drove at him in a flying tackle. He missed hitting the runner around the hips and instead got him about the ankles, was kicked in the head and knocked unconscious. Shortly after he was taken to the hospital, it was reported that Wilson had a broken neck. Six weeks later Earl Wilson died.

A similar tragedy marred Army's season.

On October 30, Harvard came up to West Point to play Army for the first time since 1906. Under the coaching of Percy Haughton, the Harvard team stressed power football, massing all of their players at one point in the line to advance the ball.

Harvard took a 9–0 lead in the second half and the next time they got the ball launched another power-crunching drive into the line. Army's right tackle, Eugene Byrne, a fiery, driving player, had already taken a great deal of punishment, and now he dove headlong into the mass of players to stop a play.

The referee blew his whistle to end the play, and the charging players slowly untangled. But Gene Byrne did not get up. He lay quietly on the ground. The players looked at him, murmuring quietly. Byrne opened his eyes for a moment.

"I can't move," he spoke softly.

Then he lapsed back into unconsciousness.

Captain John Hammer, a surgeon on the Academy staff, came out on the field to examine Byrne and ordered a stretcher. The player was carried carefully to the Post hospital.

Shortly after reveille the next morning, Eugene Byrne died.

His death stunned and saddened the Cadets. There were only 396 at the Academy then. Everybody knew everybody else. The death hit each Cadet personally.

The remaining games on the Army schedule were canceled, including the traditional game with Navy.

The Midshipmen of the Naval Academy sent an anchor of four dozen white lilies and their love to Byrne's parents.

Byrne's death was the fourteenth in football in 1909, and the National Rules Committee set to work shortly after that terrible season to develop new rules and safety standards for the game.

The new rules adopted in 1910 included:

When a player's knee or elbow hit the ground the play was over. He could not advance beyond that point.

Once down on the turf, a player was not permitted to crawl forward to gain additional yardage. This prohibited players from piling on the fallen player.

The ball was downed when the forward motion of the ball carrier was stopped.

The 15-yard penalty for incompleted forward passes was eliminated. Forward passes were now allowed from any point behind the line of scrimmage.

A field goal was reduced from 4 points to 3.

The football field, which had been marked off like a checkerboard to check on forward passes, now returned to the appearance of a gridiron.

The halves were split into quarters, with a one-minute intermission between the quarters.

The new rule changes may or may not have helped Lieutenant Frank Berrien in 1910, for after two years as Navy's football coach Berrien had developed one of the greatest teams in Navy football history, virtually destined to have a great season. And it did. Navy's 1910 players swept through a rugged nine-game schedule, undefeated and unscored on.

In putting together this remarkable unit, Coach Berrien had worked with a number of plebe stars who would make football history in 1910, and who years later would go on to make an even greater contribution to their nation.

There was the 200-pound Babe Brown, a tackle who played without a helmet and was known to tear into opponents with a frenzy that had them terrorized even before the game began. In World War II, Babe Brown received a number of the nation's highest military awards for his heroic efforts commanding a group of the "fightingest toughest Submarines in the Navy."

Then there was Richard Byrd, a fine end with great hands who helped Navy win all nine of its football games in 1910. Commander Richard E. Byrd would be the first man to fly over the North Pole and the second man to fly the Atlantic single-handed; he also commanded several Antarctic expeditions.

Last, but not least, there was Jack Dalton, one of the great triple-threat players of early football. Three-to-Nothing Dalton they would call him after 1911 for his magnificent all-around play; he could run and he could pass, and his kicking won against Army in two successive years. Experts of that day compare Dalton's gridiron exploits with those of Jim Thorpe, the immortal Carlisle Indian star.

Dalton's incredible punting, his uncanny ability to dash through openings for long runs, his great forward passing—all combined to bring a Navy victory over Army in 1910. It was a performance that sports experts declared the "finest football exhibition" seen on any gridiron in 1910.

As the game began, the Navy line, charging as a unit, opened great holes through which Dalton slashed through for sizable gains, alternating his line bucks with flashy sprints around the Army ends.

Having reached the Army 35-yard line, Dalton called for a field goal, his seventh attempt

of the day. This time the play worked like a charm. Bob Weems, the Navy center, spiraled the ball to the kneeling holder, Ingram Sowell, and Dalton took three quick steps before slamming into the ball for a perfect field goal. And a 3–0 victory for Navy.

Outside of Dalton's marvelous play there was very little to choose between the two teams. But Dalton's punting and field-goal kicking were in themselves so vastly superior to the abilities of either Bob Hyatt or Doug Keyes of Army as to end any comparison between the teams.

A crowd of more than 30,000 spectators was on hand for the game, among them many high-ranking Army and Navy officers. General George Von Meyer was an early arrival and sat in a special box. He was greeted with a great cheer from the Army Cadets and was obliged to doff his cap a number of times in response.

A few minutes after the general and his staff had seated themselves, Mr. Jacob Dickinson, the secretary of war, appeared, walked across to the Army stands, and was cheered to the skies by the Cadets and the Brigade of Midshipmen as well as the Army side. As a special salute, the Middies tossed their white hats into the air. Then a regular procession of generals, admirals, commanders, and lesser officers of the Army and Navy filed into their seats.

Promptly at one o'clock the Corps of Cadets marched out of their seats to one end of the stadium and joined with the Army band. Then as the band began to play, the Cadets briskly and in perfect formation marched to the other end of the stadium, then stepped back into their seats. Then the Middies, seemingly more than three times the number, took their turn onto the field and briskly marched to the Navy band. As the Middies passed the Army grandstand, the rear guard stopped and led out the Navy goat, covered with a blue Navy blanket that said, BEAT ARMY. The Cadets booed the goat while the rest of the spectators cheered both teams.

There was no Army mule to answer the challenge of Navy's goat this year, the animal having passed away a few weeks earlier. It

Top, left: *Dick Byrd was an outstanding end on the 1911 Navy football team. In 1926, as Admiral Richard E. Byrd, he became the first man to fly over the North Pole. Above: Byrd about to depart for the South Pole from the Ross Island hut left by the 1901–4 Scott expedition. Left: In 1945, Admiral Byrd received the Legion of Merit from President Franklin D. Roosevelt for "outstanding service to the nation."*

Three-to-Nothing Jack Dalton, whose field goals gave the Middies 3–0 victories in 1910 and 1911. Dalton could run, pass, and kick, and his exploits in baseball, basketball, track, and swimming in addition to football made him one of the greatest all-around athletes ever to compete for the Navy.

would seem he was sorely missed on that great day for Navy.

After three successful seasons as Navy's head coach, Lieutenant Frank Berrien was ordered to sea duty in 1911, and Doug Howard was named to replace him.

Howard had been a star end and captain of the 1905 Navy football team and had led his team to its finest record up to that time: 10 victories and only 1 loss, to Swarthmore by a single point.

Howard's first Navy eleven swept to an undefeated season, Navy's second in a row, and then in the biggest game of them all the Middies defeated Army 3–0 in a no-holds-rock-'em-sock-'em game that had the large crowd standing and cheering throughout the entire final quarter.

The 3–0 Navy victory, its second in succession over Army by the same score, was the Navy game of the decade.

The victory was achieved once more by Three-to-Nothing Jack Dalton, the great Navy fullback and captain, who kicked a 30-yard field goal in the second period.

Army dominated the first half of the game, and only Dalton's marvelous punting kept the Cadets from scoring. One of his punts registered 72 yards, while several others went for 55 and 65 yards, always just as Army was in position for a serious offensive move.

In the second period Navy began the lone scoring drive of the game from their 30-yard line. Fullback Monty Nicholls drove off tackle for 8 yards, then Dalton, running wide, cut in sharply off tackle and picked up 10 more yards for a first down. On the next play Dalton skirted his right end for 25 yards, bringing the ball to the Army 23.

Two linebacks failed to gain any ground and on third down, Dalton dropped back and with K. P. Gilchrist holding, kicked a 30-yard field goal to give Navy a 3–0 lead, which they held onto for the rest of the game.

Navy played a conservative game after Dalton's field goal, concentrating on their running game, making certain that their backs held onto the ball when tackled.

In the third period, Jeff Keyes, Army's fullback, missed a 30-yard field goal, and thereafter, Jack Dalton's tremendous punts kept the Army deep in its own territory.

Like Army's mule in 1910, Navy's mascot goat died a few days before the 1911 Army-Navy game. It was embalmed and stuffed after the end of that season, and currently resides as an athletic memento of that great victory, in the huge Navy field house. Its name: Three-to-Nothing Jack Dalton.

In 1912 New Mexico became the forty-seventh state admitted to the Union. . . . U.S. troops began the occupation of Tientsin, China, for the protection of American interests. . . . The steamship *Titanic* struck an iceberg on April 14 and sank. More than 1,500 persons were lost at sea. . . . The National Convention of the Democratic party met at Baltimore and nominated Woodrow Wilson for the presidency. . . . Tom Marshall of Indiana was selected by Wilson as his VP. . . . On October 14, Theodore Roosevelt was shot by one John Schrank during Roosevelt's campaign tour. The bullet struck a bulky manuscript and entered Roosevelt's chest. However, he insisted on delivering his speech before being taken to the hospital. . . . Andrew Carnegie established the Carnegie Corporation foundation with an initial endowment of $125 million. This was the first of the great charitable foundations. . . . In sports, the great Native American star, Jim Thorpe, won both the decathlon and pentathlon at the 1912 Olympics in Stockholm . . . and Navy prepared to face Army without their great star Jack Dalton.

Army's football team had not scored on Navy since the second half of the 1909 game and was determined to hand the Middies a "surprise." With the relief of Jack Dalton's graduation, the Cadets had been developing a few trick plays for Navy.

In 1912 there were a number of additional important rule changes. The field was altered to provide a 10-yard zone at either end of the field in which a forward pass might be legally caught. The kickoff was moved back to the 40-yard line, and after a touchback, the ball was put in play from the 20-yard line instead of the 25. Touchdowns were increased from 5 to 6 points.

However these changes may have improved the game in 1912, nothing Army did on the field against Navy seemed to be an improvement over 1910 and 1911. Navy continued to enjoy the advantage Jack Dalton had given them due to the development of another marvelous field-goal kicker in Babe Brown, an advantage that would again determine the outcome of the contest.

At the opening kickoff, Army drove upfield and seemed to be on the way to an early score, but the Navy defense stiffened and held at their 25-yard line. Jeff Keyes, Army's fine fullback, then dropped back to attempt a field goal, but the kick was short by a few inches.

In the third period, Babe Brown, Navy's great guard, dropped back and tried a field goal from the Army 35-yard line, but missed. Again in the fourth period, Brown attempted another field goal, this time from Army's 40-yard line, but again it was short.

With about five minutes remaining in the game, Brown dropped back for yet another field-goal attempt. But this time the ball was snapped to Brown instead of his holder, Gilchrist, and instead of kicking the ball, Brown took off to his right and sped past several Army tacklers, who seemed stunned at Brown's daring to run the ball. But on the 5-yard line, just as it appeared that Babe would cross the goal line, he was tackled from behind and brought down.

Two running plays failed to gain ground, and then Brown, with Gilchrist holding, kicked a field goal from the 12-yard line to give Navy a 3–0 lead.

Army tried every trick play in their repertoire to score a touchdown, but could get only to the Navy 25-yard line. Here Army fumbled the ball and Navy recovered.

Navy then marched up the field and once

Left: *John "Babe" Brown, a hard-nosed guard for Navy, drop-kicked a 35-yard field goal to beat the Army, 6–0, in 1912. The next year he outdid that feat by kicking three field goals in the Middies' 22–9 loss to the Cadets. In World War I, Commander Brown led numerous raids on German shipping, for which he received several decorations.* Right: *Then, in World War II, Admiral Brown led a submarine group that sank more Japanese ships than any other in the Pacific.*

more Babe Brown dropped back to the 35-yard line. This time he booted the ball straight through the crossbars for another 3-pointer, and Navy had again beaten Army, 6–0. It was the third straight Navy shutout over their bitter rival.

In 1942, Captain Homer Grosskopf, an outstanding end on that 1912 Navy eleven, was posthumously awarded the Presidential Unit Citation for heroic action as executive officer of the USS *Houston*, lost at sea on February 8 fighting against overwhelming odds.

In 1944, Vice Admiral John Hall was awarded the Legion of Merit and gold-star-in-lieu for heroic leadership as Navy task force commander during the invasion of Italy. Hall was another fine end on the 1912 Middies.

Charlie Daly Returns to Coach: 1913-14

Since leaving West Point in 1907, the great Charlie Daly, Army's All-American star in 1900 and 1901, had been backfield coach at Harvard and had helped turn out some of the Crimson's fine football teams. But after Army had suffered their third consecutive shutout at the hands of Navy, they called on Daly for help and Charlie was delighted to return to West Point.

Nineteen thirteen was the year that a little-known midwestern team from South Bend, Indiana, was first invited to West Point to play Army. Notre Dame was led by a marvelous end, Knute Rockne, and by a smart, fiery quarterback named Charles Dorais. Dorais and Rockne had perfected a little-known play that Rockne called "the buttonhook." The play called for Rockne to speed downfield, then slow down and cut back toward his quarterback just as the ball was thrown to him at a certain point on the field. Rockne and Dorais had practiced the play all summer long as the latest wrinkle in a passing game that had helped the Irish run up a string of twenty consecutive victories in the past two seasons.

Army also had a fine passing quarterback in Vern Prichard, a 158-pound star who played sixty minutes in every game Army played during his three varsity years. Prichard had estab-lished an outstanding reputation as a forward passer at Morningside College in Iowa prior to his coming to West Point, and as a plebe he had driven the Army varsity crazy with his forward passing. His favorite receiver at Army was his left end, Lou Merillat, a savage tackler and an end with a pair of uncanny hands.

But under Coach Daly, Army utilized the forward pass only as a desperation play, usually in the final quarter of a game that was lost.

But after Notre Dame's Dorais-to-Rockne combination rolled up a 35–13 upset victory over the Cadets by completing twelve consecutive forward passes and scoring five touchdowns, the Army board of strategy completely altered their offense to include several pass plays for the big game against Navy.

The 1913 Army-Navy game was held at the famous Polo Grounds in New York before President Woodrow Wilson and a number of high cabinet officials. A crowd of more than 45,000 spectators was attracted to a game that favored Navy as a 7–1 favorite to defeat Army.

The Middies had been tied by Pitt in the opening game of the season, but then went on to defeat every opponent on their schedule. With such stars as Babe Brown, Homer Ingram, K. P. Gilchrist, Harvey Overesch, Pete Rodes, Johnny Bates, and Bill Alexander, Navy was expected to have little trouble against a team that had lost to the unknown Notre Dame squad.

The game opened with Army kicking off to Navy and an alert Middie tackle advancing the ball 10 yards to the Navy 30-yard line. From there the Middies began their drive. Johnny Bates and Bill Alexander, two bull-shouldered powerful runners, cracked through Army's line for successive first downs, then continued to pound the Army guards and tackles for additional gains until they had smashed to the Army 20-yard line.

Here the tough, stubborn Army defense held off three running plays, refusing to give an inch of ground.

★ ★ ★

Letter from John P. Markoe

John Markoe entered West Point in 1910 and without previous experience made the football team as the regular end. In 1912 and 1913, his teammates included such Army players as Dwight Eisenhower, Leland Hobbs, Vern Prichard, Tommy Doe, Captain Benny Hoge, Lou Merillat, and Babe Weyand. Father John Markoe, the former football star, was at Creighton University from 1946 to 1967. He passed away several years ago.

I entered West Point in March 1910 and during my plebe year did not turn out for the football squad or team as I never played high-school or college football. But as there were only about six hundred cadets in the Corps at that time I was persuaded by upper classmen to try for the squad. This I did during the football season of 1911, trying for a place in the backfield. After the season was over a member of the Class of 1912, Gilbert Cook, told me I was no backfield man but should try for end. This I did and immediately things began to click. I not only made the squad but left end on the first team in 1912.

The season of 1913 (my last) was my best; I was first-string left end. Merillat (All-American on the Walter Camp team) was right end, Benny Hoge, a right end, was captain, John McEwan was at center, also a Walter Camp All-American. Omar Bradley (now a five-star general) was a linesman, etc.

Now comes the first Army–Notre Dame game in 1913. It was supposed to be a practice, warm-up game for the Army-Navy game to be played at the Polo Grounds, New York, a few weeks hence. I was to be starting left end in this game and sportswriters, in announcing the lineup, had me as left end. But, in scrimmage a few days before this historic game, I injured my back so Harry Tuttle, the trainer, pulled me out and Jack Jouett played left end. As a consolation prize I was made head linesman and thus watched the game from the sidelines. But for many years after I was mentioned in sports write-ups as having played left end in this game. This is one of the inaccuracies that still persists. I get tired explaining it so let it go.

Notre Dame opened the eyes of Charlie Daly, head coach, to the possibilities of the forward pass and began drilling us in the same. Two weeks later the Army team beat Navy on the Polo Grounds, New York, 22–9, mainly by using the forward pass. I played left end in this game.

This was the first victory and only victory of Army over Navy during my career as a cadet. Dalton of the Navy defeated Army in 1910, 1911, 1912 by his ability to kick field goals.

On fourth down, Navy's great kicking star Babe Brown dropped back to the 30-yard line and kicked a perfect field goal to give Navy a 3–0 lead.

Now the Cadets began to move. After receiving Navy's kickoff, John Jouett, Lou Merillat, and Vern Prichard punched their way to a series of first downs. Then Prichard surprised the Middies by faking a run and stopping dead in his tracks to hurl a perfect pass to Merillat out in the open. But with nobody near him Lou dropped the ball. Army then kicked to Navy, and a Middie halfback returned Lou's favor by fumbling on the Navy 3-yard line, where Army recovered the ball.

An aggressive Navy line led by Babe Brown

★ ★ ★

In this 1913 victory of Army over Navy, I made the tackle after Army kicked off. As I still lay on the ground, a Navy man fell hard on my left knee, badly spraining it. Time was taken out during which I cautioned Prichard, the quarterback, against throwing passes to me. He did, however, and somehow I managed to catch a few but could not run after the catch.

Between halves, Harry Tuttle (former trainer for the Detroit Tigers) taped up my knee, gave me a glass of whiskey, and sent me into the second half. How I made it, I don't know, but I played the full game. But as soon as I stopped using my knee, it began to swell like a balloon and I was hospitalized for several weeks after returning to West Point. Merillat, right end in this game, made All-American (Walter Camp) that year, 1913.

Now here comes another thing I would like to get straight. In sports articles, the remarks of others down through the years, etc., I have been referred to as an All-American left end. Here is the straight dope on this.

Never have I referred to myself as an All-American nor have I ever claimed to be one. But at the time I was playing football on the Army team, Walter Camp was the one recognized authority for picking All-American teams and during my four years at the Academy he began to lose his grip. His teams were picked almost invariably from Harvard, Yale, and Princeton. They had a monopoly. Things began to change. Coaches began to pick their own All-American teams. *Colliers Weekly* had its own. Other publications got into the game and finally, Walter Camp died.

During this time of transition Walter Camp gave me an honorable mention in 1912. In 1913 some sportswriters referred to me as an All-American. I have read this in a book on football, have been introduced to audiences many times as a former All-American Army left end, etc., etc. It is hard to stop a rumor once it gets going.

Years ago, in the *New York Herald*, I believe, Dick Vidmer, a kid at West Point when I was playing, wrote a column headed: "What Happened to the Other End?" In it he described my career as a cadet and then my hectic career as a second lieutenant in the old 10th U.S. Cavalry stationed at Ft. Huachuca, Ariz., with all our duty along the Mexican Border (1914–15), and, later as a Capt. of Co. F, 2nd Minn. Inf. along the Texas Border (1916–17) and ended by stating that I had joined the Jesuits to study for the Priesthood. This may be the best way to end this report. I am still a member of the Jesuit Order, past seventy-five years in age . . .

I have enjoyed writing the above and hope I have not unduly burdened you in the reading of it.

Sincerely,

(Rev.) John P. Markoe, S.J.

★ ★ ★

Letter from Dwight D. Eisenhower

Dwight D. Eisenhower made the Army team in 1912, his second year at the Point. Unfortunately, his football career was cut short before that season was over by a serious leg injury received during a game. He later coached the Cullum Hall squad, watched the varsity games from the bench, and never lost his love and respect for the game. Even during his brilliant military career, football had a special meaning. Here he talks about his gridiron experiences.

During my first year as a plebe (at that time plebes were eligible for the varsity team) I weighed something on the order of 155 pounds. However, I was big-boned and was strong and had average speed. I was a member of Cullum Hall Squad, which was comparable to a junior varsity at other schools. I showed up fairly well in the games we played and two or three times during the season was moved intermittently to the varsity squad, but, within two or three days, would be sent back as "too light." In high school I had played at end and tackle but was converted by the picturesque Cullum Hall Coach, Toby Zell, to a backfield position. At the season's end I was still a Cullum Hall player.

During the succeeding year I worked hard at running (particularly at starting) and indulged in every kind of gymnastic exercise that would strengthen leg and arm muscles. As a consequence I started the season of 1912 weighing about 174 and participated in West Point's first practice game, against a soldier team. In the latter half of the game, partially by good luck and partly by burning desire, I showed up quite well and for the first time attracted some attention from the varsity coaches, then headed by Captain Ernest Graves.

After completing several postgame laps around the field, I trotted toward the gymnasium, overtaking and passing the coaching group. I was some fifteen or twenty yards beyond it when Captain Graves called sharply, "Eisenhower!" I stopped, ran back, and saluted and, of course, said, "Yes, sir." He looked at me and asked, "Where did you get those pants?" They were hanging around my ankles. I replied, "From the manager." He said, "Look at those shoes—can't you get anything better than that?" Again I said, "I am just wearing what I was issued." It happened that the cadet manager, named Perkins, was in the group with Captain Graves, and the latter turned to Perkins to say, "Get this man completely outfitted with new and properly fitting equipment." He went on to say a couple of other things but actually I scarcely heard him; I was walking on air, because this was my first intimation that I would probably become a member of the varsity squad.

One amusing incident: While, at 174 pounds, I was fairly light for line plunging and line backing I so loved the fierce bodily contact of football that I suppose my enthusiasm made up somewhat for my lack of size. In any event, always playing as hard as I knew how, in one game an opposing player made a protest. He turned to the referee who was standing close by my side and said, "Watch that man!" The referee with some astonishment said, "Why, has he slugged you or roughed you up in any way?" The man, who was probably green and overexcited said, "NO! But he is going to!" I think this was the oddest thing that happened to me on a football field.

During the following season [after Ike's injury] the new head coach, Captain Charlie Daly of Harvard and West Point, asked me to take over the active coaching of the Cullum Hall Squad. As such I was invited to sit on the bench at varsity games.

(Continued)

Left and Below: *Ike at West Point. Described in the 1915* Howitzer, *the West Point yearbook, as "the most promising back in Eastern football," Dwight David Eisenhower broke his knee in 1912 in his sophomore year in the game against Tufts, ending a gridiron career that seemed destined for All-American honors. In the group photograph, taken with members of the 1913 Army team, Ike is fourth from the left; the youngster squeezing into the picture on the right is Richard Vidmer, son of the post adjutant, Captain George Vidmer, who will become one of America's premier sportswriters for the* New York Herald Tribune.

did not yield an inch of ground, and on fourth down Roscoe Woodruff kicked a field goal to tie the score at 3–3.

Later in the period an Army fumble gave the Middies another scoring opportunity, and once more the indomitable Babe Brown kicked another field goal to give Navy a 6–3 lead.

Just before the end of the half, Lou Merillat caught a magnificent pass from Prichard and dashed 15 yards for an Army touchdown to give the Cadets a 9–6 lead. But John McEwan missed the extra point.

In the third period Monty Nicholls, Navy's fullback, picked up 25 yards on three successive running plays that brought the ball to the Army 10-yard line. Here the Cadet line stiffened and once again, for the third time, Babe Brown kicked a field goal. The game was tied at 9–9.

Then, taking the kickoff, Lou Merillat, with a surprising burst of speed, shot through the entire Navy defense for 65 yards, only to be dragged down on the 5-yard line. It was the most spectacular play of the game and brought a roar from the Cadets. Halfback John Jouett then bucked across the goal line for the touchdown.

In the final period, Army uncorked a spectacular pass play, Jouett to Prichard, who then

---

★   ★   ★

The most thrilling game I ever saw was Army's victory over Navy in the fall of 1913. During the course of that season Army had taken on Notre Dame and ran into an unexpected reverse from the passing combination of Dorais and Rockne. They bewildered our defense. Sitting on the bench we got the full impact of the Notre Dame passing game, which, incidentally, featured what is now called the "option play."

Promptly after that game Daly changed some of his tactics and soon developed a fine passing combination of "Prichard to Merillat." Heavily favored Navy of course expected us to play traditional football but found themselves slightly behind at halftime. Nevertheless, such was the general confidence in their team's superiority that a Navy officer came over and visited a group of Cadets with whom I was sitting; my leg was in a plaster cast. He said he would like to bet even money on Navy. Among a dozen of us cadets we collected $65.00. He promptly took out an equal amount and left it with us saying, "If I win I will be back for the money and if you win, of course, keep it." We went on to win by 22 to 9. I think it was the first Army victory in something like four years and you can imagine the scene among Army cadets when we finally got back to West Point to rehash every play of the game.

One sequel to my football experience: thirty years after those days, I found myself in the midst of war. I had occasion, because of my position, to be on the constant lookout for natural leaders. I noted with great satisfaction how well ex-footballers seemed to fulfill leadership qualifications: among others, Bradley, Keyes, Patton, Simpson, Van Fleet, Harmon, Hobbs, Jouett, Patch, and Prichard, and many others, measured up. I cannot recall a single ex-footballer with whom I came in contact who failed to meet every requirement. Personally, I think this was more than coincidental. I believe that football, almost more than any other sport, tends to instill into men the feeling that victory comes through hard—almost slavish—work, team play, self-confidence, and an enthusiasm that amounts to dedication.

Sincerely,
Dwight D. Eisenhower

lateraled the ball to Merillat. Lou raced down-field for another Army touchdown, and the game ended with Army the winner, 22–9.

One of Charlie Daly's top assistants during the 1913 season was a former Army halfback who, in 1912, had been called "a leading candidate for All-American honors." Injured during the fifth game of that season against Tufts College, this hard-running halfback had to give up his position after starring for the Cadets, and spent the next year on the sidelines. He was Cadet Dwight D. Eisenhower.

Army's powerful and smooth-running football machine went undefeated in 1914, including a smashing 20–7 win over a great Notre Dame eleven. In this year's great service rivalry, the black, gold, and gray warriors from the banks of the Hudson hurled back and crushed the blue-and-gold players of Navy inside the historic and battle-scarred walls of Franklin Field. The gridiron superiority of the Cadets over the Midshipmen was even more marked than the 20–0 score would indicate.

Army came out of that fray victorious because it played better football. In every department save one—sheer gameness—the well-balanced Cadets smashed, hammered, and literally tore their way to a victory that would go down as one of their most decisive over the Middies. Before the kickoff, West Point was conceded to have the advantage. After five minutes into the game, that advantage was never in doubt.

Perhaps the dismal specter of World War I that had just broken out between Germany and Russia, France, and Great Britain spurred the promoters of the game to produce the most colorful atmosphere at the game. Whatever it might have been, Franklin Field had never known a more wonderful scene than it did that day. Everywhere the black, gold, and gray of West Point were flaunted. Thousands of pennants bannered NAVY or ARMY appeared on the stands, while along the sides of the gray-hued field, chrysanthemums of a rich gold were displayed in riotous profusion. Slowly but stead-

ily, the fortunate ticketholders streamed through the gates until, well after one o'clock, the real invasion of the holiday hosts—the march of Cadets and Midshipmen—began. As the turnstiles whirled and ushers guided men and women to boxes or less pretentious seats, the broad field speedily lost its amber aspect.

The setting of the scene once within the gates would never be forgotten by the 35,000 spectators. Every bit of available space was taken in both permanent and temporary stands. The competing colors of the two institutions seemed more prominent than ever before, and as supporters of the two services followed every cue of the academies' cheerleaders, the long oval-shaped stands surrounding the field were constantly aripple with the hues of West Point and Annapolis.

The din ceased for a moment when the great Army band struck up "The Star-Spangled Banner," to be replaced by 35,000 voices joining in song. Then, as the music reached its highest crescendo, pandemonium returned as the Middies and Cadets in the stands cheered and cheered until the very foundations of the stadium seemed to rock.

Secretary of War Lindley Garrison, surrounded by members of his staff, sat at the Army site of the 50-yard line, while high-ranking Navy officers, together with other distinguished Washingtonians and their families, were assembled on the other side of the field.

After the Army band's rendition of the National Anthem, the Navy band, not to be outdone, broke into "Tipperary," and the Middies still on the field did their famous two-step to the music as they mounted into the west stands while the entire Brigade of Midshipmen raised their voices in song:

It's a long way to Philadelphia
It's a long way to go.
We have come to beat the Army
With the best Navy team we know.

The music, songs, and cheering over, Army kicked off and the game began. From the very outset it was plain to see that Navy was outmatched this day, as they remained backed up in their own territory for much of the first period. The great Army line of All-American Johnny McEwan, Alexander Weyand, Ed Timberlake, Cowboy Meacham, Sandy Goodman, and Charles Herrick smothered the Middies running attack.

The final 20–0 score did not indicate the vast superiority of the undefeated Army eleven. Army might have added at least three more touchdowns had the Cadets not fumbled and lost the football three times within the Navy 10-yard line.

Army clearly had the superior firepower,

and once Vern Prichard, Merillat, Paul Hodgson, Jim Van Fleet, Omar Bradley, and Bob Neyland coordinated their passing attack with a slashing running attack, it was only a matter of how many points Army would score.

In the first period, Navy was deep in its own territory and was forced to kick on fourth down. Harry Blodgett, the Navy punter, had to leap high in the air to receive the pass from his center, Eddie Smith, and Lou Merillat came smashing in to block the attempted kick. Several players dove for the ball as it bounded into the end zone, and Blodgett finally flopped on it for a safety, giving Army its first two points.

Below: *Army's 1914 team, victorious over Navy 20–0, was led by Captain Vern Prichard (with ball). In the second row (third from left) is Omar Bradley, a tough tackle. Right: Army General Bradley in 1947.*

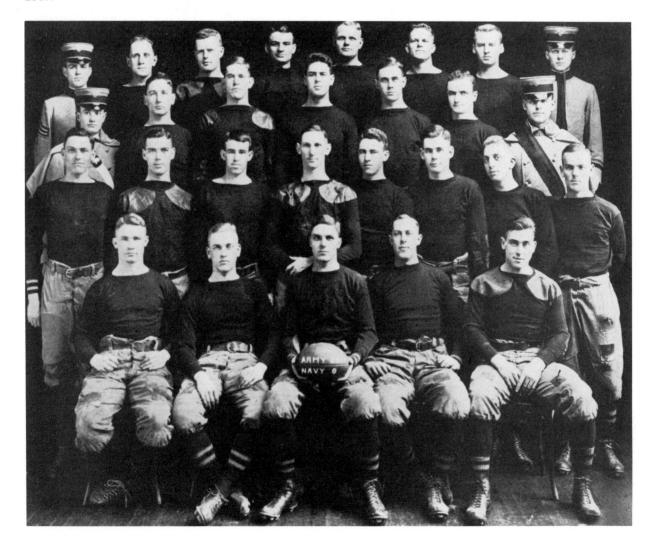

Blodgett's play was to become even more ig-nominiously prominent. In the second period the Middies could not make any headway through the Army line, and Blodgett kicked to Army. Army failed to gain after receiving the punt, and kicked right back to Blodgett, who fumbled once again, with Lou Merillat recov-ering for Army on the Navy 15-yard line.

On the very next play Vern Prichard faded back, fought off two Navy tacklers, and shot a perfect strike to Merillat, who romped across the goal line for the touchdown. The point af-ter touchdown was missed and the score stood, Army 8, Navy 0.

Once again Navy received the kickoff and tried to start upfield. But in three downs they could not advance the ball and punted. Army received the kick and punted right back to Blodgett, and poor Harry fumbled the ball for the third time. And again Merillat recovered for Army.

Two line plays by Army failed to gain, but on third down Prichard found Merillat with a bulletlike pass and Lou took the ball to the Navy 1-yard stripe. On the next play Paul Hodgson plowed through the line for another Army touchdown.

In the third period both teams resorted to another punting duel, hoping the other team would fumble the ball. As a result neither team fumbled and neither team scored.

In the final period, after another series of punts by both teams, Army started on its own 35-yard line and proceeded to move upfield.

Hodgson, Army's swiftest back and most consistent ground gainer, ran from a fake kick formation, turning and twisting his way for 35 yards and a first down. At this point, another pass, Prichard to Lou Merillat, brought the ball inside the 5-yard line. Van Fleet then picked up a tough yard, Hodgson added another, and finally fullback Charlie Bene-dict charged through tackle for Army's third touchdown.

Navy was simply being worn down by a big-ger, superior football machine. Both offensively and defensively Army was just too strong.

When Navy found they couldn't move on the ground, they attempted to mount a passing at-tack, but only two of their many passes were successful, and both came during the last few minutes of the game.

Army's 20–0 victory capped their first un-defeated season and assured their selection as national champion by the All-America Coaches Committee. And captain and center John McEwan was picked on the Walter Camp All-American team.

Several members of those 1914 Army and Navy football teams would make great contributions to their nation during World War II. Omar

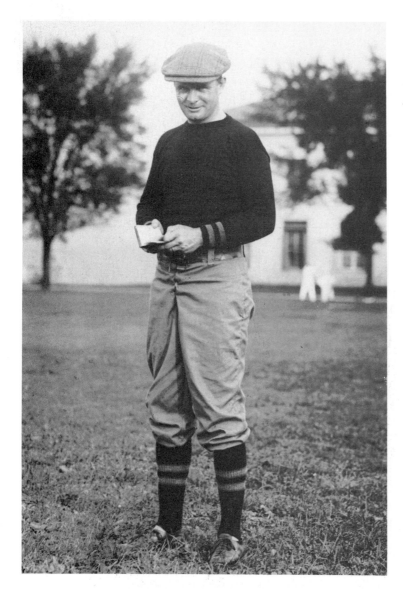

Major Charlie Daly, Army's three-time All-American, was West Point's head football coach in 1913–16 and 1919–22.

Bradley, a fiery tackle, commanded all U.S. forces in Europe; General Jim Van Fleet, a fine halfback, was in action in World War II and Korea; General Vern Prichard, a halfback, commanded two armored divisions under Bradley. And General Bob Neyland would go on to make a name for himself after World War II as one of the nation's great coaches at the University of Tennessee.

Navy football stars who also shone in World War II included quarterback Ralph Mitchell, a Marine Corps general who led the great air raids against the Japanese in Bougainville and Rabaul, and Captain Dick Bates, the team's fullback, whose own Pacific bombing raids helped recapture the Philippines in 1944. Bates was awarded the Navy Cross and the Legion of Merit.

The Oliphant Years: 1915-16

In 1915, the war in Europe became the major concern of America. On May 7, the steamship USS *Lusitania*, queen of the Cunard Company's fleet, was sunk without warning by a German submarine off the coast of Ireland. Of the 1,925 passengers aboard, 1,198 were drowned, 114 of them Americans. Indignation aroused by this act of war made American entry into the war against Germany inevitable, despite the Germans' reply that the sinking was justifiable since "the ship was armed with cannon and carried a cargo of munitions." . . . On July 21 President Wilson dispatched a third warning note to Germany saying that "any future violation of U.S. rights would be regarded as distinctly and deliberately unfriendly."

On September 21, the first transcontinental telephone call was made by the same two men who had made original telephone conversation in 1876: Alexander Graham Bell speaking from New York said to Dr. Tom Watson in San Francisco, "Mr. Watson, come here, I want you."

In sports, Ty Cobb of the Detroit Tigers set a new baseball record by stealing ninety-six bases. . . . Jess Willard won the heavyweight title by knocking out Jack Johnson in twenty-three rounds in Havana. . . . Driving a Stutz at 102 miles per hour, Gil Anderson set a new land speed record in winning the Astor Cup at Sheepshead Bay, New York. . . . And in baseball, the Boston Red Sox defeated the Philadelphia Phillies, 4 games to 1 to win the twelfth annual World Series.

At West Point, the Army football team greeted Elmer Q. Oliphant with open arms as he reported for football practice, for Oliphant had come to the Army as a plebe the year before with a sports background that defied description.

Elmer arrived at West Point from Purdue University, where he starred in football, basketball, baseball, track, wrestling; he was also the heavyweight boxing champ of the school. As football players go, Elmer was an odd-looking young man—only 5 feet 7, no neck of any sort, and weighing 178 pounds. But he was as light and fast on his feet as a ballet dancer, and with a pair of legs as thick as steampipes, it was almost impossible to tackle him. When Oliphant took the field against the Middies, every eye was on Elmer the Great, for he had starred in every phase of every game that season. When Oliphant failed to score a touchdown, he kicked 45-yard field goals. In the Georgetown game he scored all 17 points as Army won 17–0.

The 1915 Army-Navy game returned to the

Polo Grounds in New York, and a huge crowd jammed every inch of the old ballpark.

The game began with Army kicking off. Oliphant's long kick carried right to the goal line where it was scooped up by a Navy back who was then smothered on the 10-yard line. The Navy backs—Harry Goodstein, Bill Ingram, John Welchel, and Wolcott Roberts—failed to gain, and Navy punted to midfield.

Oliphant and halfback Benny Hoge picked up a couple of yards, but the Navy line was now fired up, charging in and hitting hard on every play. On fourth down Oliphant kicked and Navy took over.

After another series of punt exchanges, Ernie Von Heimburg, the Navy end, punted to Oliphant on the Army 20-yard line and Elmer darted through several tacklers for 25 yards and a first down at midfield.

Again Navy toughened and held Army, and Coffin kicked on fourth down. Fullback Harold Martin of Navy fumbled the punt and Army recovered the ball. Three savage smashes by Oliphant and Bill Coffin brought the ball to the Navy 1-yard line. On fourth down, Oliphant, carrying the ball behind an unbalanced line, ran in for the touchdown. Elmer kicked the extra point and it was Army 7, Navy 0. By now every time Oliphant touched the ball, the crowd stood and roared his name.

In the third period, Army's All-American center, 6-foot 4-inch, 218-pound John McEwan (the first center to spiral a pass to his backs) intercepted a desperate Navy forward pass and brought the ball back to Navy's 30-yard line. On the next play, Oliphant, behind some of the most devastating blocking that Navy had seen all season long, skirted off tackle and was away and across the goal line for Army's second touchdown. Oliphant kicked the extra point and it was Army 14, Navy 0 as the game ended.

Navy's 1916 football squad included some of the most famous names in the history of the Naval Academy. Names like Lyman Perry, Bob Dash-

iel, Bill Ingram, John Welchel—all outstanding backs. The line was big, tough, and strong: Eddie Ewen, Ernie Von Heimburg, George Skinner, Ed Doolin, Ed Moran, and Ben Wyatt. The Middies charged through a difficult 10-game schedule with 6 wins, a tie, and 3 losses before meeting an undefeated Army eleven that had won 8 straight, including a win over an outstanding Notre Dame team by a 30–10 score.

Just lying in wait for the Middies, the Cadets had an almost unstoppable running attack led by the All-American Elmer Oliphant and his running mate, Gene Vidal, one of the most versatile halfbacks ever to play for the Black Knights of West Point. The Army line still had All-American John McEwan at center, completing his fourth year at West Point.

Ten days prior to the Army battle, Navy coach Jonas Ingram erected a tackling dummy on the practice field with Oliphant's name and face plastered over the front, and the Middies kept hitting the dummy until it fell apart. There were pep talks and rallies at Annapolis, with secretive plans hatched on how to stop Oliphant, so when Navy trotted onto the Polo Grounds in New York for the big game, they felt fully confident they could handle their tormentor from the year before.

John McEwan of Army won the toss of the coin and elected to receive the kickoff, and Navy, in the full bloom of its confidence, kicked the ball right to Oliphant.

Ollie caught the ball on the Army 10-yard line, tucked it under his arm, and started upfield. He avoided several Navy tacklers with a beautiful change of pace, then with the aid of some marvelous blocking sped toward midfield. Time and again Elmer would thrust a hip at a Navy tackler, then swing away from him. Three or four Navy players attempting to bring him down simply fell trying to react to Elmer's puzzling running style, and it looked as if he would go the length of the field.

But out of nowhere, Tommy Fisher, a big Navy tackle, hurled his body at Oliphant and knocked him down on the 6-yard line. It was a magnificent run of more than 85 yards on the

West Point's football lettermen—"Wearers of the 'A'"—for 1915, the class "the stars fell upon." Dwight Eisenhower is in the second row, third from left; Omar Bradley is in the third row, third from the right; James Van Fleet is in the third row, extreme left.

The great Elmer Oliphant, who could do everything. He starred at West Point in football, basketball, golf, track, and as a heavyweight boxing champion. In Army's 1915 14–0 victory over Navy, Ollie scored both Army touchdowns and kicked both extra points.

opening play of the game, and had brought the crowd to its feet with a great roar of excitement, first for Ollie's great run and then for Fisher's super effort in tackling Army's one-man tank.

Oliphant and Gene Vidal then alternated in driving for a couple of yards, and on third down Oliphant penetrated the Navy line for the touchdown. The extra point was missed and it was 6–0.

Navy received the kickoff, but their attack stalled and they had to kick to Army. Once more it was Oliphant and Vidal alternating in carrying the ball for first downs, until Army had advanced to the Navy 10-yard line.

Now it was Navy's turn to shine as they held the great Oliphant on three successive thrusts at the line. On fourth down, Elmer dropped back to the 25-yard line and casually kicked a field goal. It was Army 9, Navy 0.

Returning the kickoff Navy finally began an attack of their own, but it stalled at midfield and Army took over.

Two running plays gained 15 yards and then Oliphant attempted another field goal from the Navy 35-yard line, but the kick fell short and Ingram, the Navy halfback, picked up the ball and sped upfield all the way to the Army 45-yard line before he was brought down. It was Navy's biggest play of the day.

But time was running short, as two Navy running plays failed to gain ground. On fourth down, Navy punted the ball and Oliphant ran it back to the Navy 43-yard line.

Once more Army was in fine field position. Three runs by Vidal, Oliphant, and Royal Place brought the ball to the Navy 35-yard line. Here the Middies stiffened and held. On fourth down, Gene Vidal attempted a drop kick, but the kick was blocked by Lyman Perry, the Navy halfback, who recovered the ball and brought it back to the 46-yard line.

Again successive running plays by Navy failed to gain, and Army took possession of the ball on Navy's 41-yard line. This time all three Army backs, Oliphant, Vidal, and Place, made successive first downs, driving to the Navy 16-yard line.

Army went into a kick formation. Quarterback Charlie Gerhardt knelt to hold the ball for a field-goal attempt, but instead he scooped it up, stood, and tossed a perfect pass to Vidal for the Army touchdown. The play caught the Middies completely by surprise, and after the conversion was missed, Army had a 15-0 lead.

As the third period began with their fourth straight defeat by Army staring Navy in the face, halfback Wolcott Roberts took the kickoff and behind magnificent blocking sped upfield to the Army 32-yard line. It was an advance of 55 yards, but again Army held and Navy had to give up the ball on downs.

The Cadets took over, but now it was Navy's turn to show their defensive strength as they held Army for three downs. On fourth down, Oliphant dropped back to punt. Harry Goodstein, Navy's big center, had been bearing the brunt of the Army attack all afternoon and now he broke through the Army line to block Oliphant's kick, then led the chase for the bounding ball. He scooped it up and outran Vidal, Oliphant, and several Army players for a magnificent dash of 55 yards and Navy's first touchdown of the afternoon. The kick was good and it was Army 15, Navy 7.

The touchdown seemed to give the Middies a new lease on life. Three times they penetrated to the Army 20-yard line, then to the 15, and once to the 10-yard line. But they simply didn't have that extra firepower necessary for another score, and the game ended with Navy still hammering away but failing to cross the coveted goal line. Army had once again taken a close 15-7 game from Navy.

In 1944, Admiral Art Miles, captain of the Navy team in 1915, was awarded the Legion of Merit, as director of procurement, Bureau of Aeronautics, in World War II.

And in that year, Rear Admiral Henry Mullinix of the 1915 Navy team that had battled Army tooth and nail, was posthumously awarded the Legion of Merit when his ship the USS *Liscombe Bay* was torpedoed by the Japanese off Makin Island. Mullinix was the task force commander. And in 1945, Admiral Earl Mills was awarded the Distinguished Service Medal for vital decisions in the engineering and electrical plans for all fleet units; Mills was an outstanding guard on the Middies squad.

In 1942, Commodore Ben Wyatt, a fine end on the 1916 Navy eleven, received a Letter of Commendation, for performance as commanding officer of USS *Chenango* during an assault and occupation of French Morocco. In 1943, Commodore Wyatt received a Navy unit citation for "outstanding heroism," in action against Japanese forces as commanding officer of USS *Chenango*.

In 1942, Captain Edward Moran, another fine end of the 1916 Navy squad, received the Navy Cross, as commanding officer, USS *Boise*, in night action against Japanese forces off Savo Island. Moran's ship caught fire, but heroic actions by him and other officers and men saved the ship.

After the War: 1919-21

With America's entry into the world war, the War Department ordered the Army-Navy game discontinued for the duration. Both schools, however, received approval to schedule games with other schools.

In 1917, Navy won seven of eight games against such opponents as Davidson, Carlisle, Haverford, Indiana, and Villanova, and trounced a hapless Western Reserve by 95–0. And in 1918, the Middies defeated Newport and Norfolk Navy, and annihilated Ursinus by a 127–0 score.

Army was able to play out games with Carnegie Tech, Virginia Military, Tufts, Villanova, Notre Dame, Carlisle, Lebanon, and Boston College. The Cadets won every game except the Notre Dame contest. They lost to a hard-charging Irish squad led by the immortal George Gipp as Gipp scored the only touchdown of the day in a 7–2 Notre Dame victory. In 1918, Army defeated the Mitchell Field Aviators 20–0 in the Cadets' only game of the season.

The 1918 plebe team at Navy included Emory Larson, Clyde King, John Orr, Dwight Newby, Abe Snively, and Hog Murray. The end of the war seemed imminent, and in a lighter moment after practice one day, Larson was discussing the rivalry with Army with his teammates. "Fellows," he said, "I'm going to play ball here for three more years and we're gonna beat Army every year that I'm here."

In the next three years Larson would be the star center of a Navy football team that would defeat Army all three years. And when Larson graduated, he would return to coach Navy, and his teams would defeat Army in all three years he was the head coach.

Meanwhile, West Point had a new superintendent. He was General Douglas MacArthur, and he believed in physical conditioning as a requirement for every Cadet. He also loved football more than any other previous superintendent had. The general would spend hours on the practice field, observing the drills of the teams, talking over strategy with various coaches. MacArthur's philosophy on athletics is inscribed on an arch over the gymnasium at West Point: "Upon the fields of friendly strife are sown the seeds that upon other fields, on other days, will bear the fruits of victory."

In 1919 both academies had selected new head coaches. Charlie Daly, one of the Army football immortals, had returned for a second tour of duty as head coach, and at Annapolis, Gilmour Dobie, whose persistently pessimistic forecasts about the chances for his football teams in important matches had earned him the nickname of "Gloomy Gil," was appointed Navy's head coach.

Dobie came to Annapolis from the University of Washington, where his team had one of the most remarkable records in the history of college football. The Washington Huskies ruled West Coast football from 1908 through 1916. In those nine years when Dobie coached the team, Washington won 58 games, tied 3 games, and never lost a game.

Navy opened the 1919 season with a smashing 49–0 win over North Carolina State, then trampled St. Helens training group 66–0. Another win over Norfolk was by 37–6. Then Colby was smothered under an avalanche of touchdowns, 121–0. The former plebes Emory Larson, John Orr, Clyde King, and Deetman Moore had come into their own. A week later Navy lost to Georgetown by 7–6, which made coach Dobie gloomier than ever, with the Army game approaching.

Saturday, November 29, dawned damp, foggy, and bitter cold. Promptly at 1:00 P.M., the Navy band, followed by some one thousand Midshipmen in platoon strength, marched in perfect formation through the south entrance of the Polo Grounds in New York City. Suddenly every bit of brass in the Navy band broke into a stirring rendition of a martial tune as the crowd jumped to their feet and cheered the colorful Middies as they swung majestically around the entire field in full dress blues with gold trimmings and quick-stepped into their seats in the lower stands.

As soon as the Middies were seated, the Cadets marched into the stadium through the north side entrance. Led by their own jaunty brass band, the Cadets in their gray uniforms then reversed their march, passed directly in front of the Middies, and as they paused there for one frozen moment, every cadet lifted his cap in salute to Navy, who acknowledged the gesture with three rousing cheers that filled the big stadium.

Gil Dobie, the Navy head coach, 1917–19.

As the Cadets settled in their seats, the Navy cheerleaders led out a white dummy mule with a huge gold *A* on its back. The dummy mule lay on its side, and three Navy cheerleaders attempted to revive the dead beast. Suddenly three attendants in white suits rushed to the mule and tried to pump air into the lifeless body, until one of the white-clad men pulled a string attached to the mule and several dozen carrier pigeons flew out and around the park. Each pigeon had a ribbon attached to its leg with a sign, BEAT ARMY.

Army thereupon quickly put on their own show. The pantomime consisted of an attempt to blow up a small battleship with the help of a miniature airplane. But everything went wrong; the plane flew in the wrong direction, and then something went awry with the apparatus that was to detonate the ship. The hapless Cadets tried everything, until finally one was able to wire a battery to the battleship and, as the crowd cheered, the ship was engulfed in smoke.

All this time the Middies were singing, "Don't Give Up the Ship."

Finally the game was called and referee Ed Thorp flipped a coin. Army chose to kick off to start the game.

Navy received the kickoff and brought the ball back to the 20-yard line. Navy ran a number of running plays and drove to midfield. The Middies' line was opening up wide holes for their backs, and two first downs advanced the ball to the Army 38-yard line. Here the Army defense held. Navy's Claude McQuarrie punted the ball and Army took over.

Three line plays failed to gain and Army kicked.

Once again Navy was on the move as Ed Cruise, Ben Koehler, and Lou Benoist picked up valuable yardage. The Middies smashed to the Army 17-yard line. Again Army toughened and held.

On fourth down, Clyde King kicked a field goal and Navy had a 3-0 lead.

The teams pounded each other through the second period with neither having an advantage.

Late in the third quarter, the Middies smashed to the Army 15-yard line, and when two running plays failed to gain any appreciable ground, Clyde King, the great Navy tackle, calmly booted another field goal to give the Middies a 6-0 lead.

Early in the final period, Navy slashed and cut through the Army line, but just as it seemed that Navy might drive for a touchdown, Army held and Navy was stopped on the 17-yard line. The game ended with a 6-0 Navy win.

The Middies poured out of their seats, snake-danced under the goalposts, and threw their white-topped caps over the bars to celebrate the great victory.

In 1945, Captain Edwin Graves was awarded the American Defense Service Medal for heroic service in the European African Area . . . and the Order of the British Empire. . . . Graves was an outstanding end on the 1919 team.

In 1944, Commodore Lyman Perry received

a letter of commendation from Secretary of the Navy James Forrestal for his services as aide and adviser to the secretary during the intense naval activity from January 1943 to April 1944. Perry was guard on the 1918 squad.

In the first Army-Navy game of the new decade, Navy outplayed the Cadets to take a hard-fought contest, 7–0.

Before the 1920 season began, Navy's great coach, Gil Dobie, shocked Navy officials and the football world by suddenly resigning. He had been offered a new three-year contract but had turned it down. Later, Dobie confided to some sportswriters that he "couldn't take all the crap from the officers. I had too many bosses."

Bob Folwell, a great University of Pennsylvania star before 1910, was appointed Navy's head football coach, but Folwell got such a late start with his new team—just one day's practice with his regulars, and not all of them at that, before the opening game of the season against a strong North Carolina State team—he decided to play the game with his better-drilled plebe team. As a result, Navy lost a 14–7 tussle to North Carolina.

After the full brigade had returned to school and all the regular stars had reported for practice, the Middies captured 5 of 6 games, losing only to a strong Princeton eleven by a 14–0 margin.

A week before the Army game, the Middies trampled South Carolina, 63–0. They were led by Captain-elect Eddie Ewen, the first two-time captain in Navy football history; tackle Ed Willkie, whose brother Wendell Willkie would run for the presidency against Franklin D. Roosevelt; Clyde King, the marvelous placekicker; plus a quartet of hard-running backs, Steve Barchet, Benny Koehler, Ed Cruise, and Vic Noyes. Vic Noyes sparkled against South Carolina with three dashes of 50 yards or longer to score three touchdowns in the game.

The Middies were so buoyed by their spectacular win they could hardly contain them-

Gar Davidson's three tenures at West Point: Right: As an outstanding tackle on the 1920 and 1921 Army teams. Below: As head coach, 1933–37, with Harvey Jablonsky, captain of the 1933 Army eleven. Below, right: Following a distinguished record as a commander in the European theater in World War II, superintendent of the Academy, 1956–60.

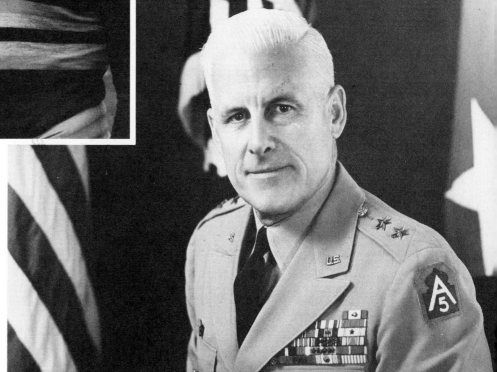

selves as they prepped for the Army game. All that week the battle cry rang out in the Yard at Annapolis, "Wait till the Gang hits the Cadets." Even the Navy fleet anchored in the Hudson that week sensed victory. As the Middies crossed the Hudson River on the Jersey Central Ferry, officers and men of the numerous naval vessels anchored in the river saluted the members of the team with tremendous blasts of whistles and cheers. The Middies then debarked at the 155th Street pier as the Navy band broke out in a stirring song, and marched through the town to Coogan's Bluff at the Polo Grounds and into the great stadium.

But as the game got under way, something happened to the Middies. The line, which had been fast and aggressive all season long, seemed lethargic. The backs were slow and their timing was off. As a result Army threatened to score on three separate occasions in the first half.

Walt French, Army's great punter, had the Middies floundering most of the first half with booming kicks of 50 and 60 yards that trapped Navy deep in their own territory.

Then, something happened between halves. The Middies came out inspired, scrapping and playing like the champions they were. Vic Noyes and Barchet led the running attack and began pounding the Army line to shreds. The Navy line now opened huge holes for the backs, who poured through until Noyes blasted to the Army 10-yard line.

As Army dug in and Army secondary moved in to give the line additional support, Victor Noyes caught the Cadets by surprise by calling for a complicated cross-buck play with Benny Koehler blasting through for a touchdown with hardly a Cadet touching him. Clyde King kicked the extra point and it was Navy 7, Army 0.

And as the game ended, admirals, commanders, and the brigade of Midshipmen swarmed out onto the field to snake-dance together. The Middies took over Manhattan that night and all over town was music . . . Navy music.

— ★ —

In 1921, the Navy football team came within one touchdown of winning the national championship. That happened when Penn State's great halfback, Glenn Killinger, outsped half a dozen Navy tacklers to score one touchdown in the second period and another in the third to hand Navy its only defeat in six games. The score was 13–7, and Killinger was the difference, sending Penn State rather than Navy to the Rose Bowl and the championship.

Two grueling weeks of scrimmages following the Penn State game had Navy players so hard and tough they could hardly wait for the twenty-fourth annual battle against their Army rivals.

The day of the big game arrived, and the Middies were greeted by a torrential downpour as they embarked at the 155th Street pier in New York City. Then, as Navy ship whistles and the Annapolis band joined in a musical salute, the Middies marched across town to the scene of battle at the Polo Grounds.

Army had a fairly strong team this year, having posted wins over Villanova, Wabash, and Springfield, but they dropped games to Yale, Notre Dame, and New Hampshire. They were led by Larry French, a fine runner and passer; Edgar Garbisch, one of the great field-goal kickers in Army history; George Smythe, a marvelous broken-field runner; and Bill Wood, who had had four years of football at Johns Hopkins before coming to West Point. So Army was primed for the Middies.

The rain continued to come down as the two teams squared off before a crowd of 50,000 at the Polo Grounds. Navy took the opening kickoff and marched downfield, with Ben Koehler, Steve Barchet, and Bull Conroy picking up one first down after another, until stopped by the Army defenders. And so it went for the entire first period: Navy continued to force the ball deep into Army territory, but each time the Cadets' defense stiffened, and Army took over the ball on downs. And each time that happened, Army's Ed Garbisch would send a tremendous punt downfield, one as long as 75 yards, and Navy would have to drive upfield all over again.

Army attempted a 43-yard field goal, but the try was far short and Navy took over with five minutes remaining in the half. Steve Barchet then carried the ball and picked up the Middies' longest gain of the day on a 24-yard sprint. Another 9-yard pickup by Barchet brought the ball to the Army 9-yard stripe. Two plays failed to gain, and on third down Barchet slashed off tackle and scored the touchdown. Clyde King, the Middie with the "automatic toe," kicked the extra point, and it was 7–0, Navy.

Navy threatened several times thereafter, but penalties and a costly fumble by Barchet, who was all over the field, cost the Middies another score.

Late in the fourth and final period, Army took the ball to the Navy 8-yard line, but they were unable to capitalize on the drive, and the game ended with Navy hanging on to a 7–0 lead.

It was the third straight shutout victory for Navy over Army.

Captain Emory Larson had made good on his 1919 promise.

In 1944, Rear Admiral Eddie Ewen was awarded the Legion of Merit for outstanding service as commander of bombing enemy aircraft off Roi Island and Naumur Island in the Marshall Islands group. Also in 1944, Ewen was awarded the Navy Cross for "extra-ordinary heroism" as commanding officer of the aircraft carrier USS *Independence* in the Pacific.

In 1942, Commander Ed Cruise, a fine Navy halfback in 1921, was awarded the Navy Cross for heroism as air officer of the carrier USS *Saratoga* in action against the Japanese at Tulagi. Cruise was promoted to rear admiral after the engagement.

Also in 1942, Captain Ed Durgin, another great star of the 1921 team, was awarded the Legion of Merit and gold star for his heroism as commander of forces in the assault on Sicily.

Into the "Golden Age": 1922-25

The twenties were one of the most notable decades in the history of the United States. It was an era of recovery after World War I, and of economic advance that ultimately led to the biggest economic crash ever in the country.

Historically, the decade was marked by the U.S. repudiation of the League of Nations and the subsequent election of Warren G. Harding as president. Former President Woodrow Wilson was awarded the Nobel Peace Prize but died shortly thereafter, disappointed by America's unwillingness to join the league.

President Warren Harding died in office and Calvin Coolidge succeeded him. In 1924, Coolidge defeated John Davis for the presidency.

In the world of sports, the twenties are still considered the "Golden Age" because of the superlative performances of such incredible athletes as Jack Dempsey, Red Grange, Bobby Jones, Bill Tilden, Gertrude Ederle, and Helen Wills.

And in 1922, Army in triumph and Navy in defeat furnished America with one of the great sports spectacles and most thrilling contests of the series.

Rarely in the history of Army and Navy football classics can be found another such dazzling contest as that staged in Penn's new stadium on this great day, and it would be hard to find in those annals a record of individual achievement surpassing that furnished by a young Cadet named George Smythe, a Muhlenberg graduate.

Few in that great multitude of 60,000 were there by right of social privilege. Rather it was a conclave of those who had achieved or attained the right. Certainly it was preponderately martial, for this was a martial event. There was General John J. "Blackjack" Pershing in the forefront of the victorious hosts, and Admiral Joe Wilson smiling in the face of defeat. There were Franklin D. Roosevelt, assistant secretary of the navy, and other military and naval dignitaries too numerous to mention.

Twice the gritty and lightning-fast Navy team scored to go into the lead, and both times a glorious Army team came from behind, the last time to ultimate victory.

Navy had scored a touchdown in the second period, and before the half ended the skillful toe of Cadet Edgar Garbisch, Army's great center, had driven the ball straight between the uprights and over the crossbar from the 45-yard line to bring the score at halftime to 7–3 in favor of the Middies.

Early in the dramatic third period, West Point had swept into a 10–7 lead by scoring a touchdown, and it looked like Army's day until

Navy unleashed a brilliant passing attack led by Ed Norris, who had replaced Steve Barchet at fullback for the Middies. Norris connected to Marvin Parr, his left end; then came another pass, Norris to halfback Carl Cullen; and finally with the ball on Army's 1-yard line, quarterback Vincent Conroy scored for the Middies to give them a 14–10 lead.

The end seemed to be at hand for Army. Navy had effectively bottled up the bull-like rushes of Army's backs, Pat Timberlake, Bud Dodd, and Bill Wood. The day had all the appearance of another Navy triumph, but that would have been reckoning without George Smythe.

There were less than seven minutes to play when Navy's Cullen punted to midfield. Smythe, back at safety for Army, waited until he'd judged the ball correctly, babied it to his chest, and then realizing that he had no running room, he decided to scramble back toward his own goal line. He faded back, back, and

Army's rooters screamed for him to cut away and dash back upfield.

And suddenly he did begin to move upfield, slipping off one Navy tackler after another. Back and forth he twisted and turned, and now he had room and was out in the open, into the clear. One last desperate Navy defender downed Smythe on the 12-yard line, while 60,000 fans screamed in excitement.

It was a brilliant run of 48 yards, one of the most exciting runs ever on a football field, through virtually the entire Navy team. Smythe did not score, but his great run put the ball in position for victory.

There were just two minutes remaining in the game when Smythe casually took a shovel pass from fullback Bill Wood, quickly darted toward his right end, then stopped dead in his tracks, for out of the corner of his eye he had spotted Pat Timberlake sprinting into the end zone all alone. Without a moment's hesitation, Smythe pitched a perfect pass to Timberlake

Fritz Breidstar, a great guard and captain of the 1922 Army team, which defeated Navy 17–14 in one of the most thrilling contests of the rivalry.

for a touchdown, and the colonels, generals, and two thousand Cadets erupted in a volcano of sound.

Then Ed Garbisch, captain of the team, whose father had wanted him to be a concert pianist, calmly kicked the extra point. Army had snatched the game right out of the grasp of a fighting, aggressive band of Midshipmen by a 17–14 score.

When the victorious Army eleven returned to West Point the following afternoon, the entire Corps of Cadets was waiting at the railroad station for the traditional ride up the steep hill in the ancient stagecoach. The Corps made Ed Garbisch sit atop the coach as they pulled it up the hill and showered him with their very own special brand of gratitude.

Tom Hamilton was the Navy quarterback who guided the Middies to a national championship in 1926 by drop-kicking the extra point that tied Army 21–21 in what was perhaps the most exciting game in the history of this thrilling interservice rivalry.

In 1934, Tom Hamilton returned to his alma mater as head football coach and guided the Middies to a highly successful season. He remained at the Naval Academy as head coach until 1936, and then returned for two more seasons in 1946–47 as head coach and later on as director of athletics.

In World War II, Commander Hamilton was awarded numerous honors and awards while serving as executive officer of the aircraft carrier USS *Enterprise* in that carrier's successful invasion of the Gilbert Islands, its raid on Kwajalein, the Marshall Islands, and the battle of Leyte.

Tom Hamilton stands as an Annapolis immortal. As a player, coach, and director of athletics, he left behind a legacy that will always be part of the Naval Academy's history. What follows is his own account of his first three years of Navy football as a star player, 1923–25.

"The year 1923 was memorable in Navy football annals as our officials adopted the '3-year rule' and prohibited freshmen from playing varsity football. But Army refused to go along with this policy and continued to allow fellows who played at other schools to come to West Point and play additional seasons. The Navy authorities were letting themselves in for a situation which would lead to the curtailment of the Army-Navy game for two years (see p. 82).

"On the bright side of the 1923 picture was Navy's selection to play the University of Washington in the Rose Bowl, a game that ended in a 14–14 tie. This was a season that is still regarded as one of the finest in Navy football history for the only team to beat us all season long was Penn State with their great star, Light Horse Harry Wilson. After three great years at Penn, Wilson would come back to plague us after he entered the Academy at West Point.

"The Army game was one of those things. Neither team could get going in the torrential rain and mud at the Polo Grounds. The footing was terrible.

"The best play of the game occurred on the opening kickoff. Pete McKee, our fine halfback, took the kick, got great blocking, and skidded, sloshed, and stumbled to midfield. It was a great run of 40 yards. Pete would have gone all the way on a dry field. I remember also how our fine punter, Carl Cullen, had two of his punts blocked inside our 15-yard line. We were lucky both times as Carl quickly recovered the ball, and since both kicks were tried on third down, we were able to kick on fourth down and get a reprise. The game ended in a 0–0 tie."

"In 1924, we lost such great players as Captain Art Carney, Bob Mathews, Sol Levinsky, Bill Brown, Pete McKee, Bill Devens, Carl Cullen, and Steve Barchet. And to make matters worse, Paul Clyde and Carlton Hutchins became ill and Charlie Shewell, a great tackle on the 1923 team, resigned from the Academy.

"But Coach Bob Folwell redesigned the 1924 offense, did a great rebuilding job with our line, and we got off to a flying start by defeating William and Mary in the season's opener, 14–7.

"I got my chance as a starter this year and I made the most of it, playing in practically every game.

"In the big game of the year against the Army, we were outkicked by Mr. Ed Garbisch of Army. All Mr. Garbisch did was to kick four field goals to beat us 12–0.

"The year 1924 was the fifth that Bob Folwell was our football coach. During that stretch we had our ups and downs, going to the Rose Bowl, losing twice to Army, winning two, and tying one game. After the season the Navy officials decided it was time for a coaching change, and Jack Owsley, a former Yale star, took over."

"We opened the 1925 season with wins over William and Mary, 25–0, defeated Marquette, tied a very tough Princeton Tiger squad, 10–10, and defeated Washington, 37–0. But then a mighty Michigan team trounced us, 54–0. However, we turned the season around with wins over Western Maryland and Bucknell, and then it was time for 'the big game.'

"The guest of honor on the 50-yard line was a former star tackle on the 1887 Navy team, Secretary of the Navy Curtis Wilbur, who cheered his head off during the game as a very strong Army team took a squeaker 10–3 win.

"Tommy Trapnell, later a great World War II hero, Bill Hewitt, and Harry Wilson ripped and tore up our line for one first down after another. But when the chips were down and our backs were to the wall, we held the Army on at least half a dozen opportunities to score.

"We came roaring back in the second period as Alan Shapley, a great halfback all season long, tossed a beautiful pass to Harry Hardwicke, and Harry smashed to the Army 12-yard line before he was downed. Four drives into the Army line brought us to the 4-yard line, and Army held.

"Then it was the Army's turn, and they took

★ ★ ★

Letter from Edgar Garbisch

Sports headlines throughout the land hailed Cadet Ed Garbisch after the Army-Navy game of 1924, for it was the strong right foot and stout heart of Garbisch that won the game for Army, 12–0. He kicked four field goals to score all the points. Garbisch made additional headlines when it was discovered that he led his squad in a prayer in the dressing room before going out on the field.

I finally have found the verbatim version of the prayer I offered with the football squad in the dressing rooms just before going out to play the game. Here it is:

"O God, help us to play the game today in the spirit of clean sportsmanship with no malice towards our opponent. Help us, also, to play our best and to acquit ourselves like men. Amen."

This prayer was offered for the first time just before the team went out on the field to play Yale in the Bowl, and it was repeated before all of our remaining games.

I want to repeat that the 1924 football team did not suffer any penalties beyond holding and offsides all season; that is, there were no clipping, unsportsmanlike conduct, roughing the kicker, etc. penalties.

Sincerely,

Ed

Cadet Edgar Garbisch was a star center for Army, 1921-24, but he made national headlines with his magnificent drop-kicking and punting. In the 1924 Army-Navy game, Garbisch kicked four field goals to defeat Navy 12-0.

over the ball and began to move upfield. With Wilson, Hewitt, and Tommy Trapnell carrying the ball on each play, the Army got the ball to our 4-yard line. Then we dug in and held. There were 4 yards to go on fourth down, and at this point Army threw the book at us. Harding dropped back as if to try a field goal, then bluffed a pass to Charlie Born (whose brother Art was our left halfback). While we were chasing Charlie Born, end Harry Baxter of Army buttonhooked back and caught a pass

from Harding for the Army touchdown with three of our guys hanging on his back. The conversion was made and it was Army 7, Navy 3.

"In the final period both teams hit each other with everything they had. Army finally got to our 12-yard line; we dug in and held them for three big downs. But then on the fourth down, Red Reeder, Army's great kicker, came in, calmly kicked a field goal, and the game ended with Army in front 10-3."

10

The Greatest Game: 1926

The economic boom that had begun after World War I continued in 1926. Wages were high and prosperity was the shibboleth. Henry Ford sent shock waves through the skyrocketing automobile industry as he introduced a revolutionary eight-hour day and a five-day work week for his employees. . . . AT&T demonstrated the first successful transatlantic telephone conversation between New York City and London. . . . On the political front President Calvin Coolidge dispatched several detachments of Marines to Nicaragua after an armed insurrection had broken out and the rebels began a march on the capital city of Managua. Once landed, the Marines quickly put an end to the disturbances. . . . A devastating earthquake ripped Florida and a number of other Gulf States with casualties numbering in the hundreds and some eight thousand injured. More than five thousand homes were destroyed with property damage estimated at over $80 million.

And in an incredible achievement, Admiral Richard E. Byrd and Floyd Bennett made the first successful flight over the North Pole. Dick Byrd had been an outstanding end on the fine 1911 Navy football team that defeated Army, 3–0.

In the sports world, heavyweight Gene Tun-

ney, "The Fighting Marine," scored one of the greatest upsets in the history of professional boxing by defeating champion Jack Dempsey. . . . René Lacoste foreshadowed the rise of French tennis by defeating the invincible Bill Tilden at Forest Hills. . . . The St. Louis Cardinals won the World Series by defeating the New York Yankees, four games to three. . . . And in 1926, Army and Navy met in Chicago in a game that the nation's sportswriters voted in 1950 "The Greatest College Football Game of the Century."

The first service game ever played in the Windy City saw the two archrivals struggle through to a 21–21 tie before a record 110,000 onlookers. For more than three and a half hours, twenty-two valiant young giants fought back and forth on Chicago's Soldier Field, until it became so dark that you could hardly tell the Army mule from the Navy goat. The teams attacked and counterattacked in a contest that enthralled even the conservative vice president of the United States, Charles Dawes, sitting among high-ranking cabinet officials, mayors, governors, gold-braided officers, and thousands of ordinary football fans.

It was a football game that never will be forgotten, this twenty-ninth meeting of the lads from the Hudson and the Middies from the Severn. Even if Chicago's Doric temple of football never sees another Army-Navy game, the windy town will always remember its one service battle, fought on a field piled high with snow only the day before. For who could forget any minute of it, from the opening kickoff to the final whistle?

Brave rallies and gallant goal-line stands, drama, suspense, and so many thrills—all were packed into this unforgettable game. Now it looked like Navy's game for sure, now as certainly Army's. And just when you had the game all charted and decided, a halfback would go tearing through the line, forward passes would darken the sky, and all your calculations would go up in smoke.

Chicago had built the huge Soldier's Field as a memorial to the dead of World War I and had arranged to have this Army-Navy game shifted from the East Coast for the first, and only, time in its history. Even before the kickoff, the game had assumed epic proportions, like all seven games of the World Series rolled into one afternoon of bitter battle.

Light Horse Harry Wilson, Mo Daly, Bud Sprague, Tommy Trapnell, Blondie Saunders, and Gar Davidson were some of Army's big guns. But their biggest gun of all was Chris Cagle.

Christian Keener Cagle ranks with Jim Thorpe, Red Grange, Tommy Harmon, Bronko Nagurksi, and Glenn Davis as one of the greatest backs in collegiate history. Cagle, raised on a cattle ranch in Marryville, Texas, wanted as a boy to become, of all things, a doctor. But at Southern Louisiana Institute he soon discovered that a premed course mixed with football, basketball, track, and waiting on tables was too much for him. After four athletic-record-breaking years at SLI, Chris was given an appointment to West Point and became an instant star.

In 1926, Army had lost but once, to a Notre Dame team that went on to enjoy one of its finest seasons. But in Chicago they would be pitted against a Navy team that still today is looked on as the greatest ever to wear the colors of the Naval Academy. The Middies boasted

such great stars as All-American Tommy Hamilton, one of the nation's great triple-threat stars; Alan Shapley and Howard Caldwell in the backfield; Frank Wickhorst and Tom Eddy at the tackle posts; and Hank Hardwicke and Russ Lloyd at the ends. The Middies had rolled up impressive victories over Princeton, Michigan, Georgetown, Purdue, and Colgate, and came to Chicago as the only undefeated major team in the nation.

Both schools had made important changes in their head coaching positions for the 1926 season. Army had called in Lawrence "Biff" Jones to take charge of the Cadets, while the Middies had tabbed Navy Bill Ingram, star halfback on

William A. "Bill" Ingram, Navy's inspirational coach from 1926—when he guided the Middies to a national championship—to 1930.

the 1916 team, as their new head coach.

Navy got an immediate break as the game got under way when Army was penalized for pass interference on their 45-yard line, giving Navy a first down. Hamilton cracked through tackle for 5 yards. Then halfback Jim Schuber tossed a beautiful 40-yard pass to end Howard Caldwell. Surrounded by three Army defenders, Howie outjumped them all to pluck the ball out of the air. He was downed immediately on the Army 2-yard line.

Two line plays failed to gain, then Caldwell smashed through Army's right tackle for the first score. Tommy Hamilton's kick was good, and Navy had a 7-0 lead.

When Navy got the ball for the second time, they turned loose their powerful set of backs in a series of plays that included a lateral pass, a reverse, the Statue of Liberty play, and a double reverse. Hamilton, Jim Schuber, Alan Shapley, and Caldwell smashed through the Cadets for 65 yards, until Schuber cracked off tackle for Navy's second touchdown. Once more Tommy Hamilton kicked the extra point, and now Navy had a commanding 14-0 lead.

At this moment you would have had to rate Army's chances as being worth something less than a plugged Mexican nickel. After five lean years without a victory over Army, the Middies appeared on a tremendous roll, seemingly on their way to a win over one of Army's greatest teams. Army fans sat determinedly grim. When would Cagle and Wilson get going?

Hamilton kicked off to Army's 17-yard stripe where Lighthorse Harry Wilson scooped up the ball and dazzled the huge crowd with a 35-yard return to the Navy 49. Then it was Tommy Trapnell and fullback Clyde Dahl picking up valuable yards. Then it was the magical moves of Red Cagle as he sped 30 yards off tackle to the Navy 16-yard line before being stopped by a horde of Navy tacklers.

On the very next play, Wilson slashed his way 16 yards on a buck lateral for Army's first score. Wilson kicked the extra point and now it was 14-7.

Army's fans roared their tribute to the Ca-

dets' game comeback, and the cheers still reverberated throughout Soldier Field as Army halfback Johnny Murrell punted after each side's attack had stalled. It was a poor kick, but Navy's Howie Ransford misjudged the ball. It hit his shoulder, bounced away, and Army's end Skip Harbold grabbed the ball and never stopped running until he fell over the Navy goal line for the Cadets' second touchdown within two minutes. Wilson's kick for the extra point was perfect to tie the game at 14-14. The crowd was in a frenzy of excitement as the gun sounded the end of the first half.

Between halves Secretary of War Dwight Davis and Navy Secretary Curtis Wilbur exchanged salutations at midfield, where they agreed that if they never saw another football game as exciting as this one had been up to now they could still die happy. At the same time Vice President Dawes crossed from the Navy side to the Army, maintaining a benevolent neutrality on a day when to maintain any kind of neutrality was a feat in itself.

It appeared that the vice president had brought victory along with him to the Army legions, for in the first few minutes of the second half Army's touchdown twins, Wilson and Cagle, went to work in earnest. Wilson spun off tackle and dashed for 25 yards, and then Chris Cagle followed immediately with a brilliant burst off his right guard, sprinting 43 yards before Navy gang-tackled him just as he crashed over the goal line for an Army score. Harry Wilson kicked his third extra point, and the crowd was in an uproar.

Army, behind at one point by 14-0, had taken a 21-14 lead, and as the fourth quarter began, they seemingly had the game under control. There were but four minutes left to play when, once again, Army was driving toward the Navy goal. But then Alan Shapley, playing his last game for the Sailors—the same Shapley who later as a Marine captain would become the most decorated officer of World War II— stopped the drive by intercepting a pass on the Navy 35-yard stripe.

Now it was the Middies' turn to go to work,

Above: *Cagle dashes for 26 yards in the second period of the 1926 Army-Navy epic.* Below: *In the 1927 game, another thriller won by the Army, 14-9, Cagle turns the other side of the line and heads downfield behind a wall of blockers. Cagle was a threat to Navy every time he touched the ball.*

There were just a few minutes left to play in the 1926 Army-Navy game, Army leading 21–14, when suddenly the Navy came to life and drove to the Army 5-yard line. There halfback Howie "Shag" Ransford slipped the ball to halfback Alan Shapley on a reverse that completely fooled Army, and Navy had its third touchdown and, following Tom Hamilton's extra-point kick, a miraculous 21–21 tie. Thirty-five years later (photo taken in 1961), Admiral Alan Shapley was one of the most decorated war heroes in the Marine Corps.

with Tommy Hamilton and Shapley driving, cutting, and slashing through Army for precious yards and first downs behind the savage blocking of Tom Eddy and Frank Wickhorst. Slowly they drove to the Army goal line, until they reached the 8-yard line. Then, three plays later, it was fourth down with but three yards to go.

The crowd of 110,000 was up on its feet, cheering, screaming . . . The Cadets pleading, "Hold 'em, Army" . . . the Middies yelling, "Score, score, score. . . ."

Dusk was now falling rapidly and the players on the field looked like shrouded ghosts outlined against the piles of snow on the sidelines.

Quarterback Eddie Hannegan, the Navy field general—one day to become a rear admiral in charge of all American atomic strike forces—called the play "a dangerous and tricky naked reverse." The ball was centered to Ransford, who faked a run to his right before quickly slipping the ball to Alan Shapley. Bent at the waist, Ransford kept driving as if he still had the ball, and Army tacklers charged after him. The deception was so smooth that not one Army player noted that Shapley had the ball until it was too late and Alan was across the goal line for the touchdown. Shapley's delirious teammates mobbed him in the end zone and pummeled him to the turf.

But wait. There was still one point to go. It was Army 21, Navy 20. As Tommy Hamilton fell back to try to kick his way into Navy immortality, the field and the stands were quiet as a tomb. Both Middies and Cadets were silently praying to the Gods of Football as Hamilton caught the pass from center, quickly but carefully dropped the ball in front of his toe, and drop-kicked a perfect extra point. The Navy thunder from the east stands was picked up by a wind from the lake and carried out over the land as the score now read: Navy 21, Army 21.

But even now, with still three minutes left to play, it was not over. Army received Navy's kick, and Wilson and Cagle proceeded to gain huge chunks of Navy ground. Just when it

seemed that Army would again score, the Navy defense turned to steel and concrete as the Middies held and took over the ball on their 16-yard line.

Tommy Hamilton tried three desperation passes in an attempt to get the ball into position for a field goal, but the Cadets defended successfully each time. Then, on fourth down, another long pass attempt was intercepted by Army's Wilson, who cut back away from two tacklers and for a moment broke into the clear for what looked like the winning score. But Navy tacklers came charging at him and dragged Light Horse Harry down on the 40-yard line as the final gun sounded.

Thus ended a game which moved 110,000 persons so powerfully that they forgot aching feet, frostbitten noses, and congealed ears. Two truly great football teams, evenly matched and perfectly conditioned, had fought to a satisfactory tie. It was, as the French would say, a game without reproach. The two Corps—1,200 Cadets, 1,900 Midshipmen—marched back to their schools with banners flying sky-high. There was glory in all.

If you think this was only a football game, you have missed the point. This was a great national event not only watched by 110,000 spectators but also followed by countless millions on radio. From the rock-ribbed coast of Maine to the golden sands of California, by land and by sea, the Army-Navy game was fought out play-by-play before an unpredicted audience. And even around the globe, the news of it was flung by wireless to all the Army and Navy posts, to the Marines and foreign squadrons, even to the very outposts of American civilization. That day, every American soldier, sailor, pilot, and marine had one ear cocked toward Soldier Field, Chicago.

And to the credit of the city of Chicago, this was the best conducted Army-Navy game in history. The record-breaking crowd was handled without any confusion or delay. The arrangements were letter-perfect.

Here were two of the greatest football teams ever turned out by Uncle Sam's academies—

two championship teams staking everything on the fortunes of a single afternoon.

Tom Hamilton has his own memories of that glorious day, and here they are:

"Much has been said of me about what I was thinking when I had to kick the drop kick for the extra point in that 1926 game—with Navy behind by one point. Frank Wickhorst drew me out of the huddle and I cleaned the mud off my shoes while the team talked to one another about blocking out the Army team. I was more concerned about getting the mud off my shoe than anything else, and when I did kick it, it was more a matter of practice than responding to a big, impending moment. I had practiced that kick so long in my room in the Naval Acad-

emy and on the field so that the actions were second nature. So actually I did not think too much about it. More significant to me than that kick was the chance I'd had to play a whole game and do the linebacking.

"This game was certainly the highlight of my playing career, and I think it was one of the best games that I have ever had a chance to be a part of. I think it is significant that the players on both teams went on to outstanding naval and military careers. All of them were prominent in service in World War II. Ask any marine about Tom Trapnell, the Army halfback. He was one of the early heroes in the Philippines when he blocked a bridge with his big truck and stood there with a couple of men behind him, firing a machine gun. He saved an

Far left: *One of the Navy's great all-time backs, Tom Hamilton kicked three extra points to tie the 1926 Army-Navy classic 21–21. Left: Hamilton's punting also kept the Army in a defensive hole through much of the game. In 1934, Hamilton returned to Annapolis to succeed Rip Miller as Navy's head coach.*

entire company as the Japanese did not attempt a crossing.

"Blondie Saunders, one of the Army's tackles, lost a leg in the fighting early in the war. One of the stories I heard about him is that he had to be transported by air back to Hawaii for surgery to save his life. They did not have blood and plasma to give him transfusions, so a coach by the name of Shooty, who had been the high school coach at Santa Barbara High School in California, made the trip with him, and they took the transfusion directly from Shooty to keep Saunders alive.

"Many times critics of sports have indicated that the intense rivalry between the Army and the Navy is not good and engenders bad feelings between the services for the rest of their careers. In my opinion, the very opposite is true. The best friends that I have in the Army were all people that I played against in football, basketball, or baseball. While we all competed as well as we could, the respect and admiration we had for each other as opponents gave us a proper outlook toward the other ser-vice. Indeed, practically the only friends I had in the Army were those I played against.

"An interesting relationship for me was with General Gar Davidson, who was on the 1926 Army team and played against us in Chicago. Then, when I returned to coach at the Naval Academy in '34, '35, and '36, Gar was the head coach at the Military Academy. Following all those years of deadly rivalry, first as players and then as opposing coaches, we had a tour of duty in Washington where our wives and families became really good friends. We were able to play golf and meet together socially. Later on, after World War II, Gar and his wife, Verone, were stationed at the Presidio, a huge Army base, when I coached the Navy team that came to Berkeley to play the University of California. It was very nice for us to have Gar Davidson and his wife to dinner with our staff and team after the game. This was in 1947. Gar then went to West Point as superintendent. I became athletic director at Pittsburgh. We had occasion to play the Army at West Point, and our meeting with General Davidson was again most pleasant."

11

Dark Times: 1927-33

*T*he nation's football fans were still talking about the 1926 Army-Navy game when it was time for the next one, the thirtieth between the archrivals, to be played at New York's Polo Grounds. More than 70,000 spectators, many paying as much as $100 per ticket, were coming to watch the 1927 game.

Everyone wanted to see the great Army stars, especially redheaded Chris Cagle, a dashing, flashing meteor of a football player who could not be stopped. The fighting Irish of Notre Dame had tried it just two weeks prior, and Red had laughingly scored twice on two sensational broken-field dashes that had had the crowd breathless as the Cadets pounded the Irish for an 18–0 victory, one of the more one-sided defeats that Knute Rockne had suffered.

Navy had lost most of the great stars of its undefeated 1926 eleven. Captain Frank Wickhorst, Tommy Hamilton, Alan Shapley, Russ Lloyd, Howard Caldwell, Howie Ransford, Jim Schuber, Art Born, and Harry Hardwicke had all graduated. The Middies did, however, have Whitey Lloyd, a marvelous runner, back for his third season, also tackle Mike Bogdanovich, and a strong backfield of Joe Clifton, Hal Bauer, Art Spring, and Captain Ned Hannegan.

It was a budding Navy squad that lost only

to Notre Dame and Michigan before the meeting with Army, whom they were determined to beat for the first time since 1921.

The Sailors took charge on their first possession as Clifton, Lloyd, and Ransford tore the Army line apart for a series of first downs, and it looked like a Navy romp as the Middies got to the 8-yard line, only to be stopped by a stubborn Army defense. Army kicked to midfield, and once more the Navy backs led by Whitey Lloyd bashed the Army line. This time Navy got to the Army 10-yard line, and again a stubborn Army defense halted the Navy thrust.

Army dropped back deep into their end zone to kick out of danger, but the Navy forwards broke through and tackle Carl Giese blocked the kick. It was ruled a safety, and Navy had a 2-point lead.

Army failed to gain the next time it had the ball, and on fourth down kicked to the Middies. Once again the Navy backs led by Joe Clifton and Lloyd crashed through the Army line for one first down after another. Then Lloyd took a handoff and passed to left end Ted Sloane for a Navy first down on the 26-yard line. Lloyd carried the ball down to the 10-yard line, and shortly Navy was on the 6-yard line with a first down and two minutes to play in

Army's Christian Keener "Red" Cagle, one of the greatest backs in the history of football.

the half. The huge crowd at the Polo Grounds were on their feet, screaming with excitement. Here was an inexperienced bunch of Navy players pushing a great, almost invincible Cadet eleven all over the field. It looked like another great upset.

On first down, Joe Clifton crashed the Army line for a mere 1-yard gain. He smashed in for another try that moved the ball to the 4-yard line. Again on third down it was a tired, weary Joe Clifton, smashing into the Army line. But the great Army fighting spirit would not give ground, and Clifton was stopped on the 1-yard line with time running out.

Now it was fourth down, and once more Big Joe Clifton slammed into the Army line behind a fierce charge that could be heard plainly way up in the stands.

Was he over the goal line?

The Army and Navy players, seemingly all

★ ★ ★

Letter from Harry E. Wilson

Lighthorse Harry Wilson's exploits on the gridiron won't soon be forgotten. An All-American at Penn State before going to West Point, he was one of Army's great stars from 1924–27. It was four years of famine for Navy as Wilson led the Cadets to three victories and a tie. During World War II, Colonel Wilson won the Distinguished Flying Cross and five air medals.

The coaches and their assistants down thru the years. . . . Biff Jones, Earl Blaik, Bob Neyland, McEwan, Gene Vidal, Paul Parker (who went to Tennessee with Neyland), Ralph Sasse (deceased), Bill Woods (player and coach now at Norwich University), these are the ones I remember most during my time at the Academy. The trainers I think deserve a word. For example Frank Wandel of my time. Sergeant Marty Maher, a fixture at USMA since time began, took care of the gym and helped the trainer by rubbing the boys down and working out the charley horses. He was full of West Point tradition and was actually a part of it.

I can remember the first time I reported to the gym for physical training. Marty got ahold of me and took me all around the place, giving me all the physical tests he could devise. The further we went the more mournful he became. After each test he would shake his head and tell me how much better Oliphant or McEwan or other Army athletes had done. I later found out who "Marty" was and that it was his habit to put the "Bee" onto any cadet who had a shred of athletic reputation before coming to West Point.

Names that stand out particularly during my years either for ability or personality are Harry Ellinger (later a coach) and Gus Farwick, guards in 1924, Garbisch at center, Bill Woods and Bill Gilmore, the hardest working backs you ever saw on a football field, Tiny Hewitt whom I played against when he played for Pitt, Moe Daly a center, class of 1927. Later he was captured in the Philippines. He refused to try to escape on the march from Bataan because he had a company of men to take care of and he thought that more important. Trapnell, a back who was with Daly when he died in a Jap troop ship (prison ship), Bosko Schmidt, '26, a guard who played his heart out and later died in an aircraft accident. Rosey O'Donnell, '28, a back—later flew the last B-18 greatly overweight out of the Philippines. Blondie Saunders, '28, a tackle, was my roommate for four years. His name was George and I always said he could hit you three times before you hit the ground. He piled on top of one another, were pulled apart by the officials, and plainly Joe Clifton was down . . . just two inches from the goal line.

Army had held . . . and the crowd roared as the gun went off for the end of the half with Navy leading 2-0. It was one of Army's finest defensive hours. They had stopped mighty Navy's fourth drive without a score.

In the third period an Army team inspired by the great defensive play of its line began to hit Navy with an explosive attack. Led by Cagle and Harry Wilson, Army ripped and tore for three straight first downs, marching the ball to the Navy 5-yard line, from where Wilson smashed across for an Army touchdown. The kick was good and it was Army 7, Navy 2.

After taking the kickoff, Navy tried a couple of successful passes. Then Whitey Lloyd attempted another pass, a long heave to his right, but Chris Cagle, playing just right, jumped

★ ★ ★

was shot down in the Pacific in Japanese territory and had to sit on the pilot's lap to land it (B-17) in the water. He was in command of the mission and Group CO at the time. Having gone out thru the window he had to go back in after the copilot whom he had thought dead. While he was doing this the airplane sank and the Lord knows how they got out. They—the ones still alive—got to shore in a rubber boat and the "coast watchers" took care of them until they could get a Navy "Dumbo" (rescue plane) in to pick them up. Later in China, Saunders crashed in a B-25 and lay pinned in the wreck all night. As a result of his injuries his leg had to be amputated.

Skipper Seaman, Charlie Born, Harbold, Chick Harding, Bud Sprague, Johnny Murrell, and Red Cagle were outstanding players in anyone's book, as the Navy will verify. Of course there are many others that deserve to be mentioned.

One thing I might comment on—it is a question I have been asked several times. Is there any difference between an Army-Navy game and, say, a Penn State-Navy game? Well, I couldn't see how there could be too much. I had played against Navy and with some success three times before going to West Point. As for rivalry we had had a pretty good thing going with the University of Pittsburgh at which we had *not* been too successful thanks to Tiny Hewitt, Davies, Peck, Frank and a few others (like Pop Warner). Anyhow come my first Army game with the Navy in 1924 and I was due for a distinct surprise. Evidently I should have studied up on the statistics of Army-Navy games. Previous records for the year should really count for something. Well of course they do—some—but far less than in any other rivalry I know of. Mediocre players become stars for a day and a more brilliant player may find himself handcuffed unless he can work himself up to the spirit of the occasion. I would say that the intense spirit which goes into this game does not increase the finesse of the play, for subtlety and strategy can be lost on someone too blind to see and all powerful with an overflow of adrenaline or whatever it is. However, if you are looking for spirit, heart, and do-or-die rock 'em, sock 'em, clean football with great uncertainty as to the results—you got it! My answer to the question is Yes. It is hardly necessary to add that the color that is part of this occasion surpasses that of any other athletic event of the year.

Sincerely,
Harry E. Wilson
Col. USAF (Ret).

high for the interception and was off, running like a deer. The redhead sped 65 yards past the entire Navy team and was finally pulled down from behind on the Navy 8-yard line.

On the next play Wilson called Cagle's signal, but Red said, "Today it's Wilson's day. He scores the points."

Quarterback Doyle Nave looked at Red, nodded, called Wilson's signal, and Harry smashed over for the touchdown. Red Cagle kicked his second extra point and it was 14–2, Army.

In the fourth period Army kept up the pressure and consistently gained ground, reaching the Navy's 15-yard line. But there Navy's stout-hearted defense rose up and stopped the Cadets cold.

After an exchange of punts, Navy took possession of the ball in midfield. There Whitey Lloyd dropped back, shook off two Army tacklers, and spotted Ted Sloane, all alone on the Army 40-yard line. Whitey tossed a perfect strike to Sloane, Ted took the ball over his shoulders, and without breaking stride pounded in for a Navy score. Ned Hannegan kicked the extra point, and it had become a 14–9 battle, Army in front.

Shortly thereafter the game ended, as did the glorious gridiron careers of Army's Charlie Born, Blondie Saunders, Harry Wilson, and Chips Harbold. All of them would become Air Force heroes in the bigger battles of World War II.

For the next two years the great game was suspended while officials of the two academies remained at odds because of a number of eligibility rules that Navy insisted upon. Eventually Navy got its way; plebes were not to be used, and each school was to limit playing to a three-year rule. Football players who had performed at other schools had to conform to this new standard when they transferred to either the Naval Academy or West Point.

By 1930 the nation was mired deep in the gloom of the most widespread depression the country had known. U.S. unemployment figures showed that more than four and a half million people were out of work. . . . The stock market's downward trend since October 1929 reached bottom as more than $30 billion in paper profits vanished. . . . In September, panic swept the banking community as more than 305 banks closed their doors, and a month later 522 banks closed up. . . . And President Herbert Hoover asked officials of the Army and Naval Academy football teams to resolve their differences and play a benefit game for the unemployed. The request was approved.

The news that the annual rivalry would be resumed was received by both football teams with incredible joy, and the entire season took on a new dimension.

Navy with such stars as Bullet Lou Kirn, Oscar Hagberg, Dick Antrim, Joe Bauer, Captain Bob Bowstrom, Howard Born, Tom Chambers, Mickey Miller, and Ted Torgerson enjoyed a highly successful season, winning six games, including a 31–0 victory over a strong Princeton team.

Army, under new coach Major Ralph Sasse, also enjoyed one of its finest seasons as the Cadets defeated every opponent before tying Yale 7–7 and then dropping a spine-tingling 7–6 thriller to the fighting Irish of Notre Dame before 100,000 fans in Chicago.

New York's Yankee Stadium was packed as a crowd of 70,000 spectators, many paying $100 per seat, jammed every inch of the huge ballpark. Mayor Jimmy Walker remarked that he could have sold half a million tickets for the renewal of this game, which had meant so much to New York through the years.

As the game began it was apparent that Army had the bigger, faster team. With Ray Stecker and Tom Kilday carrying, Army moved the ball smartly to the Navy 20-yard line. But three running plays failed to gain, and a pass just missed. The ball went over to Navy.

Navy could not gain ground and kicked to Army. A forward pass, Stecker to Wendell Bowman, Army quarterback, was good for 45 yards and brought the ball to the Navy 15-yard line. But once again Navy rose up and held . . . and took over the ball.

Early in the second period, Lou Kirn faked a pass and sped 22 yards off tackle to bring the ball to midfield. But that was the most either team could do before the first half came to an end.

The game remained scoreless well into the second half, until there were about seven minutes left to play. Then Wendell Bowman decided the moment had come for a play that the Army had practiced especially for the Navy game. He had not used it yet, being content to wait for a decisive moment. Now he called the signal for "No. 54."

It was a simple play, but it depended on the split-second timing of everyone involved. The ball went to Ray Stecker, who took a couple of quick steps as if to run off tackle, but then quickly changed direction to dart inside his own left guard . . . through a big hole created by his linemen, and as the Navy defensive backs moved in to stop him, Stecker cut away sharply to the right side, into the secondary and in the clear.

Now he was running with no one near him, speeding 56 yards for an Army touchdown. When his teammates caught up with him, they pounded him to the ground, pummeling and whacking him with joy. Finally, they picked up a happy Ray Stecker as the crowd roared.

Army missed the extra point as the game ended and the final score was Army 6, Navy 0.

Army earned the victory, but never had to fight harder on any football field.

"We had a new coach in 1931," recalled Bullet Lou Kirn, Navy's great halfback, in a letter to the author. "His name was Rip Miller, the former Notre Dame star. He put in a new offense, the Notre Dame offense, and of course that changed our entire game plan. It took us nearly half the season to find our way through all those complex Notre Dame plays, but when we did we looked like a pretty good team.

"We beat some very good teams, including Princeton, Pennsylvania, William and Mary, but lost to Maryland, Ohio State, Notre Dame, and Southern Methodist. But by the time the Army game rolled around, we were ready for them, or so we thought.

"Coach Ralph Sasse of Army had developed some outstanding backs including Ray Stecker, Felix Vidal, Bob Carver, and Tom Kilday. He also had All-American Jack Price, a big tackle, and Pete Kopscak, a fine end. Army had a great season record, including wins over an outstanding Michigan State team, Colorado College, Louisiana State University, and a big win over Notre Dame, shutting out the Irish to win 12–0. The victory over Notre Dame provided the Cadets with just the proper mental attitude that meant t-r-o-u-b-l-e for Navy."

Before a crowd of 75,000 excited spectators at Yankee Stadium the two service teams squared off in another game played for the Unemployment Relief Fund. More than $350,000 was raised.

There was no scoring during the opening period, but plenty of excitement as both teams showed promise of things to come. Lou Kirn's letter described what followed:

"In the second period, Army took possession of the ball on the thirty-yard line and on successive plays marched to our seven-yard line, before losing the ball on downs. Ray Stecker and Kilday alternated in carrying the ball and slicing through our line for huge gains.

"I then punted to Carver, who returned the ball to our thirty-seven-yard line. Now the Army backs had good field position and made the most of it. Stecker tossed a pass to Carver who sliced downfield to the ten-yard line. Three line plays by the Army netted only two yards, and then Travis Brown kicked a field goal to give Army a 3–0 lead.

"I received the kickoff after the field goal, but the Army defense stalled our attack, and then I got off a fifty-five yard kick, deep into Army territory."

Now the Army machine began to hit on all cylinders. A Navy defensive back, eager to intercept a pass thrown by Stecker, charged into

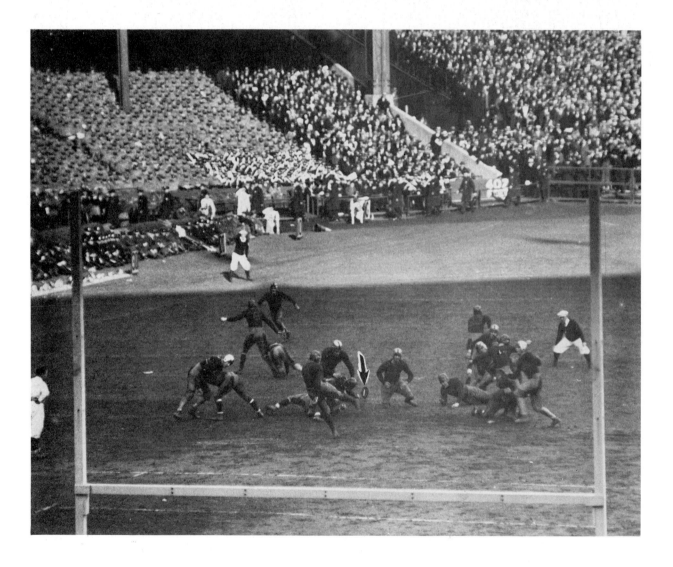

The 1930 game was yet another spine-tingler. Two successive plays in the first period provided special excitement. Opposite page, top: On third down deep in Navy territory, "Bullet" Lou Kirn fumbled the ball and, fortunately for Navy, recovered. Opposite page, bottom: On the next play, the Middies' captain and outstanding tackle, Bob Bowstrom, despite a formidable Army rush, punted the ball 65 yards . . . and Navy was out of danger. The game remained scoreless until there were six minutes to play. Left: Then Army's fullback, Ray Stecker, took the ball on his own 44-yard line, faked right, cut to his left, and dashed 56 yards for the only score of the game, and a 6–0 Army victory.

Kopscak, and Navy was penalized 15 yards for interference. It gave Army a first down on the 35-yard line. Stecker pounded the Middies for another first down on the 25-yard line. Then, in a beautifully timed reverse, Jack Buckler to Pete Kopscak got still another Army first down on the 10-yard line, from where Vidal slashed through for the touchdown. Jack Buckler kicked the extra point and it was Army 10, Navy 0.

"We finally scored a touchdown in the third quarter," said Kirn. "That was on one of the longest plays on record. The pass was at least a fifty-yarder and was caught by our wingback Joe Tschirigi on a beautiful over-the-shoulder catch for the score. After throwing the ball as far as I could, I was standing there watching the catch and was wide open. I was hit as hard as I ever was in my life, by Army's All-American Jack Price. He drove his two hundred and ten pounds into my hundred-and-fifty-five-pound frame, and I felt as if a steamroller had passed over me. As we were getting up, Price asked, 'Are you hurt, Sonny?' I yelled back at him, 'Hell no, you big ox.' Years later, I met Jack at an officers' club and we had a friendly drink together, reminiscing about the game.

"The final score was 17–7. We were lucky to play the Army so close, for they had a great team.

"After the game the football was auctioned

The 1931 Navy football team included some of the Academy's greatest stars: Lou Kirn, Howie Born, Captain Magruder Tuttle (front row, with ball), and war hero William "Killer" Kane. A great tackle, Kane (sitting on the right of Tuttle) was officer of the day at Pearl Harbor on December 7, 1942. On duty for forty-eight straight hours, Kane later shot down three Japanese planes in one day.

off for charity. It brought ten thousand dollars. The ball was autographed by the players on both teams, and when I last saw it, it was reposing in a trophy case at the Naval Academy."

The year 1932 was a trying one for the nation. President Herbert Hoover tried desperately to stem the floodtide of a terrible depression. He granted generous credits to industry, cut his salary and those of ten of his cabinet members, and planned a series of huge public works programs for the unemployed, whose ranks had reached thirteen million. . . . A Bonus Army of about seventeen thousand veterans of World War I marched on Washington and camped out on the Capitol grounds until Congress authorized immediate bonus payments. . . . Federal troops under General Douglas MacArthur drove out the veterans after weeks of dickering with them to leave their ramshackle cardboard huts. . . . Republicans renominated Herbert Hoover in their annual convention at Chicago, while the Democrats nominated Franklin D. Roosevelt over Al Smith. Roosevelt easily defeated Hoover, carrying all but seven states. . . . Charles Lindbergh's twenty-month-old son was kidnapped from his parents' home in Hopewell, New Jersey. . . . Two months later the baby's body was found after a $50,000 ransom had been paid. . . . Amelia Earhart became the first woman to fly solo across the Atlantic. She landed in Londonderry, Ireland, a distance of 2,026 miles from Harbour Grace, Newfoundland, where she started.

In the world of sports . . . the Olympic Games were held in the United States—the Winter Games at Lake Placid, New York, the Summer Games at Los Angeles. . . . Jack Sharkey of Boston defeated Max Schmeling of Germany for the heavyweight championship in a fifteen-round decision victory. . . . The Yankees defeated the Chicago Cubs as they swept the Series in four games in the twenty-ninth annual World Series. And in the annual Army-Navy game, played at Franklin Field, Philadelphia, the Middies and the Cadets battled each other up and down the field before Army

won their third straight game from their old rivals.

Army had chosen Major Ralph Irwin Sasse as the new head coach in 1930, and his first two seasons were an astounding success story with two straight victories over Navy. When Sasse took over in 1930 after years as an assistant coach, first under John McEwan and then Biff Jones, he had addressed the 1,200 Cadets and said, "I promise you fireworks." And it was fireworks he gave them.

A strong Army eleven entrained for Franklin Field to battle Navy in 1932. They had had 7 wins in 9 games and were overwhelming favorites to defeat a young, inexperienced Navy eleven with only 2 victories in 8 games.

But once the game began, Navy turned on some firepower of their own. Hugh Murray, a tall, rangy end, intercepted an Army pass and dashed to the Army 45-yard line. On the next play, halfback Bill Clark, behind some fine blocking, took the ball on a reverse and sped to the Army 25-yard line. Clark hit the line for 10 more yards and a first down on the 15.

Now the huge crowd, which had barely settled down, found itself watching an underdog Navy team pounding at Army's door. On a first-down play, they got to the 10-yard line, but a penalty moved the ball back. Then quarterback Les Slack tried a pass, but halfback Ken Fields of Army intercepted the ball and ran it to the 25-yard line. Here Army really stunned and surprised Navy with a quick kick that was downed way back at the Navy 15-yard line. Navy failed to gain and punted.

Felix Vidal took the kick and ran it back to the Navy 30-yard line. Three successive tries at the line failed to gain any ground, and the Middies punted. Now Army had the ball on the Navy 45-yard line, first down. But line plays failed to gain and Army kicked on the fourth down. Navy attempted two unsuccessful plays and kicked to midfield.

Two Cadet first downs brought the ball to the Navy 10-yard line, and then Vidal took the ball over for the first score of the afternoon. Jack Buckler kicked the extra point and it was 7–0.

★ ★ ★

Letter from Norman B. Edwards

Norman Edwards played for Army in the 1930s and vividly remembers the games—particularly the one during which he got slugged by the coach for his overexuberance. Here are his comments about his days with the Army squad.

In my day, the "B" teams learned the plays of the next opponent from scouting reports and we usually had a couple of days of scrimmage against our opponent's offense before each game. Among the scrubs of my day were Westmoreland, now general in Vietnam; Abrams, now vice chief of staff of the Army (I believe Abe later made the varsity as a substitute guard); Throckmorton, who was Westmoreland's deputy in Vietnam, and others who have gone on to great heights.

Red Blaik, who was our backfield coach before going to Dartmouth as head coach, was the finest technician I have ever seen, but Ralph Sasse, our head coach in 1930–32, had the greatest ability for bringing a team to fighting pitch before a game and during a half that I have ever seen. In 1932, before the Harvard game, Sasse had Milt Summerfelt, our captain, read a letter to the squad immediately before leaving the dressing room to begin the game. The letter was from a young invalid boy in Vermont (I suspect Sasse wrote the letter), and the lad went into detail how the Army was his greatest inspiration and the best team in the country. The letter described the lad's afflictions and requested one of the team's practice footballs if it could be spared. It was a masterpiece of writing; a tearjerker and heart wringer, and so inspired us that we tore out of the dressing room and made four touchdowns in the first half of what was supposed to be a close game. In the second half of that game, I had just come out of the fracas and was sitting on the bench behind Sasse when one of our safety men returned a punt for a touchdown. In my excitement, I jumped up and slapped the coach on the back. Whereupon Sasse turned around and slugged me, knocking me completely backward over the bench. Guess he was excited, too. Anyhow, I had a sore jaw to add to my other aches and pains.

With respect to an Army-Navy game in 1934 in the mud at Franklin Field, when Army lost 3 to 0 for the first time in 13 (?) years, Slade Cutter, the Navy tackle, thought Moose Stillman, one of our guards, was holding him and invited Moose out behind the stands after the game. Stillman, knowing that Cutter was intercollegiate heavyweight boxing champion, replied rather sensibly, I thought, "What do you think I am, a G.D. fool?" Incidentally, that game was the only game, high school or college, that my parents ever came to see me play and it was so muddy that after the first play even the numerals on our jerseys were obliterated. So, although in the stands, my parents never saw me play a game of football.

Sincerely,
Norman B. Edwards
Major General, USA
Deputy Chief of Personnel
Operations

Several plays later, Army began another drive that culminated in a touchdown when Jack Buckler passed to Bill Frentzel, who caught the ball and scored. Buckler missed the extra point and the score was 13–0, Army.

Buzz Borries, Navy's young, shifty halfback, began to move the team upfield. But Borries fumbled the ball on a reverse and Army recovered on the Navy 48-yard line. After a series of off-tackle plays, an end run, and a reverse, Jack Buckler slammed over from the 5-yard line. The extra point was made, and it was 20–0, Army, as the whistle sounded to end the game.

Guest of honor at the game that day was the former supe of the Military Academy, General Douglas MacArthur.

A slim-hipped, swashbuckling halfback from Texas named Jack Buckler led Army to its fourth victory of the decade in 1933 by defeating a stubborn, fighting Navy eleven, 12–7. It was another thrilling, pulse-tingling battle that had the crowd of more than 79,000 at Municipal Stadium, Philadelphia, standing and cheering through most of the game. Although Army had not lost to Navy since their 1921 battle, two of those ten games had ended in ties, and in 1933 Navy came close to another.

The game opened with neither team gaining an advantage in their first possessions. Then Bill Clark, Navy's fine kicker, got off a beautiful 50-yard spiral punt that Paul Johnson, the Army quarterback, scooped up and took off upfield. He got magnificent blocking, and every Navy tackler ended down on the turf before Johnson, running down the right sidelines, had sped 81 yards for a touchdown. Jack Buckler's extra

point try was blocked, and it was 6–0, Army, with the game just one minute old.

The Middies took the Army kickoff and began to move upfield in a spirited drive led by Buzz Borries and their great Hawaiian halfback, Gordon Chung-Hoon. But Army stopped the drive and Navy was forced to kick. Bill Clark's punt was a beauty—it went out of bounds on the Army 4-yard line—and the Cadets were in a hole.

Buckler kicked on first down, and then Borries and Red Baumberger, who had replaced an injured Chung-Hoon, took turns battering at the Army line. In rapid succession, two first downs brought Navy to the Army 35-yard line. Then Baumberger cut through left tackle, and suddenly he was all alone . . . down to the 20-yard line, the 15, and over the goal line for the Navy touchdown. Dick Bull kicked the extra point, and it was upstart Navy out in front by 7–6.

In the second period Army launched an attack that began on their 29-yard line. Jack Buckler's fine running and passing advanced the Cadets to the Navy 20-yard line. On first down Buckler dodged two Navy tacklers, cut through a hole in the secondary, and raced into the end zone to return the lead to Army, 12–7. The conversion was missed.

Late in the third period, Navy began a march that brought them to the Army 13-yard line. Here Army's great line, led by All-American tackle Harvey Jablonsky, stopped two pass plays and a run by Borries.

In the final period, Navy got to the 30-yard line once more, but Johnson intercepted a pass on the 10-yard line to stop Navy's last attempt. The final score: Army 12, Navy 6.

12

Hamilton Coaches Navy: 1934-36

$\mathscr{L}$et Tom Hamilton tell of his first years back at the Naval Academy:

"In 1934, after coaching the U.S. Fleet Team for three years on the West Coast, I was called to the Naval Academy as head football coach. Our squad was small but spirited and bright. We had tremendous confidence in ourselves, and above all we had two great players we were able to capitalize on to a great extent. The first was Buzz Borries who, in my opinion, was the finest football player I've ever seen. He was a running back, and our squad, although it had spirit and great moxie, was not a great physical squad able to give our backs the type of blocking needed against more physically strong opponents. So I think Borries could have made a name as an open-field runner that even exceeds what he actually did, which was plenty. He had an amazing style of running in a relaxed manner, keeping a little reserve open to give him more speed when needed. He had tremendous ability to fake a would-be tackler. No one ever hit him squarely.

"The other great player was Bill Clark. He was the best punter I have ever seen. His ability to kick the ball out of bounds inside the 15-yard line meant a great deal to this team. We never covered both sides of the field. Clark would just tell his teammates where he was going to kick

it, and he never let them down. This restricted the amount of area that we had to cover, so we were able to utilize the kicking game very well.

"Our ends were Dick Boll, Clark Hodd, and Bob Dornin, and the tackles, Slade Cutter and George Lambert. The guards were Captain Dick Burns and John Schaffer; the center, Lou Robertshaw. The backfield consisted of Borries, Clark, Dick Pratt, and Starr King. We had some excellent replacements, notably Joe Evans in the backfield and Otis Cole and Dave Zabriskie as guards. Jim Mini was an end; Carl Fellows, a back; and Rivers Morell, a guard.

"We had not beaten the Army for eleven years and came into this game with only one loss—that to Pittsburgh just the week before. The Army had a fine squad with a fine back named Jack Buckler; also Monk Myers. And their captain was Jay Stancook, an excellent ballplayer.

"The game was played in a sea of mud on Franklin Field, Philadelphia, and our strategy was to try to score as fast as we could before the ball and everybody got too muddy. Borries was able to make about a 20-yard gain early in the first quarter to give us good field position. Bill Clark took advantage of that position with a punt that Dusty Dornan knocked out of bounds on the Army 1-yard line. When the

Navy's outstanding coaching staff in 1934 was headed by Tom Hamilton (back row, far left) and included (front row) Johnny Wilson, Magruder Tuttle, Lou Kirn, Frank Foster, Oscar Hagberg, and (back row, right of Hamilton) Rip Miller, Howard Caldwell, Johnny Cross. Navy defeated Army 3-0 for its first victory in thirteen years.

Army punted out, Borries made a nice return. We then made a few first downs, one as a result of a shovel pass from Borries to Dick Pratt, and when we couldn't make the touchdown, Slade Cutter kicked a field goal from the 20-yard line which turned out to be the only score of the day.

"The game was very exciting throughout. The Army quick-kicked on us once, and Buzz Borries picked it up on the Navy 15 and ran it back about 15 more. He almost broke loose. And then the Army threatened several times. One time Starr King intercepted a pass, and Clark really saved the day for us when he punted 68 yards over the safetyman's head late in the game.

"This was a team of which I was very proud. They were not very big, but they certainly be-

lieved in themselves and they played to the limit at all times."

During World War II, Slade Cutter was one of the Navy's most decorated submarine commanders. His submarine was USS *Seahorse*. Cutter and his crew sank 141,000 tons of Japanese shipping. He received the Silver Star, Navy Cross, and Presidential Citation.

"The game of 1935 was played in Franklin Field in Philadelphia. Both teams were pretty well matched. So it was really quite a blow for us to lose the game, 28-6. Perhaps it's the first time as a coach that I have ever seen a team freeze.

"On the first play of the game, immediately after we had kicked off, the Army halfback,

Navy's 1934 victory in a sea of mud. Above: Navy's Buzz Borries carries the ball well into Army territory, led by Dick Pratt and Bill Clark. Below: On the very next play, Slade Cutter kicks a field goal for the only score of the game.

John Grove, took the ball on a reverse play and went 80 yards for a touchdown. This big play seemed to throw our team into a state of shock, and although we replaced several players, everyone seemed in a trance the rest of the day. The Army ran up 28 points in the first half.

"In the second half, we outplayed the Army completely but were only able to score 6 points. Sneed Schmidt did an especially fine job. So did Bill Ingram in the backfield.

"Our center and captain that year was Lou Robertshaw, and his substitute, Charlie Hutchins, had a most interesting experience during the war as skipper of a destroyer. He rammed a German submarine and kept his ship on top of the sub. The Germans came on deck and were firing anything they could get their hands on up at the bridge of the ship. Likewise the sailors on Hutchins's destroyer picked up anything they could grab, from potatoes to ink bottles, to throw at the Germans until the German sub sank. It's quite an epic in destroyer history.

"Thirteen members of our wonderful 1935 football team were killed in action during World War II. Their names: Dick Bull, a great end; halfback Bill Mason; Duckett Miller, center; Frank Case, halfback; Tommy Edwards, halfback; Joe Evans, halfback; Walt Bayless, tackle; Bill Hulson, end; Charley Anderson, halfback; Charles Reimann, fullback; Jim Andrews, center; Dave Sloan, tackle; and Dave Zabriskie, a fine guard."

★　★　★

Letter from Charles R. Meyer

"You're too small for Army football, son. Better try the Cullum squad." Those were the first words that Charles Meyer, pint-sized Cadet, heard from an Army football coach when he reported for football at West Point in 1934, and small he was. But when Coach Gar Davidson saw little Monk Meyer in action, he told the equipment manager to "get a special uniform for Meyer."

Meyer went on to become one of Army's finest running and passing backs, and his spectacular play in the 1935 Army-Navy game won All-American honors for the little scatback. As Brigadier General Charles R. Meyer, he wrote from Vietnam.

I would like now to go on record that I was probably the lightest individual who has ever participated in the Army-Navy contest, weighing in at approximately 139 pounds. This, I am sure, you will find unique in your rundown of Army-Navy football statistics.

Perhaps being such a lightweight and born at West Point was a natural sportswriter's delight and resulted in my getting much more credit as a football player than I duly deserved. The whole situation, I suppose, lent itself to good copy, and I often hear in reflection a well-worn line of many years ago which went something like this: "A spindle-legged son of an Army colonel, born at West Point."

I am very proud to say that my son, a third-generation West Pointer, earned his letter this past fall by playing second-string linebacker. I hope he will do better next year.

Very sincerely,
Charles R. Meyer
Brigadier General, General Staff
Chief of Staff

Navy's 1935 team, of which thirteen members were killed in action in World War II.

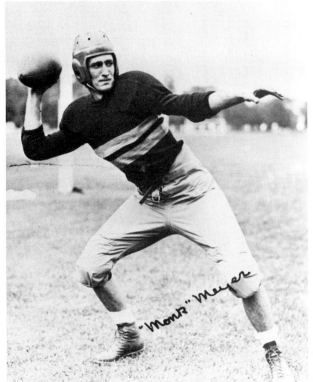

Left: *In the 1935 game, Army's Monk Meyer, a 140-pound quarterback, was all over the field. He ran elusively, kicked like a demon, and passed the ball with the accuracy of a major-league pitcher. That day, Meyer and his Army teammates ran over and around Navy to the tune of 28–6. Below: Twenty-seven years later, General Monk Meyer (with a fair bit of weight added from his playing days) met and chatted football with Captain Pete Dawkins, one of the most admired Army stars of the modern era . . . in Vietnam.*

— ★ —

"The 1936 game was played in Philadelphia's Municipal Stadium, and we won 7–0. It was a tremendous football game that was decided by a Statue of Liberty play, with Schmidt faking a kick and Ingram running about 30 yards to the Army 20-yard line. Bill Ingram then threw an incomplete pass to end Irwin Fike, but there was interference on the 2-yard line. We got the ball and Sneed Schmidt ran it over for a touchdown. The conversion made the score 7–0.

"There were many fine athletes on this team. Ed Hessel, Maurice Ferrara, and Frank Lynch were prominent on the line, and we had two ends, Bill Bringle and Arch Soucek, who were splendid. In 1944, Bill Bringle was one of our leading admirals in the Pacific. Bob Antrim was a fine wingback. Other prominent players included Ray DuBois, a guard, and Ned Thomas, a fine back. This was a good football team which won on this day in a bitter struggle.

"One feature of that team was its employment of a spread formation. Much has been said about the pro teams today with their shotgun offense. We had a team in 1936 that employed this spread or shotgun offense and it was quite effective, especially in our games with Pennsylvania and Columbia. We beat Notre Dame 3–0 and had a very good record.

"Joe Widd was a fine member of this squad who was killed during World War II. And we had a young quarterback, Smokey Manning, who as the executive officer of a submarine dur-

Turning point of the 1936 Army-Navy game: Navy's Sneed Schmidt, from a fake punt formation, hands off to Bill Ingram (son of Navy's outstanding coach of the late twenties) on a Statue of Liberty play for a sizable gain that led to the game's only touchdown and a 7–0 Middie win.

ing an engagement in the South Pacific had to perform an appendectomy on one of his sailors while submerged on a war patrol. It was quite a story in Navy circles."

The 1936 Navy football team had a rather erratic season. In the first three games, against ordinary opposition, the Middies rolled up impressive wins. But then, up against three stronger opponents, the Middies displayed a poor running attack and little defense as they dropped games to Yale, Princeton, and Pennsylvania. And then, in a complete reversal of form, and against odds of 7–1, the Middies roared back to defeat their bitter rivals, Notre Dame, in a 3–0 squeaker, and a strong Harvard Crimson, 20–13. So the Middies were primed to upset a favored Army team in their annual classic.

Army's 1936 squad was once again paced by tiny Monk Meyer, who had demonstrated that he was one of the finest running backs in college football. Jim Ryan was the quarterback on this team, the same Jim Ryan who as a major general just a few years later would command a squadron of Flying Fortress bombers on missions around the world.

On a cold, damp, chilly November 27, at Philadelphia's Municipal Stadium, more than 102,000 spectators, some of them paying as much as $250 per ticket, attended the annual service classic. There were long lines fighting to gain admission, and thousands of fans had to be turned away.

The tremendous crowd saw a hard-fought but unspectacular game in which both teams clawed and scrambled for every bit of precious yardage. It was a battle that saw Army unleash beautiful offensive marches right to the Navy goal line, only to be stopped time and again.

Little Monk Meyer, all of 145 pounds, got to the Navy 5-yard line in the first period, but on the next play was thrown for a 5-yard loss. Again in the second period Army was stopped within the 10-yard line.

Then Navy took over. Led by halfback Bill Ingram, who went on to coach Navy's football squad and then become athletic director, Navy advanced to the Army 25-yard line as the half ended, the score 0–0.

And so it continued well into the second half. Convinced that the game would end scoreless, many in the crowd started leaving midway in the final period. But then Navy began to attack. Again it was Ingram through the line for 10 yards, then for 5 more, then 8 yards.

As the teams lined up, Ingram again took the ball, but this time he bluffed a run up the right side of the Army line and threw a perfect "strike" to Bob Antrim, the big Navy end, far downfield. Jim Craig, the Army defender, was also right on target, however, and jumping into the air, Craig took the ball out of Antrim's hands and started upfield. Suddenly the play was called back. Army's halfback Riggs Sullivan had been detected pushing Navy's end Irwin Fike alongside Antrim. The penalty gave Navy the ball on the Army 2-yard line, and the exiting crowd began to rush back to their seats.

In three plays fullback Sneed Schmit cracked in for the Navy touchdown, and Bill Ingram kicked the extra point. So the game ended: Navy 7, Army 0.

The interference play was to be discussed by the Army players all year long, with threats to have their revenge "next year."

13

Army Comes Back: 1937-38

In 1937, the New Deal policies of the Roosevelt administration came under heavy attack as the President tried to alter the composition of the Supreme Court. . . . The German dirigible *Hindenberg*, attempting to land in New Jersey, exploded and crashed. . . . Spain and China were being torn by civil wars. . . . King Edward VIII abdicated and became the duke of Windsor, then married an American divorcée, Wallis Simpson. . . . And America's most popular woman aviatrix, Amelia Earhart, was lost in a flight in the Pacific.

In the sports world, Don Budge led the U.S. Davis Cup team to victory in England, bringing back the cup after ten years. . . . The New York Yankees defeated the New York Giants in the World Series to become the first team to win six World Series titles. . . . Joe Louis, Detroit's Brown Bomber, knocked out Jim Braddock to win the heavyweight title. . . . And Army's fine football team prepared to face Navy in Coach Gar Davidson's final game as coach after five outstanding seasons at West Point.

For two long years, a big farm boy from Oklahoma named Jim Craig had sat on the sidelines at Army games, his rawboned body draped in a gray Army blanket. Game after game he gazed out onto the field, perhaps with envious and impatient eyes, as he watched a scrawny little narrow-chested Cadet, Monk Meyer, playing the tailback position . . . his position.

But every once in a while the little guy would get awfully tired, or at least Coach Gar Davidson would think he was tired, and Davidson would turn and look at the big farm boy and would bark: "Craig, go in there for Meyer."

When he said that, big Jim Craig would shoot up from the bench, toss his blanket skyward, and go charging onto the field, to relieve Monk Meyer, Army's great back. But only once in a while, and only for a few brief plays (and then usually on defense, as in the 1936 game when he made the famous interception wiped out by a penalty), for somehow little Monk never seemed to get very tired and, somehow, even though he weighed only about 145 pounds, he never got hurt.

Jim Craig waited in hope, for he knew that the Little Monk would graduate one year ahead of him, and it was natural for big Jim to feel that with Monk Meyer gone he, Jim Craig, would take his place in the regular Army backfield. Jim thought about that prospect often.

Then it happened. Monk Meyer graduated. And there was Jim Craig, still on the Army bench with the rest of the subs.

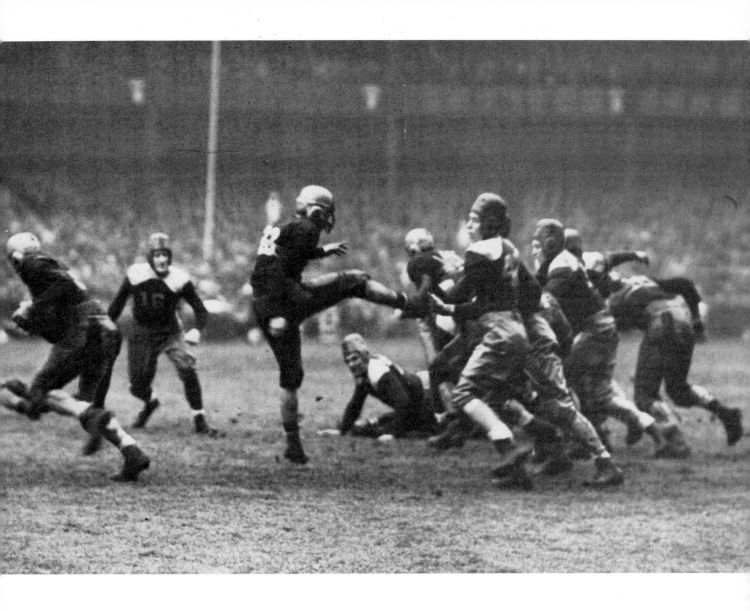

Above: *Army returns the favor in 1937: the Cadets' Woody Wilson fakes a punt after deftly handing the ball off to halfback Huey Long, who picks up 8 yards. But the game remained scoreless until well into the fourth period, when a special drama unfolded. . . . Right: For three years halfback Jim Craig had been sitting on the bench waiting for an opportunity to play against the Navy. At last in the 1937 game, Craig got his chance and came in to score the touchdown that defeated Navy 6–0.*

And so it was again on November 27, 1937, at Municipal Stadium, Philadelphia. As 102,000 spectators peered down through the rain and mist that hung above the stadium, the Army and Navy teams got ready to face each other in their traditional battle for the supremacy of the services, with Jim Craig on the sideline while the Army stars—Woody Wilson, Huey Long, Jim Schwenk, and Jack Ryan—took their places in the backfield.

Jim Craig sat there and fidgeted as neither team could gain sufficient yardage to move the ball for a score, and probably thought to himself, Gosh, if they would just let me get out on the field—if they would just give me a chance to get the ball—I could smash across the Navy goal line. I know I could do the job.

Back and forth the two teams battled through most of the first quarter, failing to gain, exchanging kicks.

★ ★ ★

Letter from Garrison H. Davidson

Gar Davidson was a member of the Army team in that classic battle with Navy in 1926 which ended in the 21–21 tie. When he was appointed head football coach at West Point in 1933, he was the youngest ever in that position. After military service that included numerous campaigns, honors, and awards, he became superintendent of the Academy. Now retired, General Davidson recounts the high spots of his days as both player and coach.

First, a few personal comments. On the train back from the Chicago game in 1926 (incidentally, I was listed as a tackle instead of an end in the newspaper accounts of that game), Ralph Sasse who coached the ends, with Biff Jones's concurrence, invited me to come back the following fall as end coach of the plebes. I served three seasons in that capacity before becoming the head scout and coach of the "B" squad for two years and head coach of the plebes for one. It was also Ralph Sasse who, in the summer of 1932, recommended me to succeed him when he departed the following January. There was quite an exodus of football players at graduation in June of 1933, and the prospects were not bright.

In September of '33, we really only had a few college-size players, but the fifteen cadets who bore the brunt of the season had a tremendous spirit and a firm determination to live down the forecasts. As you know, we went undefeated until the last two or three minutes of the season when the old machine just wore out and several players made a mistake on a punt, any one of which, had it not occurred, would have made the play a success. In retrospect I often wonder how bad a mistake I made in not having the team take deliberate safety, but we had never had a punt blocked all year. It was many years later when we both were officers before I could disabuse Ozzie Simons, our kicker, of his worry that he had been at fault, which was not the case. It was the protection. However, I lay a great deal of the cause to our first major game against Illinois. It was a hot day and the evening before Bob Zuppke, in an address to the Illinois alumni, had waxed extremely confident. We scored a touchdown and later kicked a field goal which was disallowed "because the holder of the ball touched his knee to the ground." It was not until the half that I was able to collar the referee and have him read the rule. He admitted his mistake, said he was sorry, but there was nothing he could do. Anyway, our outmanned team had to play practically the entire game under sweltering condi-

Suddenly Army switched tactics and took to the air. A pass from Wilson to Schwenk brought the ball into Navy territory. Another pass from Long to Jack Ryan put the ball on the Navy 5-yard line. Big Jim Craig's backfield mates were doing all right without him. But two line smashes by Army did not gain an inch, and now a third down.

Just at that moment, as the huge crowd stood and cheered Navy's great goal-line stand, Coach Davidson turned, as he had turned so

seldom over three long years, and said the most glorious words Jim Craig had ever heard: "Craig, get in there and get that touchdown."

And so, his heart bursting with pride and happiness, big Jim Craig came bouncing off the bench and charged onto the field in his last game as a Cadet. When his teammates found him in the backfield, they were as happy for Jim as he was for himself.

On the very next play, quarterback Jim Schwenk called Craig's signal and the ball came

★ ★ ★

tions. It took a great deal out of them and each succeeding Saturday they came back a little more short of their capacity at the start of the Illinois game. By the time we reached the Navy game the smaller members of our team were playing pretty much on their nerve. Nevertheless we were able to hang on, as newspaper accounts show, on the strength of Beanie Johnson's fine punt return and Jack Buckler's nice run on our cutback play off tackle.

The next year was an in and outer, and of course we lost to the Navy for the first time in a long time under impossible conditions. As I remember it, the total number of first downs was five. Navy scored early and that was it. Despite the going, at one point in the game we again broke our cutback inside tackle clean through the line and had every Navy man taken care of. It would have produced a long run for a score had not Borries gotten up off his back and slithered across the field in the mud to drag down our ball carrier from behind just as he was in the clear. Monk Meyer, whom I saw off to Vietnam last week, got his first crack at the Navy in this game. He fumbled at a critical stage, for which I did not blame him a bit, but he took it greatly to heart and swore he would never do so again. I don't remember him fumbling during his next two years despite the fact that he bore the brunt of our offense, handling the ball on two-thirds to three-fourths of the plays.

The Army-Navy game in 1935 was a coach's dream. The newspaper account could have been written prior to the game from our written quarterback instructions. I wish I could find them and send them along. Red Reeder, with the able assistance of Blondie Saunders, who lost a leg during the war, and Eddie Doyle, who was killed in the North African landings at Algiers, did a superb job so that we knew just about what every member of the Navy team had for breakfast. Consequently, everything we attempted turned to gold and we scored twenty-one points in the first sixteen minutes of what was expected to be a tight ball game. We managed to get every cadet on the squad who made the trip into the game as well as one who didn't but left his seat in the stands and got dressed to sit on the bench.

Monk Meyer was our threat and we had rarely run to the weak side when he received the ball. My instructions to the quarterback were the first time he had the ball if he was in position to call a reverse in which Monk handed the ball to Whitey Grove on first down, or if he wasn't in position, to get in position and call the play on the second down. Billy Grohs did the latter and Grove went over eighty yards for a touchdown. He had also been instructed the first time he got a first down near midfield to throw a special pass to Whitey Grove from formation left which we had not used a back to Jim. He tucked it under his huge left arm and started to move. His teammates blocked out several Navy tacklers, but Jim charged ahead oblivious of any hole. Digging in his cleats, he cut through his own left tackle, was met by three Navy tacklers, and carried them over the goal line for the Army touchdown.

That touchdown in the first quarter by Jim Craig was the ball game, the only score of the afternoon. The point after touchdown was missed, and Army ended up winning 6–0.

And Jim Craig, the big farm boy from Pauls Valley, Oklahoma, had scored those 6 points. In all likelihood he still feels today that those three years sitting on the sidelines were a price well worth paying for that one moment.

After all, it isn't every man who can go through his military career, rising from a lieutenant to captain, captain to major, major to

★ ★ ★

great deal. He did, and in a few minutes we had a second score. We instructed him the next time he got in Navy territory to throw a running pass to Clint True, our fullback. This also worked for a long score and a happy day was well begun. This pleasant victory was in no small degree due to the superb leadership of Bill Shuler who took advantage of proximity of the Navy goat to the sideline during the game to pluck some of his whiskers for a souvenir.

1936 was a nightmare for us. A very severe epidemic of the flu hit our squad about midseason. For a couple of weeks the players dropped literally like flies and our team never recovered. I had a particular problem throughout the year with the quarterbacks. Finally, for the Navy game, I decided to select the player with the most poise, experience, and leadership and instruct him intently and in detail for ten days before the game and rest our hopes on him. I selected Stan Smith, a guard, who is now the academic dean of the Coast Guard Academy at New London, and he called a practically perfect game, his first and only effort at quarterbacking. Another difficulty we had to overcome was the lack of a competent wingback and we converted an end, Riggs Sullivan, later commandant of cadets at the Air Force Academy and now a major or lieutenant general in the Air Force, into a halfback for that game, and he did a very superior job. It is still my opinion that there was absolutely no interference when he was called for that penalty which gave the Navy possession of the ball near our goal (incidentally, to this day I am still convinced that neither was there any interference against Milner in the Notre Dame game of the previous year).

1937 was my swan song and the Navy game loomed as an exceedingly tough one. We weren't sure how well we could run against them inside the twenty- or twenty-five yard line; therefore, we cooked up a special reverse pass in which our spinning back, Jack Ryan, now commanding general of the Strategic Air Force, spun, gave the ball to Huey Long, a left-hand passer we had not used very much, who faked a reverse play and then turned and threw diagonally back across the field to Ryan. We instructed the quarterback to use this play when he got in the vicinity of the Navy 25-yard line. He did, and Jack carried the ball to the Navy 3. To get added power, we had adopted also for this game the two inside and outside tackle plays from a 5–1 unbalanced line and the quarterback was told to use them in succession close to the goal. This he did and Jim Craig scored the only touchdown of the game.

Sincerely,
Garrison H. Davidson

colonel, and always have the satisfaction through the years of knowing that he scored the winning touchdown against Navy.

That one great plunge across the Middies' goal line in 1937 is something that Jim Craig will remember vividly throughout the rest of his life. All the rest, the weary backbreaking secondary scrimmages, the tough practices, day after day for three years, all has been forgotten. . . . For Jim Craig beat Navy in 1937.

Jim Craig was graduated from the Academy in 1938 and commissioned as a second lieutenant and assigned to the Quartermaster Corps. Serving in this area, Craig rose in rank and in 1958 was sent to Korea. He served with distinction in that country, and in 1965, Colonel Jim Craig was reassigned to the States, and then left the Army as a full colonel. He now lives in retirement in California.

Coach Tom Hamilton was transferred to sea duty in 1937 and was succeeded by Hank Hardwicke, a crack end on the 1924–26 teams.

Hardwicke's first season, 1937, began impressively with victories over William and Mary, Virginia Military Institute, and Virginia. But then losses to Yale and Notre Dame marred what could have been an outstanding season . . . that is, up to the Army game.

Army also had a new head coach in Bill Wood, plus a bevy of outstanding linemen and several fast scatbacks. The Cadets opened the season against Wichita and trounced the visitors 32–0; following that win, there were victories over Virginia Polytechnic Institute; a close but losing battle against Columbia, 20–18; an easy win over Boston College, 40–0; a loss to Notre Dame; and wins over Franklin & Marshall, Chattanooga, Princeton.

Thus with a 6–2 record, Army was heavily favored to defeat a Navy eleven depleted by injuries to key players, particularly Bill Ingram, an offensive star for the past two seasons.

As a downpour threatened to engulf the field, the teams faced each other in the annual classic at Philadelphia. The capacity crowd saw an exciting, closely contested game, with the underdog Navy at first battering Army all over the field, threatening to score on several occasions only to see the huge Army line, led by tackle Harry Stella, rise to the occasion and stop the Middies' attack.

The Cadets scored first. Navy's Lem Cooke sent a beautiful 48-yard punt upfield where Huey Long took the ball on a run. Gathering speed, picking up blockers on his way, Long cut to the right sideline and outran three Navy tacklers to complete an 80-yard touchdown run, one of the most exciting in the history of the classic series. Long added the extra point, and it was 7–0, Army.

But then the Navy attack began to click. Halfback Lem Cooke passed to end Lucian Powell and Dick Cooper for short gains. Another pass to Powell was caught at the 50-yard line, and Powell kept moving, cutting and slicing until he was stopped by three Army tacklers on the 1-yard line. On the next play, Cooke scored the touchdown, and Bob Wood tied the score by kicking the extra point as the half ended.

In the second half Navy continued to dominate, pounding the Army line with savage thrusts by Cooke and Powell. But a fumble on the 18-yard line cost the Middies a possible score as Harry Stella of Army recovered the ball.

With that the tide of battle turned. Inspired by their break, Army began to strike back. The Cadets pounded the Navy line for 10 yards. Another dash by Wilson advanced the ball to the Navy 27-yard line. Then a beautiful end-around play completely fooled the Navy defense and picked up another 15 yards. Fullback Art Frontczak smashed off tackle for 8 yards, down to the 4-yard line. On the next play Woody Wilson cracked through for the Army touchdown. Huey Long kicked the extra point, and it was Army 14, Navy 7 for the final score.

14

The Larson Years: 1939-41

*A*mong the hundreds of thousands who came pouring into the United States in the floodtide of immigration around the turn of the century were two young men: one was a husky Italian, the other a German. They were poor and eager to make their mark in this new land, and both ended up in the small but thriving Midwest city of Kankakee, Illinois.

One of the new arrivals was an engineer, the other a skilled carpenter. Both found good jobs in Kankakee, saved their money, and got married.

In time, each of the men had a son.

The engineer named his son Alan and the boy grew and grew. He had wide, sloping shoulders, a slim waist, and good coordination, and he began to play a lot of baseball and football.

The carpenter also had a son, named Harry. He turned out to be much shorter than Alan, but he was stocky and strong, and he too played a lot of ball.

Alan Bergner and Harry Stella first met when they attended Kankakee High School and reported for practice on the football field. When the coach spotted burly Alan he gleefully greeted the boy, and after he watched him run through a few drills, the coach shouted for all to hear: "There's my new star." But when he

saw Harry and noted his slight build, he snorted and told an assistant coach: "This kid's not strong enough. Too slight. Not built for football."

With all his physical advantages, Alan developed into a shining star. A tackle, he could hit an opponent with one savage shot of his shoulders and send him to the ground. He was a good blocker and could pull out of the line to lead his halfbacks on power sweeps.

Harry idolized Alan, and the two boys became great friends. Alan encouraged Harry's attempt to make the team. Harry did have courage and determination, and finally the coach had to recognize Harry's growing ability and allow him to make the team.

In their final year the two boys were named cocaptains and led Kankakee to one of its finest seasons. And after they'd played their last high school game, the boys made plans to go on to college.

Alan was appointed to the Naval Academy, and the city was soon delighted to hear that Harry would attend West Point. And when, a year later, both boys made their respective football teams, the entire city celebrated.

Sophomore and junior seasons passed, and both boys became standout players. The two friends didn't have much contact during the school year, except, of course, when Army and Navy met on the football field.

One cold, wintry day at the close of the 1938 season, the news spread like wildfire through Kankakee: Harry, their little guy who played with Army, had been elected captain of the Army football team. And now people in town began to speculate. "Those two kids Harry and Alan are great pals, like peas in a pod. Their families are friends," they said. "Harry's family must be bursting with pride."

In a few days, there was more news. News that sent this small Midwest city into a frenzy of joy and civic pride. Alan had made it, too! He was elected captain of the Navy football team.

The 1939 football season was a grueling and difficult one for both elevens.

Major Emory "Swede" Larson, United States Marine Corps, was back at Annapolis as Navy head coach. Larson had played on three Navy teams and had coached three others. In none of those six years had Navy lost to Army, so as the season opened, the Middies had high hopes that this would be another great Navy year.

The opening game was a good practice test as the Middies romped over William and Mary by a 31-6 score, and when Navy defeated a strong Virginia eleven, 14-12, it looked as if the Middies would indeed have an outstanding season. But then Dartmouth played them to a 0-0 tie, and as Notre Dame, Clemson, Penn, Columbia, and Princeton successively defeated Navy, the team seemed to have lost all desire to play winning football.

On December 2, Coach Larson led his oft-beaten Navy team to Philadelphia for the fortieth game against Army, a 5-1 favorite.

Before more than 80,000 hushed fans, including high cabinet officials, Army and Navy brass, Cadets and Midshipmen, the two kids from Kankakee, Alan Bergner, captain of the Navy eleven, and Harry Stella, captain of the Army team, walked out to the center of the gridiron and shook hands. "Good luck, Harry," murmured the Navy captain. "And good luck to you, Alan," said the Army captain.

And in a box seat on the fifty-yard line, in a world the like of which they'd never known, sat the parents of Alan Bergner and Harry Stella, surrounded by generals and admirals. President and Mrs. Franklin Roosevelt could not be there, but sitting with the Stellas and Bergners were the President's two sons, James and Elliot. Each of the two couples sat very close together, squeezing each other's hands tightly, and each said a silent prayer.

And all over the world, Army and Navy officers and enlisted men took time from their duties this day to listen to the shortwave broadcast account on radio.

As play down on the field began, an inspired Navy eleven, infuriated at being downgraded by most of the sportswriters, tore into the highly regarded Cadets. Before confident Army knew what was happening, Navy and their big, hard-charging fullback, Cliff Lenz, were tearing up huge holes in the Army line. Army couldn't seem to stop Lenz, and just to vary the attack, Ed Gillette, Navy's quarterback, would send halfbacks Phil Gutting or Ulmont Whitehead for a reverse or power sweep and pick up additional yardage.

Finally Army's defense stiffened, and when the Navy attack stalled, Bob Leonard, injured and aching all season long, got off the bench and calmly booted a 25-yard field goal to give Navy a 3-0 lead.

The two teams battled each other up and down the field, and on almost every play it was Bergner at tackle for the Navy who steadied the Navy line. And when Army had the ball, Harry Stella, also at tackle, would pull out of the line to lead interference for his ball carriers.

Following Bob Leonard's field goal the two teams played even-up football through the first three quarters.

In the fourth quarter, a Navy halfback, 155-pound Dick Shaefer, was sent into the game. Just three weeks earlier Shaefer had been shunted to the Navy B squad, then was brought back up to the varsity after he'd made a shambles of the first team in a practice session. Now Shaefer proceeded to tear up the Army line as he had the Navy varsity.

"IT'S A SMALL WORLD"

Top, right: *"Two Kids from Kankakee"*
meet in the 1939 classic. Above: Army captain Harry Stella with coach Bill Wood.
Right: *Navy captain Alan Bergner with*
coach Swede Larson.

It was Shaefer for 5 yards up the middle, Shaefer around the end for 7 yards, Shaefer for 10 yards over the middle, until finally like a wild colt pent up for three years as he sat on the bench waiting for his time, Dick Shaefer pounded across the Army goal line for a touchdown and Navy had a 9–0 lead. Bob Leonard again came off the bench, kicked the extra point, and it was 10–0, Navy, for what proved the final score.

When the game was over, delirious thousands flowed out of the stands onto Franklin Field in a wild celebration of victory for Navy. And pushing through the dancing, wildly cheering Middies came Harry Stella to congratulate his Navy buddy, Alan Bergner. The two captains shook hands warmly. They had battered each other throughout the long day, but in the end, as Harry Stella had to concede, it was Navy's day, and a tremendous victory.

Schooldays and football were over for the two friends from Kankakee, and duty now called. Off they went into the service of their country, one on land, the other at sea.

Harry Stella served with great distinction in the South Pacific during World War II, earning numerous awards for his gallant service under enemy fire, including the Silver Star, the Legion of Merit, and two Bronze Stars. During the Korean War, Captain Stella further distinguished himself by winning another Legion of Merit medal. Later, promoted to colonel, Stella became assistant chief of staff with the Eighth Army in Korea.

Ensign Alan Bergner was stationed at Pearl Harbor when the Japanese attacked on December 7, 1941, and survived to serve the Navy with distinction. On active duty in mine-infested waters in the South Pacific for more than three years, he was decorated on numerous occasions and promoted several times. On one occasion Bergner voluntarily risked his life to transfer an injured sailor to another submarine in dangerous waters, using a rubber boat to row the man to safety on board the sub while enemy fire raked the area of his boat. Lieutenant Commander Bergner was personally decorated by Navy Secretary Jim Forrestal and was

Halfback Dick Shaefer scored the only touchdown in the 1939 game, but it was all Navy needed. Final score: Navy 10, Army 0.

awarded the coveted Navy and Marine Corps Medal.

Captain Alan Bergner later returned to duty in the Pentagon, working in the antisubmarine warfare program.

And so the story that began more than fifty years ago in the small city of Kankakee, Illinois, when two boys formed a friendship, played high school football together, went to West Point and Annapolis and played football against each other, continued on to greater and heroic service to their country.

The fiftieth anniversary of the Army-Navy game had to be a major national event, with a greater host of dignitaries than ever.

The parade of notables included Secretary of War Henry Stimson, Navy Secretary Colonel Frank Knox, Chief of Staff of the Army General George Marshall, Chief of Navigation Bureau Harold Stark, and Admiral of the Navy Chester Nimitz.

To the 102,000 who luxuriated in Philadelphia's Municipal Stadium on one of the most perfect days ever for the Army-Navy classic, it was an afternoon compounded of all the familiar elements of terrific and savage action, color, pomp, and beauty.

But there was a new solemn note this November afternoon of 1940, a spine-tingling echo of impending war over the lovely emerald field. For these were not ordinary young men celebrating a half century of football rivalry between two great academies; they were the future officers of the Army and Navy of the United States upon whose initiative and courage and splendor of spirit the fate of the nation would likely rest in the coming years.

The crowds were still pouring into the stadium when, at precisely 12:15, the Cadet Corps marched in companies of platoon strength and swung through the east gate behind the brilliantly uniformed Army band. In perfect alignment they passed the Navy box seats with eyes right, officers at hand salute, then circled the field to end up facing the Navy stands in full formation.

Following them came the Midshipmen, 2,596 of them, the white of their caps and the blue of their coats unwinding on the field like a huge polka-dotted scarf, until they faced their rivals from up the Hudson.

Then Cadet Jack Norton of Virginia, first Cadet captain, and Midshipman L. E. Larsen of Wisconsin, Midshipmen commander of the regiment, advanced across the center-field stripe and exchanged salutes.

As the field literally froze, with the only movement the fluttering of pennants on trumpets and of wind-whipped capes, the band broke out in the last bars of "Columbia, the Gem of the Ocean," those bars with the words "The Army and Navy forever, three cheers for the Red, White and Blue."

When the two young commanders broke from rigid attention and shook hands warmly, Army gave out a great yell for the Navy, and Navy's young men responded with a shattering "four-N" yell that rocked the stadium.

Then came the entrance of the Army mule, followed by another mule with a gold Army football helmet perched on his head. Both mules strutted briskly around the stadium as the crowd cheered them on.

Suddenly an armored car drove in from the east gate and circled the field. The doors opened and four armored guards with shotguns hopped out, pulling out the Navy goat, Mr. William Whiskers VII.

Finally the two teams trotted onto the field, ran through a few plays and warm-up exercises, and the referee blew the whistle for the business at hand . . . the fiftieth Army-Navy game.

There was a great roar from the crowd as Army kicked off and the Middies' great halfback, Bill Busik, a key man in Navy's attack all year long, took the ball and sprinted upfield for 25 yards before Army could stop him.

Then Navy opened up their game plan.

Busik and Sherry Werner hit the Army line for gains, then the left-handed passer Bob Malcolm faked a pass and ran for a first down. Navy was moving, hitting the Army tackles and guards with savage line smashes. Then Busik went to the air, tossed a pass to Malcolm for another first down on the Army 23-yard line. On the next play Busik was stopped hard at the line by a savage group of Army tacklers.

Now Navy resorted to guile.

Busik took the ball, started to his left with solid interference in front of him, then unobtrusively slipped the ball to Malcolm, driving back in the opposite direction for 18 yards to the Army 5-yard line. Three drives by Busik and Navy had its first touchdown. It looked as if Navy could score at will. The game was only two minutes old, and Navy had run through and around Army from one end of the field to the other.

But Army played tough and held Navy through the rest of the first half.

In the third period, halfbacks Busik and Malcolm took turns driving for first downs. Again Army held and took the ball on downs. But the Cadets were not able to move and had

They called him Barnacle Bill Busik, and in 1939, 1940, and 1941 he ran, passed, and kicked Army to a frazzle. Left: Busik (63) blasting through the Army line for a touchdown in Navy's 14–0 victory in the 1940 game. Right: In 1962, former All-American halfback Bill Busik was Commander Bill Busik and the new athletic director of the Naval Academy.

to punt. It was a short kick that Bill Clark caught on his 37-yard line and advanced for 9 yards.

Now it was first down on the Army 28-yard line. Clark took the ball on a fake reverse, picked up blockers, and sped to the Army 21-yard line. Three plays—by Busik, Malcolm, and Busik again—and it was another Navy first down on the Army 9-yard line.

The Cadets dug in, their backs creeping in close to stop another Navy thrust, only to have Clark quickly flip a short pass over their heads to Malcolm, who dashed over for Navy's second touchdown.

The game was winding down when Army had reached the Navy 31-yard line as a result of a long pass from quarterback Joe Maupin to end Joe Grygiel. But on the next play, another long pass, Hal Harwood of Navy intercepted and the final whistle blew to end the game with Navy the winner by a 14–0 score.

Pearl Harbor lay just a week ahead, and the war in Europe was intense, but the eyes of the nation on this November 29, 1941, were on a

Marine officer about to land in Philadelphia's Municipal Stadium and try to keep the situation well in hand. Awaiting were 98,000 soldiers, sailors, marines, Army and Navy officers, high political bigwigs, and ordinary citizens, all thrilling to the pomp and pageantry that formed a glamorous background for what would prove the greatest Army-Navy football game in many years.

The Marine officer was Major Emory "Swede" Larson, the hearty Swede from Minneapolis, whose great playing and coaching career would come to a close this day as Navy battled brilliantly to defeat a rugged Army foe, 14–6.

Six times Larson had faced Army—three times as a center on great Navy teams and three times as head coach of the Middies football team.

Not once in those six years had Swede known defeat at the hands of a West Point football team. A month from this date Larson would begin studies at the Naval War College, Newport, Rhode Island. With him would go the blue and gold Navy coverlet which bears the following lettering and numbering around a

The 1941 Navy football squad poses before the Army game in front of the Naval Academy's statue of the Indian chief Tecumseh, considered a good luck charm. Wearing a bright coat of war paint, Tecumseh must have helped: Navy won the game 14–6.

huge letter *N:* 1919, Navy 6, Army 0; 1920, Navy 7, Army 0; 1921, Navy 7, Army 0; 1939, Navy 10, Army 0; 1940, Navy 14, Army 0 (and to be added by Swede's wife this week), 1941, Navy 14, Army 6.

Larson agreed after the game that the turning point occurred in the hectic third period when Navy had advanced the ball with Barnacle Bill Busik carrying on nearly every other play for three successive first downs. On the last play of the series, Bill had smashed to the Army 16–yard line for fourth down and 6 yards to go. It was the most critical point in the game, with Army out in front, 6–0.

"I sent in quarterback Wes Gebert with instructions to take the ball and scoot around end," said Coach Larson, "and did he ever carry out those instructions? Nope, that son of a gun, he gave the ball to Busik and Bill crashed through the Army for fifteen yards to the one-yard line before five Army guys brought him down. Busik was the key all afternoon, a threat to score every time he carried the ball.

"On the next play I sent in Phil Hurt with instructions to use our thirty-seven buck, a short-side plunge, and he went right through Army for the score. It was wonderful to see those boys play so well.

"Howard Clark's ten-yard run for our second score was supposed to be the same kind of play," said Swede, "but it didn't develop as we thought.

"That score resulted when little Howie Clark set off around end, broke free, and was out in the clear and away for the most beautiful play I'd seen in years. Clark galloped sixty-eight yards and went in for our second touchdown. Leonard converted and we had the fourteen points we needed to win."

After the final whistle had sounded and the Navy was celebrating down in the locker room, Swede Larson said to the scores of reporters, "This is my last game of football for a while. There's a bigger game coming up and I aim to be right in it."

The Swede was right, for when the Japanese attacked Pearl Harbor, all hell broke loose. Weeks later, in the thick of the fight in the South Pacific, Emory "Swede" Larson was killed in action.

15

The War Years: 1942-44

In 1942 the entire world turned upside down after the United States suffered the shock and disgrace of the Japanese attack on Pearl Harbor. The officers and men of our armed forces were at work, battling the enemy on all fronts.

At Annapolis and West Point, the football schedules were allowed to continue—President Roosevelt having announced in agreement with the War Department that the continuation of college sport would be good for the "morale of the nation"—but because of war conditions the Army-Navy game would be held at Annapolis and attendance would be restricted to no more than 10,000 to 12,000 fans. The Office of Price Administration said it would check all vehicles at the game, and any spectator not from the immediate vicinity of Annapolis would be barred from entry to the stadium.

Navy's new football coach, Captain John Welchel, having just been recalled from a tour of sea duty, had little time to install a new offense before Navy opened against a William and Mary team that was one of the best that small college had ever produced. As a result, Navy suffered a 3–0 defeat, only the second time in seventeen seasons that a William and Mary team had beaten Navy.

But once coach Welchel had his new system working "on all six cylinders," and with a fine

group of players led by 145 pound Hal Hamberg, Ben Martin, Captain Alan Cameron, and Joe Sullivan, Navy settled down and played outstanding football.

They defeated a strong Virginia team, 35–0; lost a close encounter to a very good Princeton eleven, 10–0; then defeated Yale, 13–6.

Key injuries hurt the Middies in their next two games as they lost to Georgia Tech and Notre Dame, but then they came back strongly to defeat Pennsylvania and Columbia.

Meanwhile, Army's great coach Earl "Red" Blaik was in his second season and had problems of his own. The Cadets opened with four victories in a row, but then slumped badly, losing the next three games to Notre Dame, Harvard, and Penn before eking out a 1-point win over Virginia. They began furious preparations for a highly touted Navy team, favored to win by two touchdowns.

The game began with Navy carrying the ball up the field for several first downs, literally sweeping the Cadets off their feet. But then Army called for a time-out, talked things over,

Coach Earl "Red" Blaik, Army's head coach, 1941-58. Blaik's extraordinary record: 121 wins, 33 losses, and 10 ties.

and settled down. On a fourth-down play, Navy was stopped for no gain, and punted to Army.

The Cadets brought the ball back to midfield on a fine 20-yard return by Bill Mazur. Then halfbacks Mazur and Ray Hill, bearing the brunt of the Army attack, drove to the Navy 1-yard line. But the Middies showed how really aggressive and tough they were and stopped Army on four successive plays into the line. When the last pileup of players had been pulled apart by the referee, it showed the football just two inches from the goal line!

Navy's quarterback, Hal Hamberg, kicked the Middies out of danger, and now the teams took turns challenging each other's defense without either gaining advantage. The first half ended with the score 0–0.

The third period began with Army punting. Navy brought the ball back to the 40-yard line and on two plays quickly picked up a first down. Then, on third down, Sullivan blasted through tackle, cut away from Army's defenders, and raced into the end zone. The kick was good and Navy had a 7–0 lead.

In the fourth period, Hillis Hume, Navy's halfback, intercepted Bill Mazur's pass and sprinted 20 yards. On the next play, little Hal Hamberg tossed a perfect pass to Ben Martin for a touchdown, and it was Navy 14, Army 0.

From there to the end of the game, each team battled furiously and threatened to score, but wonderful defensive play on the part of both lines stopped every drive, and Navy came away with its fourth consecutive win over Army.

Once again the Navy football team said it with touchdowns for its retiring coach, just as it had for Captain John Welchel's predecessor, Lieutenant Colonel Swede Larsen of the Marines in 1941.

In 1943, for the fifth successive year, the Middies defeated Army in the comparative privacy of some 15,000 fans at West Point's Michie Stadium. As was the case the year before in Annapolis, attendance was restricted to those fans who lived within the fifteen-mile area permitted by the wartime restrictions on travel.

And for the fourth time in five years, the Cadets were shut down without registering a single point against the power-laden Middies.

The same little ball-carrying halfback, chiefly responsible for ruining the day for Army in 1942, was the 150-pound Lonoke, Arkansas youngster who ran the Cadets ragged on this day in 1943, with his brilliant all-around play. Hal Hamberg did not score a point.

But it was Hamberg with his beautiful deceptive running, marvelous pinpoint passing, and all-around brilliance directing the Navy attack from his quarterback position that made the big difference. And it was Hamberg's magnificent punts, 60–65 yards in length, and very often kicked out of bounds inside the 15-yard line, that caused the Cadets the most grief, keeping them constantly in their own territory.

With the teams hopelessly deadlocked in the third period, Hamberg got off a 60-yard punt that went out of bounds on the Army 8-yard stripe. A speedy Army back from California named Glenn Davis, playing his plebe year, was thrown for a 6-yard loss by Navy's Johnson. Then George Maxon, the Army punter, kicked to Hamberg on the 45-yard line, and little Hal dashed 10 yards before he was tackled. On the next play Hamberg smashed off tackle for 10 additional yards, to the Army 30-yard line. On first down, Hume advanced the ball to the 20-yard line on a clever lateral pass from Hamberg, and on the next play Bob Jenkins, "the Alabama Flash," cracked over from the 2-yard line for the score. Vic Finos kicked the extra point and it was 7–0, Navy.

The Army team fought like a band of tigers to make up those points. Doug Kenna, one of the best backs in Army history, but hobbled by injuries late in the season, came off the bench at this time and passed for 10 yards to Glenn Davis. The play was good for a first down.

But then two successive penalties took the Cadets back to their 10-yard line. Maxon punted the ball to the 45-yard line, and it was from there that Navy regained its momentum.

A whirling, spinning dervish of a back, Hillis Hume began this advance. He cracked

Glenn Davis in 1943, playing in his first Army-Navy game, takes a pitchout from quarterback Tom Lombardo and behind fine Army blocking picks up 18 yards.

through the line for 15 yards to the 35. Jim Pettit picked up 5 more, then another 5, for a first down on the 10-yard line. Yet again Pettit took the ball, and spurted 9 yards to the 1-yard line. On fourth down, Hume flung his body toward the goal line and just got across. The extra point was missed, and it was 13–0, Navy.

It was sheer power, plus deception, that brought both Navy scores.

Once again, the Cadets came back fired up. Taking the kickoff on the 40-yard line, they pounded Navy's line to midfield. Here it was Kenna, on the run, tossing a pass to end Ed Rafalko. Interference was called on Navy's Pettit, and Army had a first down on the 27-yard line.

The Corps of Cadets, who had been yelling themselves hoarse all afternoon, now broke into a wild outburst. But just when it seemed as if Army might score, the cheers turned to groans as Pettit intercepted Kenna's pass.

As the game wound down, Glenn Davis, who was to be a thorn in Navy's side for the

next three years, passed to Tom Lombardo for 24 yards. Then Lombardo himself hurled a fine pass, his first of the season, to Maxon for 17 yards. But Army, getting close to pay dirt, lost yardage on two reverses, and shortly thereafter the game ended.

Navy had done it again, this time by a 13–0 margin.

By September 1944, the progress of the Allied armies in Europe was the big news. France had finally been liberated from the Nazi hordes, and the Germans would make their last bid for victory in the Battle of the Bulge. Russia was exerting pressure from the east and freeing much of the territory captured by the Nazis. General MacArthur invaded the Philippines, and finally the Allies were on the road to triumph in every battle area of the world.

In the sports world, a sorry exhibition of baseball resulted in a World Series victory by the St. Louis Cardinals over their local rivals

A bed sheet copying the cover of Time *was hung out on the West Point campus a week before the 1944 Navy game.*

the St. Louis Browns, 4 games to 2. . . . Horse racing had seen a tremendous boom, with $2-million-betting days the rule at New York tracks. . . . Byron Nelson became the biggest one-year money winner in golf, taking most of his prizes in War Bonds. . . . And Sergeant Joe Louis, heavyweight champion of the world, began a series of exhibitions in Boston, Detroit, Chicago, Washington, and Los Angeles, with the gate receipts turned over to the Army-Navy Relief Fund.

And in college football, Army's superlative football team completed its first undefeated season since 1914 by trouncing Navy 23–7. Let Glenn Davis, one of the greatest stars in the firmament of Army-Navy football, tell the story of that glorious Cadet victory.

"Of the many thrills I've had in my career, I guess the Army-Navy game of December 2, 1944, was my greatest. We at West Point con-

sidered that victory the high point of our undefeated streak.

"Yes, that game was my greatest thrill, especially coming after what I'd have to call my 'greatest chill,' the time I flunked out of the Academy.

"Not many people are familiar with the fact that I was dropped from West Point after my plebe year as a result of scholastic trouble. Fortunately, the Academy enables you to take a makeup exam if you desire to continue at the Point, so all through that summer I crammed and crammed. The tedious studying paid off when I passed the test and was readmitted to school. Otherwise I wouldn't be in a position today to relate the thrill I got out of the Army-Navy game of 1944.

"The game was played in Baltimore and $58 million in War Bonds were bought by a sellout crowd as the price of admission. Army won 23–7, but there was more to it than just the score, and more to it than just a victory over Navy.

"We had, after all, lost five straight games to the Tars. And rubbing salt in that deep wound was the fact that Army had scored but one touchdown in those five games. Plus, we were on the threshold of Army's first unbeaten season since 1914. Navy was the only team standing in the way of our winning the national championship. But what an obstacle. . . .

"They were a great team. As Coach Earl Blaik said after the game: 'I think it was a case of the nation's number one team beating the country's number two team.'

"Navy was considered to have the nation's best line—Leon Bramlett, Don Whitmire, Jim Carrington, Jack Martin, Captain Ben Chase, Gail Gilliam, and John Hansen. But that day we had greater linemen in Dick Pitzer, Archie Arnold, John Green, Robert St. Onge, Joe Stanowicz, Nemetz, Barney Poole, Hank Foldberg, and Tex Coulter.

"I can't remember ever having worked so hard in preparation for a game. The two-week practice period was spent in brisk, long drills, during which we had repeated scrimmages. Coaches Blaik, Herm Hickman, Andy Gustafson, and Stu Holcomb pounded us through offensive and defensive maneuvers, leaving no stone unturned, pointing to hope that if we could handle Don Whitmire, a mastodonic tackle and All-American at both Alabama and Navy, we would win.

"The job of stopping Whitmire belonged primarily to Hank Foldberg, and Hank proceeded to play one of the greatest games of his career. Nobody envied his job that day. Whitmire had been tossing opposing linemen around like spitballs.

"Coach Red Blaik was so worried about Navy, he was pacing up and down on the sidelines just before the game was to start. This was not like Blaik, who was usually quite unemotional.

"Coach Blaik issued a few last-minute pregame messages to the team, then silence . . . until after a full minute, while looking each starter full in the face, he reached into a pocket and pulled out a telegram.

"It was from a buddy of his, General Robert Eichelberger, former supe at West Point and now one of the top generals stationed in the South Pacific. The wire asked us to "win for all the soldiers scattered throughout the world," or words to that effect. That's all Coach Blaik said, but it was enough. . . . "Win for all the soldiers . . . fighting for us." A chill went up and down our spines, and we charged out fighting mad.

"We played great team ball that day. Our blocking was just outstanding. The way our forwards cleared out and racked up those Navy tacklers made it almost simple for us backs. Not that fellows like Felix "Doc" Blanchard, Doug Kenna, Dale Hall, Tom Lombardo, Max Minor, and Robert Dobbs couldn't help themselves when the situation arose.

"Our big break came early in the first period when Don Whitmire hurt his knee from the severe pounding he'd received from Hank Foldberg. The courageous Whitmire stuck it out until late in the second period, but then had to be helped off the field. When Don left he seemingly took the Middies' hopes for a victory.

"We scored first as Doug Kenna and Dale Hall pounded away at Navy. Then a shattering block by Foldberg, and Hall was away, twisting and turning, fighting 28 yards for the first Army score. Dick Walterhouse kicked the extra point and we had a 7-0 lead.

"As the third period began, Joe Stanowicz blocked John Hansen's punt, and both Hansen and Stanowicz raced for the ball as it rolled into the end zone. Hansen fell on it for a safety, and now we had a 9-0 edge.

"But Navy fought back like a bunch of scrappy tiger-cats, with little Hal Hamberg in charge. Hal ran and passed to the Army 1-yard line, and then Clyde Scott smashed over for a Navy score. Vic Finos kicked the extra point, and now it was tight as a drum, 9-7.

"A few minutes later, crashing runs by Bobby Jenkins and Scott brought the ball to our 33-yard line. There Jenkins faded back to pass. He tossed a beautiful aerial to his receiver, but I was right there, too, and picked the ball right out of his hands. I got to the 48-yard line before I was stopped.

"That was virtually Navy's last opportunity. Doc Blanchard took over and began to run over and through Navy. There was no stopping the 235-pound fullback. He either picked up his interference, or he just ran right by it. From midfield, Doc smashed his way single-handedly inside the Navy's 10. From there Max Minor jumped off to his left, faking possession of the ball; instead Lombardo handed off to Blanchard, and Doc crashed over guard for another score.

"We got a third score after blasting 56 yards in five plays, with me and Doc carrying the ball most of the way. Then with the ball in midfield, and with Doc and Minor on either flank, Tom Lombardo, our quarterback, faked to both men, then flipped me a lateral pass. I followed Big Doc around right end and right down the sidelines for a touchdown. On that play Minor cut across the field and in one tremendous block wiped out two Navy tacklers. It was easy for me, with that kind of marvelous blocking. From that time on my teammates called that play, 'The California Special.' It was the first time we had used the maneuver, and it helped me get my twentieth touchdown of the season and clinch the title as the nation's leading scorer."

Later that night in Baltimore, Coach Earl Blaik received another wire:

THE GREATEST OF ALL ARMY TEAMS. WE HAVE STOPPED THE WAR TO CELEBRATE YOUR MAG-NIFICENT SUCCESS. SIGNED, MACARTHUR.

After the season, a booklet was given to each member of the squad by Coach Blaik, and in it was inscribed this message:

Seldom in a lifetime's experience is one permitted the complete satisfaction of being part of a perfect performance.

To all the coaches, the 23–7 is enough.

16

The Culmination of Blanchard and Davis: 1945-46

On December 1, 1945, the West Point Cadets defeated Navy, 32–13, for their eighteenth victory in succession, marking the first time they had ever gone through two perfect seasons in a row.

The most distinguished gathering that had yet attended a sports event in this country assembled in the Philadelphia Municipal Stadium, filled to its capacity of over 100,000 for the forty-sixth meeting between the service Academy rivals.

This was the first time since the 1941 contest, played a week before the attack on Pearl Harbor, that the climactic spectacle of intercollegiate football was allowed to return to its prewar setting, invested this day with all of its old glamour and glitter.

In honor of the happy occasion, President Harry Truman attended as commander in chief of the Army and Navy, along with a host of war leaders from both branches of the military, as well as most of the President's cabinet. Among the brass that day, all of them famous as artisans in the winning of the Second World War, were Generals George C. Marshall, Omar Bradley, Henry H. "Hap" Arnold, James Doolittle, Jacob L. Devers, and Carl Spaatz; Admirals Chester W. Nimitz, William F. "Bull" Halsey, and Ernest J. King; and British Air Chief Marshal Sir Arthur Tedder and Fleet Admiral Sir James F. Somerville. Also among the star wearers that day were Brigadier Generals Blondie Saunders, who lost a leg in the war, and Rosey O'Donnell. Both of them had been football heroes at West Point and both of them had great records in the Pacific with the Twentieth Air Force, whose B-29 Superforts were the terror of Japan. Seated up in the stands as well was one of the most brilliant young pilots in the Pacific command—Lieutenant Charles Bolton. Recently returned from Saipan, Bolton was wearing almost every decoration except the Congressional Medal, including two Presidential Citations won in bombing missions over Japan.

It was a brilliant constellation around the President that vied with the play on the field for the crowd's interest. As a matter of fact, the outcome of the game was decided before the President changed his seat from the Army to the Navy side during the intermission between the halves. By that time the renowned Doc Blanchard and Glenn Davis had gone across three times for a 20–0 lead in the opening quarter.

The scene during the intermission, as the President left his family to transfer his allegiance to the Navy side, was one of the most

Above, right: *Army's touchdown twins, Glenn Davis and Doc Blanchard, who together scored ten of Army's eleven touchdowns versus Navy in 1944, 1945, and 1946.*

Above: *Glenn Davis, "Mr. Outside," All-American 1944–47.*

Right: *Felix "Doc" Blanchard, "Mr. Inside," All-American 1944–46.*

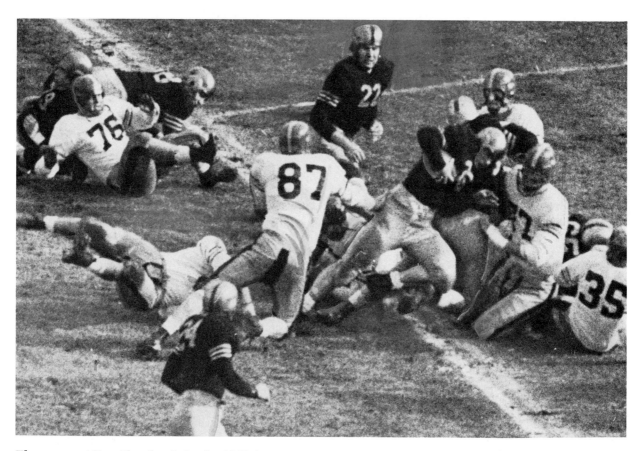

The power of Doc Blanchard: In the 1945 Army-Navy game, Blanchard scored three touchdowns, the first player of modern times to achieve the feat in the service classic. Here he has just bulled over the goal line for Army's first score in a 32–13 victory.

impressive of this almost ideally perfect football afternoon.

A hundred bluecoats formed in two lines to afford a protecting lane for Mr. Truman's march. Surrounded by Secret Service men and escorted by Secretary of War Robert P. Patterson, Major General Maxwell D. Taylor, superintendent of the Military Academy, and Brigadier General George Honen, commandant of cadets at West Point, the nation's Chief Executive left his box in front of 2,400 cheering Cadets. As he walked out on the playing field, greeting servicemen and wounded war veterans seated along the sideline, the police all came to a hand salute. Waiting in the center of the field for the President were Secretary of the Navy James V. Forrestal, Vice Admiral Aubrey W. Fitch, superintendent of the Naval Academy, and Rear Admiral S. H. Ingersoll, commandant of midshipmen. Under their escort, Mr.

Truman proceeded across the field, and now 2,700 Midshipmen cheered as he took his assigned seat as a Navy rooter.

The President was backing a loser from then on, but a loser who was as game as any service unit, whether on the football field or the fighting front.

Everyone had known from the start that the Midshipmen were a hopelessly beaten team, that their line was not quite good enough to match the powerful forwards of Colonel Earl Blaik and, above all, that Navy had no lasting, consistent answer to the depredations of those twin football scourges of modern times, Blanchard and Davis, who in the first quarter had raced 46 and 48 yards, respectively, for two of the Cadets' three touchdowns.

But if everyone else sensed the hopelessness of their plight, the white-shirted stalwarts of head coach Commander Oscar Hagberg refused to accept the inevitable. The game had gone against them from the very outset, as everyone had predicted, and into the second quarter it had indeed seemed that Navy would be humiliated by a far greater margin than the 27 points by which Army was generally favored to win.

But, after that first period, Navy did make a fight of it every inch of the way, and when they scored, six seconds before the end of the half, on a tremendous 61-yard pass from quarterback Bruce Smith to the blazingly fast Clyde Scott, racing the last 40 yards as Davis sought

to cut him down from behind, an element of uncertainty had developed for the first time that afternoon with the score, 20–7.

It was the only time, however. Forty-eight seconds into the second half, Blanchard was stampeding 46 yards with an intercepted pass for a touchdown, with blockers springing up all around him. That lightning bolt of heartbreaking adversity sealed Navy's doom.

Though Navy came back to go 26 yards for a touchdown by fullback Joe Bartos after Smith had intercepted a pass by Davis, the breaks of the game went against the Middies. Pass inter-

Autographed team photo of Army's undefeated 1945 national champions.

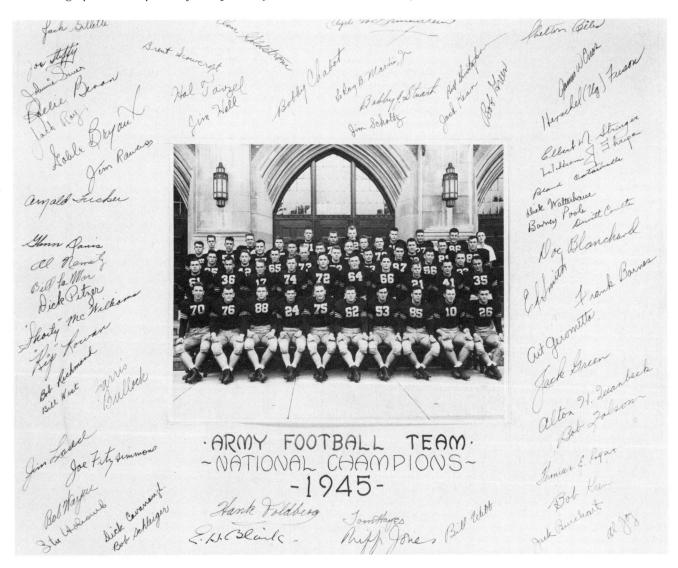

ference by Navy was ruled—questionably it seemed—to give Army the ball on the Middies' 31-yard mark, and Davis went 27 yards for the final touchdown two plays later.

There was no question that the better team won, and won decisively. Blanchard, Davis, quarterback Arnold Tucker, Bob Chabot, who started in place of Shorty McWilliams at right half, Captain John Green, Art Gerometta, Tex Coulter, and the other members of the Cadets' line will long be remembered and acclaimed for their deeds this day, as throughout that glorious season.

But not all the honors belonged to Army that day. Navy did things to Blanchard and Davis that no other team had done. Time and again it stopped the two terrors of the gridiron or threw them for losses, especially Leon Bramlett, the best end on the field, who gave Glenn Davis, the fastest back of his football era, scandalous treatment on one play as he broke through to nail him 8 yards behind the line.

Although Blanchard and Davis might be checked again and again, it still was not enough. They had to be stopped every time. To miss them once was to invite disaster, for, with their power, speed, and elusiveness, they were backs likely to go all the way if given the smallest chance to get started. And it was beyond Navy's strength and capacity to meet so exacting a requirement. One moment the crowd would be rubbing its eyes at the sight of the twin engines of destruction being manhandled like ordinary flesh-and-blood backs, the next moment it would rub them again as, suddenly, there was Doc or "Junior" streaking across the goal line.

In the dressing room Colonel Blaik finally broke down and admitted that this Army team was the greatest West Point team of all time—at least of all he had seen. Of course he hadn't seen them all, but no one was about to challenge his statement.

It would be difficult for the colonel to say good-bye to this great team and begin all over again next year. Only eight members of the regular starting lineup would be back, including Blanchard, Davis, Tucker, and Coulter.

But let Red Blaik tell of that 1946 game in his own words.

In 1946, Captain Tom Hamilton returns to coach the Navy.

Navy's heartbreaking '46 loss to Army's last Blanchard-Davis powerhouse team, 21–18. . . . Left: Blanchard bursts through the Navy line in the second quarter at the start of a 64-yard touchdown sprint. Right: Navy scores its third touchdown on a pass from Earl (after a quick pitchout from Baysinger, number 36) to Leon Bramlett, who catches the ball in the end zone directly in front of Arnold Tucker. The difference in the game, in which each team scored three touchdowns, was Navy's failure to convert on any of its extra points.

— ★ —

"We went down to the finale with Navy in 1946 owning a twenty-seven game defeatless string that had begun with the opener against North Carolina in '44. Nobody gave Navy a chance . . . except their coach, Commander Tom Hamilton, the Navy players, and the Army coaches. I don't mean the Army players were overconfident, but defeat was not part of their thinking.

"We were a weary, used-up ball club. Added to his bad shoulder and a knee which he had hurt against Penn, Arnie Tucker turned an ankle a few days before the game. Blanchard, whose normal playing weight for us was 207, had been drained down to 198. There is a photograph in Philadelphia's Municipal Stadium the afternoon before the game which shows how Doc's sunken cheeks made him look thinner than Davis, Tucker, or even myself. We took no workout that day. The players just walked up and down the field a couple of times

in their cadet-gray overcoats. It was obvious to writers on hand, and even a Navy official remarked, that we looked washed out, peaked, strained. Well, we were.

"It would be just hell, I thought, to have this gang come this far with the effort they'd made and then have the three-year record spoiled in the last game—and by the Navy. We sure would never hear the end of that.

"Get them down fast and keep them there. That was our plan, as in 1945.

"We started well. Arnie Tucker passed to Davis for 30 yards. Then Glenn took a pitchout from Arnold and snaked his way 14 yards to a score. Jack Ray kicked the extra point. That first conversion was to prove vital, though nobody suspected it at the time. Navy reacted strongly. Sparked by an unsung quarterback, Reeves Baysinger, the Midshipmen marched 81 yards for a touchdown, but missed the point.

"Fortunately for us, we were able to play about as well in the second period as we had at any time all year. Blanchard and Davis were in fine form. They alternated in moving the ball from our 19 to our 48. From there, Doc shot over the middle, veered by a linebacker to the outside, and outraced all pursuers down the sidelines. On that run, Doc looked more like the Blanchard of '44 and '45 than he had at any time all fall.

"Presently, Bill Yeoman intercepted a pass on Navy's 38, and we went on to score on a 26-yard pass play from Davis to Blanchard. This was a deep pass breaking out of a buttonhook fake. Doc executed the fake about 10 yards downfield. After luring the defender out of position, he whirled suddenly, broke downfield again, and took the lead throw from Glenn, who had bluffed the shorter throw. This was the last scoring effort of Blanchard and Davis for Army, but nobody anticipated that at the time. To the stands, it looked as if we could call our shots.

"On the bench, however, we were not feeling secure. An early block had aggravated Tucker's knee injury and we had to take him out while we were on defense. To keep the leg from stiffening on him, he had to keep walking up and down the sideline. He was in much pain.

"Tucker's condition certainly contributed to our misadventures in the second half. We not only missed him defensively, but his leg prevented him from dropping back to pass. He had all he could do to get the ball away on hand-offs.

"That was our side of it, but far from the whole story. Navy caught fire and threatened for a long time to run us out of the stadium and to run off with the game. They ran and blocked like furies and mixed in good passes. They went 79 yards for a second touchdown and 30 yards for a third. They were trailing only 21–18, when they took the ball on their 33-yard line with seven and a half minutes to play.

"The crowd of 100,000 had gone hysterical. They had come to sit in on a final Blanchard-Davis walkover. Now they were seeing what threatened to become the most dramatic upset of all time. The day was unseasonably warm and humid. For us now, on the Army bench, it began to turn gray and cold. Navy had been

Captain Felix Blanchard. On July 2, 1959, by then Major Blanchard was cited for bravery for staying with his burning aircraft over the village of Wethersfield, England. He brought down the plane safely, without injury to himself or any civilians.

June 27, 1947: Commencement exercises at the U.S. Military Academy. The three backfield stars of the great Army teams of the mid-forties are shown on parade after receiving the Academy's highest athletic awards. Glenn Davis got the Army Athletic Association Trophy, the Edgerton Trophy, the Hughes Trophy, and the Baseball Team Award; Felix "Doc" Blanchard won the Edgerton Trophy and the Football Team Award; and quarterback Arnold Tucker got the Eber Simpson Memorial Trophy.

marching without letup. I sensed they would march some more, and I did not know what, if anything, we could do about it. They had wrested the momentum of the game away from us. We were fighting for our lives. Yet our team, scorched by many fires that year, was concentrating on the job with all the poise the situation demanded. Still, they were stealing frequent looks at the clock.

"It would be just like the Navy, I thought, to spoil everything, to make us swallow a bitter, almost poisonous ending. Then, much of all this courageous Army team had done would be forgotten.

"And now they were down on our 24. And now Lynn Chewning, their big fullback, came charging around our left side for 23 yards. They were down on our 3, and there was a minute and a half left to play.

"There was nothing I could do. On top of all else, I had lost phone connection with my press-box spotters, Andy Gustafson and Herman Hickman. I thought something was wrong mechanically. It was not until sometime later that I learned from Gerry Counts, Army assistant coach, who was sitting near Gus and Herman, just what happened. There was nothing wrong with the phones. Gus and Herman were ignoring the plaintive ringing. Their emotional state had overcome them. Gus just sat there, staring blankly off into space, afraid to look down on the field, or maybe afraid to miss the spaceship he was praying would come and take him away from the awful scene. Herman wasn't looking at the field either. He had his head down on folded arms and was softly moaning, 'O God, don't let it happen!'

"It was here 'the brave old Army team' stood fast like the Federals of General George Thomas at Chickamauga. Chewning drove at our right side, but Hank Foldberg and Goble Bryant met him head-on. Chewning tried the other side. This time Barney Poole hurled him back. Navy was penalized 5 yards for taking a fifth time out for the half, which set them back to the 8. That was a break. But there was still time for one more play. It was third and goal to go.

"Fringes of the half-crazed crowd, unable to restrain themselves, had come down out of the stands and pressed against the sidelines at the southwest corner of the field, to see at close hand the climax of the almost unbearable denouement.

"Bill Hawkins, a stalwart for the Midshipmen all day, offense and defense both, took the snap from center, faked a buck into the line, and flipped a lateral out to halfback Pete Williams. Williams drove 4 yards around our left end, but he was still 4 yards from home when Barney Poole dragged him down. Barney never made a better tackle than that one.

"There were seven seconds to play when Tom Hamilton sent in a substitute to stop the clock. But before the officials saw the substitute, the clock ran out, and there was considerable argument at the time. Even had the officials seen the sub earlier, the clock would have been stopped only long enough to accept the substitution. It is doubtful there would have been time enough for Navy to run another play.

"In the confusion and excitement of the last few seconds, in the traditional American eagerness to salute a gallant underdog who had come so close to achieving a tremendous upset, it was some time before there was full appreciation of what we had done. We had stopped them with the game on the line, after they had been marching unceasingly. We had stopped them twice on our 3-yard line and once on our 4. And that was the season-long story of that Army team of 1946; when the Cadets needed it most, they had it.

"Willard Mullin did a typically humorous cartoon on the game. It shows atop the monument a bronze foot symbolizing the 3 points' difference in our 21–18 victory, the three extra points kicked by Jack Ray. Inscribed on the base of the monument: TO COMMEMORATE WEST POINT'S GREAT FOOTBALL TEAMS. UNBEATEN . . . 1944 . . . 1945 . . . 1946. Walking along, looking up at the bronze foot, are two cadets. One says, 'Weren't there a couple of other men on that team back there in 1946?'

" 'Yeah,' replies the other cadet, 'couple o' guys named Doc Davison and Glenn Blanchard, or something or other.' "

17

From Hamilton to Erdelatz: 1946-50

Tom Hamilton had been asked to return to the Naval Academy and coach the team in 1946, and he has his own memories of that season and its incredible final game from the Navy side, as well as the 1947 game, which would be his last at the Naval Academy.

"I got a fine staff together with Rip Miller, Johnny Wilson, Lou Bryan, Bob McNeesh, Eddy Erdelatz, and McGruder Tuttle. It was a trying period because at that time the GI Bill brought all the veterans from the war years back to our opponents.

"The Naval Academy, which had been operating on a three-year program, had only three classes and allowed a great many of the Midshipmen who were in there during the war to resign if they did not want to continue. This meant the loss of quite a few of the outstanding players of the previous year. Yet I have never been associated with a group of young men who had the character and guts of this squad. They went through a season of frustration and hard luck that was almost unbelievable. We won only one game coming into the Army game, though we had Georgia Tech in trouble. They were in front 21–20, but we were headed for a touchdown, late in the game, and had a good drive going. We got to Tech's 8-yard line, but

as Bill Hamilton was tackled the ball squirted out of his hands into the hands of Mathews, a Georgia Tech back, and he ran the length of the field for a Tech touchdown which made it 28–20, Tech. This illustrates the kind of luck we had all year long.

"We faced an Army team which had been national champions the year before and which had half a dozen superstars in Blanchard, Davis, Rowan, Tucker, Poole, etc. Army was undefeated coming into the contest. The game was one of the most thrilling I have ever seen, really a wonderful battle. The Army scored three times in the first half to the Navy's once, and led 21–6 at the halftime.

"In the second half, led by our great Captain Leon Bramlett, with Reeves Baysinger at quarterback, we took the ball on a fourth down and went on to score. Then we scored again, closing the gap to 21–18. And again, we took the ball to the 2-yard line, but unfortunately the crowd ran out on the field. Play was halted while the officials tried to get the people off the playing field. It took so long to get plays off with the noise and confusion that we did not score. Time ran out on us with the ball on the Army 2-yard line.

"We had lost 21–18 to one of the great Army teams in history. To me, this squad was unbelievable that day. They deserved a victory which they should have had. This team showed the most remarkable spirit of any that I've had and I think exemplified the finest traditions of the game and of the service by their continued dedication and work, even though they had not too many moments of success. I should mention a few other people that were prominent that day. Bill Hawkins was a great halfback and Pistol Pete Williams was very effective. We had Dick Scott, a great center who became All-American in '47, and there was Billy Earl, a small scatback, as well as an outstanding guard named Scott Emerson.

"This was a never-to-be-forgotten game. The spirit of the Midshipmen was probably the highest I ever saw during the week preceding this Army game. This had a great deal to do

with these lads playing over their heads and is typical of the Army-Navy spirit that precedes every game. A sidelight on that incredible game was that after it was over, Admiral Halsey, who had planned to return to Wilmington, Delaware, to have an operation on his eye, could not leave until he had come to the Bellevue-Stratford Hotel to talk to the Navy team. This was greatly appreciated by everyone."

"The 1947 game was a heartbreaker for the Navy. Our team was captained by Dick Scott, an All-American center and as fine a ballplayer as I have ever seen. We had a great opportunity early in the game. Our Al McCulley returned the opening kickoff 25 yards, and we really went to work. Starting from our 35-yard line,

★ ★ ★

Letter from Leon Bramlett

Leon Bramlett captained the Navy team in 1946 when time literally ran out for the Middies. Elsewhere he has given his account of that memorable day. Here he adds a few comments about old football friendships.

I saw Tom Hamilton in New York at the Hall of Fame banquet. He and I had a great time together recalling old times. Also saw Rip Miller, Don Whitmire, Dick Duden, Ben Martin, Doc Blanchard, Glenn Davis, Doug Kenna, Arnold Tucker, and quite a few others. We had quite a get-together and spent much time talking over the Army-Navy games of the forties.

Everyone agreed, including the Army people, that Army was "saved by the bell" in 1946.

Tom Hamilton has told me many times and he repeated it when we were together last week that the 1946 Navy squad had the finest team spirit and determination to overcome the staggering odds of any team he had ever coached. In his words and he told us this after the game—I can still remember it—"You are the greatest bunch of guys I have ever known. You took it on the chin week after week and you kept coming back for more. You were down but never out and you never let your flag down. The Navy will always remember what you did today."

Of course to me what I remember and cherish most from these Army-Navy games was the company and companionship of some great men—opponents and teammates alike. As with most old football players, those joining together in these great struggles enjoy the firm and solid bonds of friendship and mutual respect that the years never seem to dim.

Sincerely yours,
Leon Bramlett

quarterback Bobby Horne picked up 11 yards on a bootleg play, Hawkins picked up 6 more, and then Al McCully cut off tackle for 15 yards and we had a first down on the Army 35-yard line. Then in two plays, a fumble by Horne and a great play, a tackle by Yoeman of Army cost us 12 yards. Then another fumble, this time by Hawkins, and Bryant of Army recovered the ball. Jack Stuart and Rip Rowan then pounded the line for big gains and suddenly the Army was threatening. Two cross bucks and Army had the ball on the 35-yard line. Then Rip Rowan faked a pass, suddenly dashed around end and picked up a first down on our 23-yard line. Then after a couple of cross bucks, Rowan faked another line play, faded back, and tossed a pass to halfback Bill Kellum, who went in for the first Army score. The kick was good and it was 7–0, Army.

"We came right back, picked up some good yardage, then Horne tossed a long pass. It looked like a great play, but quarterback Arnie Galiffa intercepted on the 7 and brought it back to the 30. And our second big drive was over.

"On the next play, we got lucky and recovered a fumble by Stuart. Then in two plays we were down to the Army 8 and it looked like a great opportunity to get back in the game. But we couldn't move the darn ball. Army took over and that was our last chance.

"On the very first play, Rowan got the ball from center, and before we knew what happened, he was through the line, into the secondary, and in the clear for the biggest run from scrimmage in Army-Navy history. Rip sprinted 92 yards for another Army score and it was 14–0, as Joe Steffy kicked the extra point.

"Late in the game we got moving once again and got to the Army 15. Then another big mistake. Myron Gerber tried a pass into the flat, but an alert Johnny Trent of Army, who had followed the play all the way, picked the ball out of the air and was across the goal line for another Army score and a 21–0 win for the Cadets. We had more first downs than Army, but we made mistakes and we couldn't seem to stop that speedy Rowan who gained a record 148 yards in eighteen carries. He was outstanding."

— ★ —

On November 27, 1948, a slight, well-dressed bespectacled man stood on tiptoe near the Navy's 40-yard line at Municipal Stadium in Philadelphia, his pearl gray hat bobbing like a floating cork as he craned and twisted and strained to see over the wall of blue Navy coats and white Navy caps.

Harry Truman of Independence, America's commander in chief and a former haberdasher who always had wanted a big league baseball career, was struggling to focus his camera on the "hopeless" Navy football team, a team that had lost 13 successive games and now, with just 58 seconds left to play in the game, stood tied with undefeated Army, champions of the East, third-ranking power in the nation, and a 21-point favorite to win.

Fifty Secret Service men fidgeted as protocol went down the drain. For security's sake it had been their custom to get the President clear out of the crowd before the end of the game.

But Harry Truman wouldn't budge. Like the 102,580 others at this forty-ninth meeting of the service schools, Truman simply had to see Navy fire the last shot in its arsenal.

Halfback Pete Williams, Navy's fine ball carrier, took a pitchout, but he was hit immediately and lost 5 yards. On the next play, Bill Hawkins went twisting and churning through the Army line for 8 yards. Now the clock showed 33 seconds left. Quarterback Slats Baysinger tried to sneak around end, but was stopped before he could reach the line of scrimmage. Now Navy huddled once more, rushed up to the line for one more play . . . but the referee stepped in, waving his arms.

The red hand of the clock stood at exactly zero, and the best, most exciting, and least plausible Army-Navy game in at least twenty years was over.

Navy had accomplished the impossible. They had tied a mighty Army team, 21–21.

It's doubtful that any one person in that enormous stadium had expected such a result before the game began. The crying towels had been hung out for Navy's first civilian coach in fifteen years, George Sauer, for the Middies had lost eight consecutive games prior to the Army game. It looked as if Navy would finish the season against Army without a victory, for the Cadets had one of the nation's strongest teams, had posted a solid ten-game winning streak, and were a lopsided favorite to rout the Middies.

Army kicked off to open the game, and Navy's Pete Williams brought the ball back 15 yards. Halfback Jim Green smashed through the line for a first down on the 40-yard line. Then halfback Pete Williams took a pitchout from Baysinger and sprinted around his own right end. Behind fine blocking, Pete twisted and turned his way through, around, and over half a dozen Army tacklers as he thundered his way 59 yards downfield to the Army 10-yard line. The crowd was still roaring at the suddenness of the Navy attack when quarterback Baysinger faked a pitchout but kept the ball himself and plunged over the Army goal line. The kick was good and Navy was out in front, 7–0.

Army's outstanding backs, Bobby Jack Stuart and Gil Stephenson, were injured on the next few plays, and Army's running attack was practically destroyed for the balance of the game.

Again Navy had the ball, and again it attacked Army with a ferocity that the Cadets hadn't seen all season long. With Hawkins, Green, and Williams carrying the ball, Navy reached the Army 15-yard line, apparently headed for another score. But suddenly Army's big line stiffened and stopped Navy cold. On three successive rushes, Army hurled back the Navy runners for losses totaling 25 yards.

Then Army took over and began to move.

Arnie Galiffa, Army's future All-American quarterback, coolly pitched passes to Bill Parrish for gains of 10 and 14 yards. Then halfback Rudy Cosentino bulled into the line for 10 more yards, reaching the Navy 5-yard line. On the next play Harold Schultz smashed over the goal line and, after the kick, it was a 7–7 tie.

The next time they had the ball, Army again thrilled the crowd with their marvelous passing game. Galiffa tossed a pass to Parrish for a gain of 40 yards, and then Cosentino bulled across from the 5-yard line to score. The kick was good and now it was 14–7, Army.

In the second half both teams moved the ball well as the teams seemingly exchanged their offensive styles, with Navy passing and Army staying on the ground. Navy moved to the Army 35-yard line, but was stopped on successive plays. Then Army rushed to the Navy 19-yard line, but Navy held. Finally, Navy, encouraged by their tough defense, scored a touchdown as Powers, Purvis, and Hawkins picked up successive first downs. Finally Hawkins smashed in from the 5-yard line and scored. Roger Drew kicked the extra point and Navy had tied the score at 14–14.

After the fighting-mad Middies had held Army scoreless through the third period, Army put together a fourth-quarter drive capped by Arnie Galiffa's magnificent 66-yard gallop for a touchdown and the Cadets took a 21–14 lead.

With only five minutes to play, it looked like a certain Army victory.

But then Navy forced Army to punt deep in its own territory. Navy had the ball at midfield, and the big crowd suddenly began to chant: NAVY! NAVY! NAVY! . . . And the Middies responded.

Carrying the ball on nearly every play, fullback Bill Hawkins cracked into the Army line. One plunge gained 4 yards, another a first down. Then it was Hawkins for 8 yards, and again for another first down. Navy drove on and on—to the 25-yard line, the 20, and then it was first down on the 10-yard line. Hawkins ran another smash into the Army line, and now the ball was on the 5-yard stripe.

On the next play, Baysinger faked a handoff to Hawkins, pivoted sharply, and carried the ball into the center of the line for a Navy touchdown.

The score was now Army 21, Navy 20.

Slowly Roger Drew came onto the field, cleared a pebble or two from his placekicking site, and got set to attempt Navy's biggest point of the season. The ball was snapped to the Navy placekick holder, and Drew calmly stepped into

Above: *One of Army's great all-time ends, Johnny Trent, captain of the undefeated 1949 team that shattered Navy, 38–0, congratulates the 1950 Captain-elect Dan Foldberg. Right: Earlier, Trent and quarterback Arnold Galiffa, Coach Earl Blaik looking on, received the Lambert Memorial Trophy awarded annually to the outstanding college football team in the eastern United States. A few months after his graduation from West Point, Lieutenant John Trent was killed in combat in Korea.*

the ball and booted it. Over it went for the point that tied the game at 21–21 as thousands of Midshipmen flipped their caps up into the air, roared for their team, jumped up and down for joy. Admirals and vice admirals, captains and ensigns, all were shaking hands and batting each other on their shoulders to salute the marvelous play of their 20–1 underdogs. And on the field, with a few minutes left to play, the dog-tired Middies battled a furious Army team to a standstill as the final gun sounded to end one of the great service games of all time.

— ★ —

In 1949 the Middies fared considerably better than they had in 1948 over their pre-Army schedule, winning 4 out of 9 games, and they were expected to give Army a real battle. It had been a tough schedule, with victories over Princeton, Duke, Tulane, and a strong Columbia University eleven. But the Cadets, still smarting from the humiliation of the tie game, rushed and passed the Middies until they were dizzy, scoring six touchdowns in a 38–0 rout.

The game, as they say in nonmilitary circles, was not as close as the score might indicate. In less than five minutes for the first of its six touchdowns, Army rushed for 87 yards, and the

Middies never got any closer to a score than the Cadets' 47-yard line.

Army's fine back Gil Stephenson alone gained more ground than the entire Navy squad, and Arnie Galiffa, the Cadets' All-American quarterback, tossed the ball at will to Stephenson, Frank Fishl, and ends Bill Kellum and Dan Foldberg, the future All-American end.

Army thus extended its streak to twenty consecutive wins without a defeat. Not since a loss to Notre Dame in 1947, by a 27–7 margin, had the Cadets gone down. The win over Navy was the tenth this season and enabled the Army to register their ninth undefeated football season since Dennis Michie organized the first Army team in 1890.

The game began with Navy kicking to Army, and the rout began as Bobby Adelman returned the kick 20 yards. In twelve plays, with Galiffa, Fishl, and Stephenson ripping off gains of 5 and 10 yards on every carry, Army moved upfield like a battering ram, blasting everything in sight until they crossed the Navy goal line. The kick was good and it was 7–0.

In the second period, Galiffa found Stephenson with a beautiful 32-yard bomb, and Army was off again. Stephenson knifed through for 14 yards, then Fishl broke out for 12 yards, then Galiffa gained 10 yards. Then it was Stephenson over left tackle for a first down, and Gil again, smashing across for another Army score from the 8-yard line. It was 13–0 as the half ended.

For some reason Coach Red Blaik did not feel too secure with a 13–0 lead and urged his players to go all out. "Remember how they played us last year. Let's not have another tie game. Let's tie it on them."

At the kickoff, Army halfback Bobby Vinson took the ball, tucked it under his arm on the 8-yard line, and gathering a head of steam headed for the right sideline. He got a couple of beautiful blocks, hurdled over a pile of Navy players, and suddenly was in the clear, all alone on the 50-yard line and heading for a touchdown. A 92-yard sprint, it tied Rip Rowan's run in the 1947 game as the longest in the modern-day series of Army-Navy football. (In 1901 quarterback Charlie Daly had run the length of the field to score on a 105-yard run, but the field was longer in those days.)

The rest of the game was a nightmare for Navy as the Cadets dominated totally. Stephenson scored two more touchdowns, and in the third period Bob Blaik, Coach Blaik's son, entered the game with the rest of Army's second platoon. And still Army continued to pound Navy all over the field, scoring twice more in the final period.

As usual in the annual classic, Navy fought back with everything they had. But all they had that day was Bobby Zastrow, a 209-pound quarterback with a rifle arm, and Bobby's passes were not very successful this day. Usually when he spotted a Navy receiver for a pass, three or four Army defenders would also be there either to intercept the pass or to knock the ball away.

So in 1950 Navy had a new coach. His name was Eddie Erdelatz, and he had been end coach at the Naval Academy from 1945 to 1947.

Somehow in 1950, Eddie Erdelatz's first Annapolis team managed to overcome the humiliation of 1949 and defeat Army, 14–2, in the

fifty-first game of the rivalry. And they did it before President Harry Truman and a near capacity crowd of 100,000, shocked and dazed into disbelief or delirium, depending on which side you were rooting for.

The unfathomable stalwarts from Annapolis took the game by marching 33 and 63 yards late in the second period for their touchdowns, scored first by 209-pound Bobby Zastrow, quarterback from Algoma, Wisconsin, on a 7-yard sneak and second on a 30-yard Zastrow pass to end Jim Baldinger; Roger Drew, Navy's placekicking specialist, made both conversions.

The Middies gave Army its only points in the middle of the third period on a safety, when Zastrow, fading back to pass from his 13, was rushed all the way into the end zone and dumped there by end Bill Rowekamp and guard Bob Velonnino.

"Miracles" such as this one may be a dime a dozen in football history, but you still have to call it that, a miracle. Navy had lost 6 of its 8 games in one of its most disastrous seasons, and had been beaten as badly as 22–0 by Northwestern and 27–0 by Tulane only a month previous. Yet somehow the Middies managed to come up with a fantastic performance that no one could have believed possible.

Of course, this game was against Army, which meant that Navy was starting a brand-new season from scratch. Forget the past. Still . . . they were playing an Army team believed to be the finest in the land, another all-conquering Army team that had won eight straight this year without being extended; an Army team that had gone twenty-eight games without defeat (two of the games were ties) and had won their last seventeen in a row; an Army team favored by many touchdowns to conclude its second straight perfect season and its fifth unbeaten season in six years; an Army team, finally, that had assailed its opposition for an average of 400 yards a game and whose wonderful defense had strangled the enemy all year, permitting only twenty-six points.

How, then, could such an Army team, bursting with health, boasting advantages in

In the 1950 classic, Navy won a spectacular 14–2 upset victory. Here, Navy back Bob Zastrow moves through a gaping hole for the Middies' first touchdown.

every department of play, infinitely deeper in manpower, lose to such a badly beaten Navy foe?

The answer, of course, is simple. Football is, as Red Blaik has said, a game of transcendent spirit played by American youth who will not concede anything in competition, no matter what the odds may be. In this case, two teams of equal size and muscle met in a game, and the team with the greater emotional urge and drive came through with a victory it wanted more than anything else in the world.

As President Truman, his guests, members of his cabinet, generals and admirals by the bushelful, and the other eyewitnesses of this thrilling contest slowly started out of the stadium in the semidarkness of a gray, misty day, as the hysterical brigade of blue-coated Midshipmen swarmed onto the field of battle, as the winning players hoisted their new coach, Eddie Erdelatz, to their shoulders, a wild-eyed fan, obviously a Navy rooter, faced the press box and shouted, "Don't you dare call this an

upset; Navy finally played the game it was capable of playing."

That was it, in a nutshell. Thank you, Navy fan.

Navy hit and ran and drove with a controlled fury that was overwhelming, churning the turf for 2, 3, 4 yards even after Army's fine defense had, to all purposes, stopped the play. Navy defended with eleven tacklers who swarmed over, gauged, and smothered Army swift runners, including even—and especially—the fullback, Al Pollard, rated one of the outstanding fullbacks in the country.

Navy's secondary covered Army pass receivers like leeches, so that even Captain Dan Foldberg, one of the greatest offensive ends in Army's history, was never for a moment unguarded. Foldberg was restricted to just two catches.

The pattern of the game was established early and never varied.

Zastrow, a quarterback who had so often been tagged the goat in Navy defeat, had the sort of game a boy plays in his dreams. He directed Navy's T-formation attack, with its brand-new spread features, with boldness and superb skill, deftly handing the ball to his backs—Dave Bannerman, Frankie Hauff, and Bill Powers—who would then ram through for short, consistent gains inside and outside Army's tackles; and for short, consistent gains inside tackles and through the middle, Zastrow would run himself for important yardage.

In a duel of bruising, violent line impact, Navy in that decisive first half gained eight first downs to Army's one, and outpassed Army as well. Navy made this margin of superiority pay off for two touchdowns, while Army could not mount an attack, rarely crossing midfield. Even when Army recovered a fumble and had a first down on Navy's 22 in the early minutes, it could not break Navy down. The Cadets had to give up the ball on the 15 and did not get inside the enemy 30 for the rest of the half.

Between the halves everyone marveled at Navy's almost foolproof and fumble-free play, wondering whether the Middies could maintain their burning flame against an aroused Army foe. For Army did rouse itself in the second half, and Navy did make a few errors, including the third-down pass try that led to a safety.

But for all its opportunities, its relentless attack through the fourth period, Army could not shatter Navy's valorous defense. Navy never lost its poise, or its control. Backed up against its goal through all of the last period in defense of its 14–2 lead, with Army at the 20 or even closer, Navy hung on to score its first victory in the series since 1943.

That victory, in all probability, marked the dawn of a new era in football at Annapolis.

Back in the locker room Eddie Erdelatz was the man of the hour. With tears pouring down his ruddy cheeks, "the kid" kept shouting, "The greatest team effort I ever saw."

When the team arrived back at Annapolis the next day, more than ten thousand had turned out to greet Eddie and his Middies. With Coach Erdelatz perched jauntily atop the fire engine, the Middies paraded about the campus, and when the fire engine and team reached the Academy, both the traditional Japanese victory bell and another bell donated by Admiral Bull Halsey were hauled out to be rung as the team roared, "Anchors Aweigh."

Grantland Rice in his syndicated column the next day closed his description of the game with these words: "On December 3, 1950, Navy had the greatest college football team in the land."

18

The Scandal and the Long Road Back: 1951-54

On August 3, 1951, news was released from West Point that ninety Cadets were being dismissed from the Academy for infractions of the Cadet honor code. It was later revealed that sixty of those ninety Cadets were varsity athletes, with thirty-seven of them members of the varsity football squad.

Newspapers across the country reacted with huge front-page stories:

WEST POINT FIRES 90 FOR BREAKING HONOR CODE. . . . SEN. FULBRIGHT URGES FOOTBALL BAN AT WEST POINT AND ANNAPOLIS. . . . CRIBBERS ON FOOTBALL SQUAD. . . . COACH BLAIK'S SON AMONG CRIBBERS. . . . SENATORS SET INQUIRY. . . . MORE CADETS ACCUSED.

So screamed the headlines that day, and for weeks afterward the expulsions were a subject of news and editorial comments across the nation.

The infraction of the code of honor did not involve carrying illegal notes, or copying from any books. In most instances it involved Cadets tipping off other Cadets on the subject matter involved in the tests given.

While thirty-five of the thirty-seven football players involved had been recruited for their football as well as their officer potential, all of

the players were generally outstanding Cadets, and since their acts had not involved cheating in the classroom, there was no direct evidence against most of them. Some Cadets were advised to say nothing. Others insisted they knew nothing about any "tipping."

On June 8, the Tactical Board at West Point recommended that all the Cadets charged be dismissed. The board's recommendation was then passed on to the very highest level, Secretary of the Army Frank Pace. Mr. Pace in turn appointed a committee of former judges and Army officers, and their report shortly came back to West Point supporting dismissal of the Cadets.

"I also thought about resigning as football coach," said Red Blaik, "but after discussing the matter with a number of my friends, including General MacArthur, I was urged by all to stay and fight on. So I did just that."

Coach Blaik went on to tell of that unhappy season.

"We put together a team that lost four more games than we had in the previous seven seasons put together. We lost to Villanova, Northwestern, Dartmouth, Harvard, Southern California, and Penn by a one-point margin. And then we got ready to play 'the big game.'

"I had an idea I thought might work against

The coaching staff at West Point in 1951. To the right of head coach Earl Blaik is assistant coach Vince Lombardi, who would go on to achieve one of the greatest coaching records in professional football with the Green Bay Packers of the 1960s.

a Navy team that had won one game, lost six and tied one. If we caught them by surprise at the opening, we might be able to hold them, perhaps even win. So I started the defensive platoon with orders to try an onside kickoff. Navy was not asleep, however, and got the ball on the kickoff. So our surprise was nipped in the bud.

"Having gained possession, Navy with Raster doing most of the work quickly scored, and kicked the extra point.

"We then received the kickoff and fumbled the ball. And of course Navy recovered. On the first play Mike Sorrentino passed fifteen yards, and Navy had another touchdown and conversion. Now it was 14–0.

"The play settled down after that. Then we recovered a Navy fumble and slowly began to move the ball for the first time in the game. Freddy Meyers passed to end Lowell Sisson for a fifteen-yard advance. Then Meyers dropped back and attempted a long pass into the end zone. But Raster, one of the Navy's bright new stars, jumped high into the air, plucked the ball out of the hands of our receiver, and by the time we were able to react, Raster had zipped his way to midfield and was headed for a touchdown.

"Nobody had a chance to catch him, and he sprinted a hundred and one yards for Navy's third score. This was the longest run in the modern Army-Navy series. Navy now had a 21–0 lead, and it still was only the first quarter.

"Vic Fine led a Navy march for another score late in the second period, and it was 28–0 at halftime.

"We finally scored our first points late in the third period as Meyers climaxed a fifty-yard march to bring the score to 28–7.

"Two more Navy scores in the final period gave the Middies a resounding 42–7 victory over our green team. This was the biggest margin of victory for either side in the series until that time.

"Navy went to town that day," said Blaik. "They had waited a long time for the opportunity."

Coach Blaik also recalled much about the seasons immediately following the notorious "cribbing scandal" season of 1951.

"It was something of a pleasant surprise that our 1952 record for the season showed four wins and a tie in the nine games. With quarterback Jerry Hagan providing a most unreal keynote, returning an opening kickoff 85 yards to provide a marvelous start, we beat South Carolina, 28–7. Then we went on to defeat a strong Dartmouth team, 37–7, V.M.I., 42–14, and Penn, 14–13. Columbia played us to a 14–14 tie. We then lost games to Southern California and Pitt,

and to Georgia Tech by a whopping 45–6 margin.

"So we could not wait to get at the Navy."

Eddie Erdelatz, the Navy coach who had taken over the reins at the Naval Academy in 1950, was after his third win over Army in a row, something few Navy coaches had ever achieved.

And this season Erdelatz had the talent.

Fred Franco was one of the top fullbacks in the East. Bobby Cameron was a fine quarterback with a good arm and had a large target in fullback Phil Monahan, who had a knack for catching the ball and "running for daylight."

"The Middies had started the season off strongly," said Blaik, "tapered off, then came back by playing a scoreless tie with a very strong Duke team, and they were ready for us.

"And we were ready for them. I wanted to try a bit of strategy at the opening, just to give us an edge over this very strong, cocky Navy bunch. It was the same thing we'd tried the previous year—an offside kick on the kickoff—but this time it worked.

"Rox Shain kicked off for us, and the Navy bobbled the ball. Howie Clark fell on it for us

President Harry S. Truman wishing both captains well—Navy's John Gurski and Army's Al Paulekas—before the 1952 game.

Left: *The Army head coach Earl Blaik and the star quarterback of the 1950 Army eleven, his son Bob.*
Right: *Tom Hamilton, Jr., son of the Navy All-American player and two-time coach, was a fine punter for the 1952 Middies.*

on the Navy thirty-one-yard line, and we were in business.

"But then we could not advance the ball beyond the twenty-yard line."

A series of fumbles by both teams—in the space of five minutes the ball changed hands six times—stalled any advances and stymied the ball at midfield.

Near the end of the first period, Frank Brady returned an Army punt 15 yards to the Cadets' 30-yard line. On three smashes into the line he advanced to the 15-yard line. Then, on fourth down, Navy tried a pass into the end zone, but the ball was batted down.

After an exchange of downs, Navy began a drive from the 35-yard line, and with Franco and Monahan pile-driving into the Army line the Middies picked up 10–21–5 yards. Then

Monahan on a reverse drove to the 5-yard line. Two plays later, Phil Monahan smashed off tackle for the touchdown, and Ned Snyder kicked the extra point. Now it was 7–0, Navy.

Throughout the remainder of the game, Navy kept hammering away at the Army defenses. Six times the Middies were in scoring range and six times the tough, scrappy Cadets, playing their hearts out, fought off the charge of the aggressive Middies.

Finally, in the waning moments of the game, Navy smashed and battered the Cadets to put the ball on the 1-yard line. Here the Cadets held once again. Then time ran out and Navy had its third straight victory over Army by a 7–0 margin.

Coach Blaik was thoughtful about the end of the game.

Above: *In the 1952 game, Army quarterback Pete Vann gets off a short pass to Mario DeLucia (33) over Navy defender captain John Gurski. Left: The Cadets fought hard but were undone by a series of fumbles and lost 7–0.*

"We'd come a long way since 1951, but not long enough to beat Navy."

By 1953 the end seemed in sight for Army on the long road back to football normalcy after the cribbing scandal of 1951.

"After our opening victory over a strong South Carolina team in 1952," said Coach Earl Blaik, "I received this telegram:

A GOOD START EARLY. THE BEGINNING IS AL-WAYS THE HARDEST PART OF THE ROAD BACK. GO ON AND UP TO THE PLACE WHERE THE BLACK AND GOLD BELONGS. MACARTHUR

"That wire," said Blaik, "may have implied a more immediate climb back than was possible. But it bore an inspiration applicable to the season of 1953. And, for that matter, to football at West Point as long as it is played.

"When I come to describe the team of 1953, what they meant to me and, far more important, what they meant to West Point, I cannot praise them enough. Of them Granny Rice wrote with eloquent simplicity, 'They came up the hard way, and there probably has never been a squad with a finer spirit.'

"True, we had reason to look for better things than in 1951 and 1952. Players of the class of '54 and '55 had been to the wars. The

Ten days before the 1953 game against Army, Navy's All-American Steve Eisenhauer (66) and Captain Dick Olson interrupt practice drill by leading out the Middies' mascot, Billy XII.

upcoming plebes of the class of 1956, while as few in numbers as their immediate predecessors, were of high quality and able to give us some badly needed help right away.

"As the season advanced we had a number of costly injuries. Fred Attaya, a hard-nosed halfback and solid kicker, was hurt. Mike Ziegler, a fast end, center Godwin Ordway, and a few other steady players were also on the sidelines due to injuries, and by the time we got down to the Penn and Navy games, the starting eleven and about four subs were carrying the full load.

"At quarterback we had Pete Vann, who shared the job with Jerry Hagen. But as the season advanced Vann became the number one man for that position. Against Penn, the backfield of Vann, halfbacks Pat Uebel and Tom Bell, and Gerry Lodge at fullback played the entire sixty minutes.

"As a plebe in 1951, Vann was an immature youngster, very boyish in his ways and thinking. On our return trip from the Northwestern game that year, he missed our plane and had to be flown back in the superintendent's plane. Pete's being a fellow passenger of the supe gave us all a fleeting grin in a time of bitterness. I am quite sure it prompted me to say of Pete to the newspapermen: 'Why, he's just a boy, that's all. Just a boy.' And even after Pete began to settle down on the football field in 1953, I continued to refer to him as just a boy.

"But by diligent effort Pete became a very fine quarterback. He was a more than acceptable passer and field general, a solid defensive back in a crisis, and as a ball handler and faker he was one of the best we've ever had at the Academy.

"Tom Bell, the right halfback, was a strong, swift runner from Mount St. Michaels in the Bronx. He ran with the power and speed of a steam engine. And when he ran, he snorted and grunted. His teammates called him 'Train.'

"At fullback, after Attaya got hurt, we converted Lodge who had been a guard. He did not have the speed that I would have wanted, but he could power into the line with more than enough drive to get us a lot of yardage.

"At left half, Pat Uebel must have scored as many key touchdowns in big games for us in 1953 as almost any other back in Army history. In '53 and '54 I would have to place both Uebel and Bell among the top echelon of all-time West Point halfbacks.

"Our defense, inexperienced and ragged in spots at the beginning of the season, gradually achieved a tightly knit cohesion and peaked for our big game against Navy. The heart of our defense was linebacker Bob Farris, a Vanderbilt transfer, and his play in the Navy game was as fine as any I have ever seen in that game. Unfortunately, Bob played with such ferocity that he suffered a detached retina and had to leave the game. Nevertheless, Bob was to captain the 1954 squad and help out with the coaching that season. The guards were Ralph Chesnauskas, who also could kick the extra point, Captain Roy Lunn, and Mike Ziegler.

"Our end play was handled by Bob Mischak, Lowell Sisson, and a yearling of unusual potential, Don Holleder. Sisson did the punting. Mischak developed into a fine pass receiver, and Don Holleder became a top receiver with outstanding speed, hands, and competitive fire. By 1954 Don was just about the most dangerous offensive end in college football.

"At tackle, we had two yearlings, Ron Melnik and Howie Glock. A reserve who played a good deal was Joe Lapchick, Jr., son of the great St. John's basketball coach.

"I faced a strange psychological problem in 1953. For two years these boys had seen the roughest action. They had lived under the coaching lash, with dirt, blood, and constant defeat. Yet they were afraid of nothing, eager to do anything I asked. But in the two years they had played, they had lost eleven games and won only one big game, against Penn in 1952. Yet the next week they had been badly beaten by Navy, even though the 7–0 score did not show it. In that fall of 1953, nobody in the Corps had ever seen an Army team beat Navy. I had to convince our team that they not only could be, but should be, winners. I myself was far from convinced for a long, long time that what I was trying to sell them was actually the truth. But I knew I must still try to sell them. And the strange thing is, I not only convinced them, but by the end of the season they convinced me.

"Each Monday I would set the tempo of thought and work for the upcoming game. I would sum up the scouting report they had heard on Sunday morning. Then I would ask, Just who the hell are they anyhow?

"After romping through Furman in the opening game of the season, we lost to a strong Northwestern eleven at Evanston by a 33–20 score. I was somewhat to blame for having put in a new pass defense that caught up with us. But we were much improved the following week, beating Dartmouth 27–0, even though we were not very impressive in the scoreless first half. Then, in one of the season's big surprises, we defeated a strong, experienced Duke team by 14–13. It was Mischak's marvelous last-minute tackle that stopped Duke's Red Smith after a seventy-three-yard, last minute dash that would have won the game for the Blue-Devils. Mischak tackled Smith on our seven-yard line and there we held them. Four times Duke smashed at our line, but we ended up taking over the ball on the two-inch line. Then we kicked out of danger and the game ended with Duke trying desperately to fill the air with passes, trying to get a final score. The "brave old Army team" had held fast, and the Corps, a delirium of gray, swept onto the field and carried off the team.

"This was the gang now that was going to be hard to stop. Next was Penn. Then Navy. . . .

"Three periods of smashing football saw Penn and us tied at 14–14, and then Pat Uebel smashed over for the final touchdown and we had a great victory.

"In the dressing room after the game, I told the players that if they beat Navy, I would sing them a song afterward.

"WE COULD NOT WAIT TO GET AT NAVY!"

On the other hand, Navy, with a very strong plebe team moving up to join a veteran unit, had started the season strongly, tapered off by losing a couple of games, tied two games and

then won four in a row. With that they were picked as one of the strongest teams in the East and were heavily favored to defeat the Cadets for the fourth straight year.

"I couldn't resist trying the same little trick that had worked for us in '51," said Coach Blaik, "only this time we'd disguise it more. I recalled Rox Shain, a B-squad player who had been our 1952 converter, and I had him practice a short diagonal kickoff. Something with a little more finesse than the straight-ahead onside kick that we'd been lucky to recover in '51, and that had failed so miserably in '50.

"We won the toss, and since we chose to kick off, Navy suspected the same thing as before and had their entire team bunched up in the middle. Shain just sliced the ball with his big toe extended, and the ball went crazily off to the side in the direction of Navy's left end Jack Riester. Riester could not field the ball properly and fumbled on the thirty-one-yard line, and tackle Howie Glock fell on the ball for us.

"Now we went to work and scored in seven plays. Bell slanted off tackle for eight yards. Vann missed with a forward pass, but on the next play Uebel took a pitchout from Vann and sped twenty-five yards to the Navy twenty and a first down. Then Lodge plowed right through the line for eleven and another first down on the nine. Then he added four more yards. On second down Navy stopped Lodge cold. Then Vann called play fifty-four. He took the pass from his center, faked beautifully to Lodge, then just eased the hidden ball to Uebel and Pat was across the goal line. Chesnauskas converted and it was 7–0.

"A few plays later there was a magnificent sequence. George Welch, then a Navy youngster but later to become one of their all-time quarterback greats, had one of his passes intercepted by Uebel on the thirty-three-yard line, and Pat began to run the ball back. At about midfield, Jack Perkins, a Navy tackle, just stole the ball right out from Uebel and ran it back to our nine-yard line, where Mischak knocked him out of bounds."

By this time, with the ball moving up- and downfield as quickly as the eye could see it, the big crowd of more than 100,000 spectators were up on their feet, roaring with each and every move.

"Navy tried a couple of running plays that barely picked up a couple of yards. Then Bell intercepted a pass by Welsh and we took the ball over on the one-yard line and returned it to the six-yard line.

"In the second period, Vann did what he dearly loved to do. He fired a tremendous fifty-one-yard pass to Mischak who leaped over three Navy defenders to snare the ball on the Navy eighteen. Uebel picked up ten yards in two plays, then Lodge smashed in to the three-yard line. Now it was up to Vann and old fifty-four. Once more Uebel was handed the ball after Vann faked, and once more he shot into the end zone, untouched. After Chesnauskas missed the extra point we had a 13–0 lead.

"Before the half ended we had an opportunity for a field goal from the twenty-one-yard line, but missed."

In the third period Navy battled back furiously. They stopped the Army attack cold on the 14-yard line, and again on their 4-yard line. Then Jack Weaver of Navy punted to Uebel on the 30-yard line.

"Pat took the ball over his shoulder, swept past two Navy tacklers, cut to the sidelines, and behind marvelous blocking dashed some seventy yards for another Army score. There were Navy tacklers on the dirt all over the stadium; key blocks had been thrown by Farris, Mischak, and Glock. This time Chesnauskas kicked the extra point and we led 20–0."

In the fourth period a determined Navy team slashed and cut into Army's line and reached the 32-yard line where they lost the ball on downs. On an exchange of kicks, Navy once again roared downfield to the Army 6-yard line, and once again Army's great defense stopped Navy cold. Then, for the third time, Navy cranked up and began a march downfield. This time Welsh drove the team 65 yards to the Army 7-yard line, and from there Jack Garron smashed through for Navy's only touchdown.

But that was all for Navy. The Cadets won the game, 20–7.

Back in the dressing room after the game, Coach Blaik talked to his players:

"I never have coached a team that has given as much satisfaction," he said. "Considering all the conditions since 1951, you people have done more for football at West Point than any other team in the history of the Academy. And now I'm going to keep my promise. I told you if you beat Navy, I was going to sing a song. So here goes:

"Down, down, down went the NAYvee—"

"That was as far as I got," he told me later. "The roar of the players drowned me out. But somehow I didn't mind. I never could carry a tune."

No recent football game between the West Point Cadets and the Middies of Annapolis had so fired the imagination as the fifty-fifth renewal in 1954 of the service classic at Municipal Stadium, Philadelphia.

Neither team was undefeated but both were acknowledged as ranking powers in the East, with Army the nation's leader in offense and Navy having all of the defensive records. So, something had to give when they met head-on.

Army, which had scored its first win over Navy in four years the previous season, entered the fray a slight favorite, although there were plenty of experts who liked Navy after its easy win over Penn by a 52–6 margin, while Army had downed the Quakers by a mere 35–0 score.

An aggressive Navy team—alert, ready, and inspired by the Brigade of Midshipmen— received the opening kickoff and began to move the ball upfield. But the Army fought back, held the Middies, and forced them to give up the ball.

On their first play, Army fumbled and Navy recovered on the 25-yard line. Quarterback George Welsh, a fine field general, ball handler, and all-around star all season long, tried two running plays. Then, on third down, Welsh lofted a lateral pass to halfback Bob Craig, who bolted the remaining distance to the goal line. Johnny Weaver kicked the extra point and the Navy was out in front, 7–0.

Above: *On the eve of the 1954 game. Army coach Earl Blaik, only recently recovered from a bout with pneumonia, huddles with his backfield—Tommy Bell, Captain Bob Farris, fullback Pat Uebel, and quarterback Pete Vann. Right: Navy coach Eddie Erdelatz makes a point to his quarterback, George Welsh, and halfback John Weaver. Both Welsh and Weaver were outstanding as the Middies defeated the Cadets 27–20.*

Then it was Army's turn, and the Cadets gave a beautiful exhibition of power football as Bell and Pat Uebel smashed the line for successive first downs. Then Bell, who had been the center of an eligibility controversy all week long, capped the Army drive by sprinting the final 10 yards to give Army a touchdown. The conversion was missed and now it was a 7–6 game.

The Navy fullback, Dick Guest, fumbled the ball early in the second period, and Don Holleder recovered for Army on the 15-yard line.

But on the next play Pete Vann bobbled the ball and this time Navy recovered.

Two plays later, Pat Uebel intercepted a Welsh pass and raced to the Middies' 42-yard line. On the first play from scrimmage, Pete Vann faded back and tossed a bomb to halfback Ed Kyasky, who caught the ball in stride and scored Army's second touchdown.

Army then kicked off, and Navy, starting on its 41-yard line, began to flex its offensive muscle. They reached midfield, but Army held and on fourth down, Weaver dropped back for a

punt. But Weaver faked a kick, and before the startled Cadets realized it, he had tucked the ball under his arm and was streaking down the sidelines for a first down deep in Army territory. By the time the Cadets had recovered their poise, Navy had scored as quarterback George Welsh dropped back and calmly tossed a pass to end Early Smith in the end zone for a 14–13 Navy lead.

Army took the lead sixty seconds later.

After taking the Army kickoff, Welsh tried a long pass, a wobbly one that looked as if it might go out of bounds. Pat Uebel, racing in from his defensive spot, plucked the ball out of the air and dashed to the Navy 40-yard line. Here Pete Vann faked a run, stopped in his tracks, and tossed a long lofty pass to Kyasky, deep behind the Navy line. Outmaneuvering the Navy defenders, Kyasky raced in for Army's third touchdown, putting them out in front 20–14 after the extra point was missed.

That lead quickly melted in the fire of Navy's lightninglike counterattack.

Army tried an onside kickoff, but Navy re-

Navy coach Eddie Erde-latz and team captain Phil Monahan receive the 1954 Lambert Trophy, emble-matic of eastern U.S. college football supremacy.

covered the ball at midfield and in six plays moved to the Army 5-yard line. Then Welsh on two tries into the line smashed in for the touchdown and now Navy led Army 21–20.

The huge crowd was up on its feet time and again as each team battered the other, each team scoring, with the lead seesawing back and forth. It was explosive football and the crowd loved every minute.

In the third period, Navy seemed to take control of the game, marching right down to the Army 10-yard line only to lose the ball on a fumble.

Army drove back to midfield, but Bell fumbled and Navy recovered on their 40-yard line.

This time they went all the way.

Welsh passed to Earl Smith for 20 yards, and Smitty powered his way through two Army tacklers before diving into the end zone for the touchdown that gave Navy a 27–20 margin.

The game ended with Army battering its way to the Navy 10-yard line, only to lose the ball on a fourth-down incompleted pass. Navy had won the biggest game of the year.

After it was over the Middies accepted a bid to play the University of Mississippi in the 1955 Sugar Bowl (and would beat them 21–0). It was the first postseason playoff game for the Middies since 1924, when Navy had played in the Rose Bowl.

Navy won the Lambert Trophy that year, awarded to the best team in the East, and there were many who insisted that Navy was the best in the country.

19

From Holleder to Dawkins: 1955-57

The Army team that Navy just managed to defeat in the thrilling 1954 game included a great many outstanding players. Any list of such Army stalwarts would have to include the name Don Holleder. Holleder's story is a very special one in the great football annals of West Point, and there is no better person to tell the story for the year 1955 than his coach, Red Blaik.

"The saga of Don Holleder stands unique in Army, and perhaps, in all college gridiron lore. At the end of his second-class season, Don was ranked the most dangerous end in college football. Although he had substituted in 1953 and missed two games in '54, his two-season pass-completion totals were thirty-two for 781 yards and 9 touchdowns. Quick and competitive at 6 feet 2 and 187 pounds, he was also above average defensively and was selected for most All-American teams.

"Yet it is not as a great end that we remember Holleder so much as a boy who gladly gave up personal glory for the good of the team. This took place in 1955 when I asked him, although he had never played in the backfield, to become our quarterback.

"In the end Holleder won a personal satisfaction that would not be matched if they had ush-

ered him into the football Hall of Fame. He led a dedicated Army team to a victory few people thought possible in a manner that will always seem incredible.

"From 1951 through '58, we never had enough tools to do the job right; no, not even in the undefeated Lonely End season of '58. The seasons of '55 through '57 especially—and the expulsions by that time were four to six years in the background—found us in predicaments which the average coach of a non-military college would chafe at as untenable, if not downright intolerable. My assistants realized this acutely at the time, and reemphasized it later in many letters they wrote me after they became head coaches elsewhere.

"Much of the time we lacked such essentials as quarterbacks and linebackers. Between Pete Vann's last season of '54 and the development of Joe Caldwell in '58, there was nobody in the Corps with the training and potential talent to take over at quarterback. The one or two plebes of ability who did show up were lost by academic failure. We experimented again and again. Finally, we had to take men from other positions and try to remake them into quarterbacks.

"It was because I had no alternative that in 1955 I turned to Holleder.

"George Welsh would be back at quarterback for Navy again in 1955. This problem transcended all others for us. It loomed especially formidable by contrast with our own quarterback situation. Pete Vann would not be back. There were no 1954 reserves for the job. There was nobody up from the plebes to be developed. I experimented with several backs at the position the first week of spring practice. It wasn't working out. It was then that I thought of Holleder at quarterback.

"Though Don had never played quarterback, had never even played in the backfield, he had been an All-American end, a truly great pass receiver, in 1954. Normally, he could be expected to be even more brilliant as a first-classman. Yet, I had nobody to throw the ball to him. He himself threw left-handed. I knew that in the one season of eligibility he had left, he could not possibly develop into a superior passer, but he might do well enough to get by.

"On the plus side, Holleder was a natural athlete—big, strong, quick, smart, and aggressive. A competitor. I knew he could learn to handle the ball well and to call the plays properly. Most important, I knew he would provide bright, aggressive, inspirational leadership at the key position of the game.

"No matter what might happen before the Navy game, I reasoned that we would have no chance to win the big one with Welsh as the Navy quarterback unless we had a quarterback who could match him at least in dynamic leadership. This was a quality I knew Holleder to be rich in.

"On a Sunday afternoon in April, I asked him to come by my office.

" 'Don,' I said, 'I am worried about the quarterback position. I have nobody to fill Vann's job. I have looked and looked without success. How would you like to take a shot at it?'

" 'Colonel,' he said, 'I never have played in the backfield in my life.'

" 'I am well aware of that,' I said. 'But I want you to go back to your room and think this over. Then come back to see me tomorrow. One other thing. Do not say a word about this to anyone. Keep it entirely to yourself.'

"Holleder told me afterward he did not sleep much that night. He tossed and turned, and the problem tossed and turned with him. He wanted morning to come quickly, and he didn't want it to come at all. He looked a little haggard when he came up to see me after his first class Monday morning. He said that if I thought he could do the job, he was willing to make a try at it. I told him if he should become unhappy in the experiment, he could always go back to end. We talked some more. As he left, I said, 'Turn in your old end number and get a new one for the quarterback position.'

"So Don Holleder turned in number 48 for number 16. Sixteen is a football number I'll never forget.

"From the beginning, the experiment seemed jinxed. Holleder needed every second of practice he could get in his new and taxing assignment, but he was at it only a week when he cracked an ankle in scrimmage and had to wear a cast until the end of May.

"That spring and fall, the switch of the All-American end to a position he never had played before—to, of all places, quarterback—dominated every story written about the Army team. In the past, I had made many switches in personnel without undue questioning or doubt by press, public, and Academy people. The reaction always had seemed to be that they felt I knew what I was doing.

"In our first games the heat was off temporarily as we trounced Furman in a warm-up, then beat Penn State, 35–6. Against the Nittany Lions, Holleder passed for one touchdown and ran for another. More comment was excited, however, by our holding Lenny Moore, their brilliant halfback and later Baltimore Colts star, to 65 yards and just one touchdown.

"The following Saturday we played Syracuse in Michie Stadium, in one of the heaviest rains in Academy history. The storm blew in on Wednesday and raged for five solid days through Sunday. We were not a very good team under any conditions, but on a wet field we were

All-American end Ronnie Beagle of Navy was named the outstanding lineman in the nation in 1954. An honor student and one of the most popular men on the Navy team, Beagle starred for three seasons, 1953-55.

psychologically impaired before we started. Quickness and speed, the hallmarks of our football, suffer on a slow terrain. Against Syracuse, we could do nothing in the slippery quagmire. Jim Brown, who would become the paragon of professional running backs, was approaching stardom as a junior. Jim showed a sure foot in the messy going and set up their two touchdowns with his key gains. The score was 13-0.

"On Sunday night it was still raining. As Holleder left the mess hall with his roommate after supper, he heard more Cadet conversation critical of his quarterbacking. A brief furlough by the grandstand quarterbacks followed the next two games, however, as we beat Columbia, 45-0, with Pete Lash making a 72-yard touchdown run, then knocked over a good Colgate team, 27-7. In the Colgate game, Holleder threw three touchdown passes—to Chesnauskas for 30 yards, to Art Johnson for 42, and to Mike Zeigler for 17. And himself ran for the other score. The Post and the newspapers even chirped a little that maybe Blaik was right after all.

"Then we lost to Yale, 14–12, at New Haven. We encountered more miserable weather in the Yale Bowl, and our play was even sloppier than the rain and mud. We fumbled repeatedly, giving Yale one opportunity after another, and finally they capitalized. The grandstand quarterbacks returned from furlough.

"The farewell game with Penn the next week, a 40–0 victory over a weak team, carried no more meaning than the 35–0 triumph of the year before.

"So we were distinct underdogs going into the Navy game. The Midshipmen had a 6–1–1 record, including a thumping victory over Pittsburgh. Their big edge lay in the poised, experienced George Welsh at quarterback, the nation's leader in passing statistics and a smooth ball handler, clever play caller, and fine leader.

"The night before the Navy game, we bivouacked as usual at the Manufacturers Country Club outside Philadelphia. Around nine-thirty, after we returned from the movies, I took the team for our usual pre-taps stroll around the golf course. At one point, I stopped. It had been my habit over the years to tell the squad a bedtime story.

" 'I have grown weary,' I said, 'of walking across the field to offer congratulations this year to Bennie Oosterbaan of Michigan, Ben Schwartzwalder of Syracuse, and Jordan Oliver of Yale. Now I'm not as young as I used to be, and that walk tomorrow, before one hundred thousand people (and fifty million more on television), to congratulate Eddie Erdelatz, would be the longest walk I've ever taken in my coaching life.'

"There was dead silence for a moment or two, and then Holleder spoke up quietly: 'Colonel, you are not going to take that walk tomorrow.'

"I never saw a more savage-hitting Army-Navy game than that one. At the beginning and for some time afterward, it appeared they were going to run us right out of the north end of the big horseshoe. From the opening kickoff, they marched 76 yards to a touchdown.

"They had prepared especially for us a tricky, double-flanker pattern out of the split T. Welsh directed the drive, one of the best I ever saw a Navy team make, with faultless judgment. He was hitting his receivers, among them the ineffable end Ronnie Beagle, he was running the ball cleverly on quarterback-keeper numbers, he was even utilizing a Statue of Liberty play. It looked like a long, tough afternoon. Even when they missed the extra point after that first touchdown, it didn't seem to matter much.

"In the first twenty-five minutes of the first half, they so controlled the game that they had thirteen first downs to our one and 208 yards gained to our 39. But they could not crack us. Twice we stopped them at our 20. The first time, Holleder slammed into Beagle so hard as he caught a fourth-down pass, Beagle couldn't hold it. The second time, Navy fumbled and Holleder fell on the ball.

"With five minutes left to play in the half, Navy punted to our 13. From this point, we began to wrest control of the game away from them. Pat Uebel, always at his best against the Navy, began tearing inside and outside their tackles. Holleder called his own number on an occasional sneak or keeper. Dick Murtland and Pete Lash, two unsung halfbacks, began biting off useful chunks of yardage.

"Without throwing a single pass we marched 86 yards all the way to their 1-yard line. But then, before we could get off another play, the clock ran out on us and we had to leave the field at the half trailing 6–0.

"In the second half, the charge of our line so throttled their running game, Navy was forced to resort almost entirely to passing. Welsh completed eighteen out of twenty-nine passes for 179 yards that day, but all he got out of it was one touchdown.

"We threw *two* passes, and completed neither.

"In the third period, we marched 41 yards for our first touchdown. Uebel, appropriately, slammed it over. Chesnauskas converted, and we had a hard-won lead, 7–6.

"Navy hove anchor in the last quarter for the

last time. The superb Welsh hit his receivers unerringly and they went 72 yards. But they fumbled on our 20, and our guard Stan Slater recovered.

"Then we began ramming it down their throats again and went all the way, 80 yards. The last bite was the fatal one and the big one. Lash, after a fake by Holleder to Uebel up the middle, slanted over their right side, outside their tackle. Their right end was playing so tight, to relieve the beleaguered inside, that Lash's course actually took him outside the end. It was an off-tackle run that looked like a half-back sweep. When Lash shot into the open, the secondary had lost any decent angles of pursuit on him and he raced 22 yards for the score. Chesnauskas converted again and we had it nailed down, 14–6."

After the game General MacArthur wired:

NO VICTORY THE ARMY HAS WON IN ITS LONG YEARS OF FIERCE FOOTBALL STRUGGLES HAS EVER REFLECTED A GREATER SPIRIT OF RAW COURAGE, OF INVINCIBLE DETERMINATION, OF MASTERFUL STRATEGIC PLANNING AND RESOLUTE PRACTICAL EXECUTION. TO COME FROM BEHIND IN THE FACE OF APPARENT INSUPERABLE ODDS IS THE TRUE STAMP OF A CHAMPION. YOU AND YOUR TREMENDOUS TEAM HAVE RESTORED FAITH AND BROUGHT JOY AND GRATIFICATION TO MILLIONS OF LOYAL ARMY FANS.

Don Holleder was gone in 1956, and for what happened in that aftermath we have Red Blaik to continue the story:

"It is something of a paradox that the Lonely End team of 1958, toasted for its dynamic, colorful, 'mysterious' attack, was primarily, as all outstanding teams must be, a tough, sound, alert, dedicated defensive unit. We allowed, by running and passing combined, an average of 182 yards to a game. That was the third-best statistically in the nation. I believe that when we were in condition, our first team and a few subs put on the *best* defense of that season.

"But we also had backfield problems which we never did solve. We had one talented back

in Kyasky. He could do everything. Even after knee surgery, he was outstanding. Then, Gene Mikelonis, the talented yearling runner, hurt his knee in the Virginia Military Institute opener and never played again.

"With Holleder gone, the biggest backfield poser was to find a quarterback. For a while I tried Kyasky there, but later moved him to fullback. I then called on Dave Bourland, who was not a natural quarterback, but was the best we had in '56 and '57 and never gave me less than 100 percent effort.

"Early in 1956, our backs were perilous on pass defense, but they improved and in the Navy game were excellent.

"What killed us was our fumbling. We were the fumblingest team I ever coached. We had forty fumbles during the season, and opponents recovered half of them. One reason for the fumbling was lack of sufficient practice time. I concentrated on defense, because I realized if I did not, our backfield deficiencies on offense would get us murdered. This left me relatively little time to devote to offense, and that prevented the development of the cohesion that reduces fumbling.

"The fumbling, of course, not only broke up our attack continuity but frequently gave the opponent prime field position. This, added to our early-season pass-defense venalities, combined to put terrific pressure on our line—except at Michigan, where the line acquitted itself very well.

"In our 14–7 victory over Penn State (which had a 6–2–1 season, including a victory over Ohio State), Kyasky was outstanding, although new to the quarterback post.

"In losing, 48–14, at Michigan the next week, we were atrocious. We committed eight fumbles. They recovered six, five of them leading directly to touchdowns.

"Well, we were hard-nosed enough, and I thought we earned and should have had a tie against Syracuse instead of a 7–0 defeat. It seemed to me Vince Barta, our fullback, got over the goal line on fourth down in the second half, before halfback Jim Ridlon hurled him back, but an official ruled otherwise.

Above: *In 1954, Don Holleder was an All-American end for Army, but the next year he was asked by Coach Blaik to switch to quarterback for the good of the team, although he had never played the position. In the 1955 classic, Holleder's play was a key factor in the Cadets' 14–6 upset of the Middies.*
Right: *He has just handed off to fullback Pat Uebel, steaming into the end zone for Army's first score.*

"Our 60–0 victory at Columbia the next week had no significance, other than it was our farewell, for the foreseeable future, to the Ivy League.

"The Colgate game that followed is memorable in Michie Stadium chronicles for odd reasons. The score was Army 55, Colgate 46. We couldn't stop their passing and they couldn't stop our running.

"Fumbles again contributed to our 20–7 miseries at Pittsburgh, although the Panthers were stronger than we were.

"So we had a 5–3 record and only one decorative victory, Penn State, as we came down to Navy. The Middies had lost only one game, and their 7–1–1 record was their best since 1945. We faced the opportunity, as in 1955, to make it a big year by upsetting them.

"In the game, we reverted to form—eight fumbles, five recovered by Navy—and it was a crime, because we outplayed them and should have won. We outgained them on the ground, 200–81, and our defense, sparked by tackle Flay Goodwin and center Jim Kernan, prevented them from getting beyond their 39-yard line on their own power. Kyasky, the best back on the field, gained 77 yards and scored our only touchdown from the 4 after Bourland intercepted a pass and returned it 27 yards. Dave

also punted superbly. But when we fumbled once too often, on our 27-yard line in the last period, they finally capitalized with a scoring drive and the game ended in a 7–7 tie.

"The tie convinced Rear Admiral W. R. Smedberg II, superintendent of Annapolis, that Navy should not accept a bid to the Cotton Bowl, which apparently was still available to the Middies. This was small consolation to us. We felt we had beaten ourselves.

"We went into the 1957 season with more hope than in '55 and '56. Not that we were without problems. Our defense was not stable. Except for Captain Kernan and Slater, we had to rebuild a new line. Our reserves were acutely vulnerable against topflight opposition. Then the blue-chip injury jinx made its annual visit. Bill Carpenter, then a yearling but already an outstanding end, suffered a serious leg and ankle injury in a late-summer jeep accident, which also put two other players out for the season. Carpenter got in briefly late in the year, but not enough to win a letter.

"Our offensive picture, however, was interesting, even exciting. Our line, while inexperienced, especially at tackle, was our biggest since 1950 and could open up holes. Bourland im-

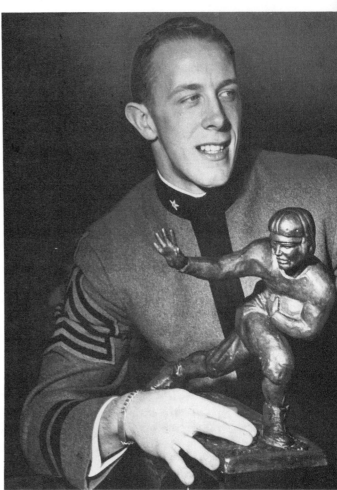

proved at quarterback. At fullback, Vince Barta now had two years behind him and was being pushed by a yearling firecat named Harry Walters. Most of all, the spring drills had revealed a pair of halfbacks to bring crowds to their feet: Bob Anderson and Pete Dawkins.

"Anderson, nineteen years old, 6 feet 2, 205, from Cocoa, Florida, was the best all-around football player at the Academy since Blanchard and Davis. He did everything well: running, blocking, tackling, passing, catching passes, defending against them, punting. He was also one of the most self-effacing and selfless team players I ever encountered.

"Pete Dawkins, as a second-classman in '57, was nineteen, 6 feet 1, and 195. Although football was the focus of the spotlight on his unique versatility as a Cadet, even without the show-case of the gridiron he would have had to be considered one of the most remarkable Cadets in the history of the Academy.

"In his senior, first-class year, Dawkins rose to an unprecedented achievement: first captain or brigade commander, the highest military rank in the Corps; academic star Cadet for being in the top 5 percent of the class; and football captain. He was also outstanding on the hockey team and was president of the class. Despite his onerous schedule, Pete still found time for social activity. His facility with the guitar and other instruments made him a leader of informal barracks musicales.

"The best team we met in 1957 definitely was the Navy. The second half of our schedule, however, was not as tough as the first half. On successive Saturdays, we opened against Penn State at University Park, then met Notre Dame in Philadelphia's Municipal Stadium, the first

The Pete Dawkins saga: Opposite page, left: *Two-time All-American halfback in his three years at West Point (1956–58), team captain in 1958, honors student and Rhodes scholar.* Opposite page, right: *Winner of the 1958 Heisman Trophy for best college football player in the nation.* Left: *Outstanding service in Vietnam as combat adviser to the South Vietnamese.*

of a home-and-home renewal with the Irish, and the next week took the traditionally rugged Pitt Panthers at Michie.

"We beat Penn State, and after losing 23–21 to Notre Dame, getting ready for Pittsburgh was a happy alkaline. An overflow crowd of 27,900 at Michie saw us play our finest game of the year in defeating the Panthers, 29–13.

What with one thing and another, "we still had a 7–1 record (which should have been 8–0) going down to play Navy. This strong Navy team, unaccountably defeated by North Carolina, 13–7, and tied by Duke, was to go on to hand Rice a decisive 20–7 beating in the Cotton Bowl.

"It was a miserable, rainy, muddy day in Philadelphia, and Navy's day all the way. They won, 14–0. Ned Oldham, their fine back, climaxed his three years by scoring all their points

on a 6-yard run, a 44-yard punt return, and two conversions.

"Their strong, laterally mobile defense did us in. Anderson, handicapped by a first-period leg injury and not much blocking, was held to 18 yards in eleven carries. Dawkins felt the pressure of his first Navy game as a regular and mussed up several assignments. One of them caused us to fumble on their 9, which we had reached on a 60-yard drive with Pete doing most of the gaining, helped by Anderson's heavy blocking. We also reached their 15 after recovering a fumble, but were stopped by an interception.

"Navy's impressive defense was featured by Bob Reifsnyder, a linebacker transplanted from tackle, and right guard Tony Stremic.

"As a sophomore in '55, Tony had been given a rough afternoon by our Holleder-directed infantry. In '57, he exacted full retribution."

Red Blaik's Last Year: 1958

It was November 1958 and the colonel sat in his spacious office in the gymnasium at West Point, plotting the football game on Saturday as if it were a battle. The "lonesome end," the mobile Army backfield, the sprinting line—these are some of the concepts Earl "Red" Blaik introduced to college football. Whenever he philosophized it was with the assurance of a soldier accustomed to many victories.

"Good fellows are a dime a dozen," Colonel Earl Blaik said, "but an aggressive leader on the field is priceless. There never was a champion, who to himself was a good loser. And there is a vast difference between a good sport and a good loser.

"Football is a marvelous game because of its limitless permutations and combinations of men in action. It is a game which cannot be played without courage."

All the previous week, as Blaik drove his unbeaten Army team through fierce workouts for its fifty-ninth game against Navy, November 29, West Point had swarmed with reporters and photographers. For the Navy game would complete Blaik's twenty-fifth year as head coach. Blaik put in seven outstanding years as Dartmouth's head coach, plus eighteen years at West Point. Yet even after all those years as a national figure, he presented an image of aloofness, more like that of a dedicated chess player than that of a backslapping head football coach.

But to the men who knew him best, Red Blaik was a warm and inspiring man. The late Frank Leahy, whose Notre Dame teams won three and tied two games with Army, once said, "It's a good thing for the nation that a man like that is teaching our future officers."

On the practice field above the Hudson, Blaik was not concerned with tributes to his past as he drove his men through their daily paces just a week before the Navy battle. The coach was looking ahead to the game.

"This game is different from all the rest," he said. "And if you lose you have a whole winter to think about it."

This year, 1958, Army, which had defeated Notre Dame and had been tied only by a strong Pittsburgh eleven, was ruled a strong favorite over twice-beaten Navy.

Because of the demands West Point makes on its Cadets, Blaik's squads could practice only ninety minutes a day (most major teams drill more than two hours). To compensate for this drawback, Blaik relied on organization. Just twelve days before the Navy game, Blaik split his squad into five units, all working under experienced assistant coaches (one of them Vince

An All-American halfback in 1957 and 1958, Bob Anderson teamed with Dawkins to give Army its most potent one-two punch since Davis and Blanchard.

Lombardi, who would go on to the pro New York Giants and establish new records with the Green Bay Packers). Then as the different squads bent to their tasks, Blaik wandered from group to group. When a manager called out that forty-five minutes had ended, Blaik formed two platoons and began directing a scrimmage.

"Now on three!" he said to quarterback Joe Caldwell, and whispered a number.

Caldwell announced the play to his huddle, and the regulars, in black shirts, broke to face the subs in white shirts. "This is a beautiful play," Blaik told the subs, "a tough one to stop."

The center snapped the ball to Caldwell on the third "hike," and Joe handed the ball off to halfback Bob Anderson. The play was halted when a sub tackle hit Anderson just as he got past the line.

"That tackle," Blaik said to a blocker, "got past you like the Flying Dutchman."

"Yes, sir," the blocker said, wincing.

Blaik called the play again and this time Anderson made 20 yards.

A few minutes later, with the subs running, a pitchout went awry and a sub linebacker intercepted the ball.

"What do you know," said the sub, "we got a score."

Blaik grinned, then his lean face grew stern.

"What happened to the ball?" he asked a back.

"I didn't get it, sir."

Blaik's voice was pure ice. He said just one word: "Augh."

Early in the scrimmage the ball was returned to the 30-yard line after every play. Now, as the afternoon waned and the sun fell behind the bare trees on a rolling hill, Blaik put the ball on the 20.

"Let's see you regulars take the ball over in just two plays," he said.

Captain Pete Dawkins and Bob Anderson carried the ball on two plays, and the varsity scored.

"Not too bad," Blaik said. "You're getting the spirit. Let's see what the other men can do." A second-string back limped toward the huddle. "Here, now, I don't want anyone limping through a workout. If you have to limp, don't work out. But if you work out, don't limp. Is that clear?" Half a dozen cadets nodded.

Later Don Bonko, a sub fullback who had been having trouble with a blocking maneuver, approached Blaik. "You can't do it that way, sir," he said.

"Can't you?" Blaik said.

Then Earl Blaik, a trim sixty-one years of age, charged against Don Bonko, twenty-one and 210 pounds, and knocked him off his feet.

"You see?" Blaik said.

"Yes sir," Bonko replied. "Guess I do."

Back in the office, Blaik sat beneath a photograph of MacArthur and talked about his years at the Point.

"Football and education are compatible," he said. "We've made mistakes in the game. Biggest has been the isolation of the players, having them live together and eat together as though they were set apart from the rest of the students. They aren't here at the Point. They're part of campus life."

Blaik sat back and considered. "Movies have also changed the game," he said. "Years ago whatever the coach said he saw happening was gospel. Maybe he didn't see a great deal more than anyone else, but no one knew whether he was right or wrong. Now films are the proof. Now there's time to analyze, to check the fine points, things like blocking angles. The game is complex; players must be intelligent."

He swung his chair and leaned forward. "There's no end to ideas. I sleep with a pad alongside my bed. Sometimes I think of something just before I go to sleep. Sometimes a thought actually wakes me up. The lonesome end idea? I was down in Miami and the monsoons came. I was watching the rains when the thought struck me."

Suddenly there came the sounds of a bugler blowing retreat and the colors came down at West Point. But the big game with Navy was just ahead. And in his office Red Blaik, teacher and schemer, worked on through the night.

"After that rainy, gloomy day in Philadelphia when Navy's great defense beat us 14–0 in 1957, and racked by a heavy cough, I went to Key Biscayne, Florida, for a brief vacation," Coach Red Blaik said after the game. "And it was here that I decided to utilize the idea of splitting the defense of our opponents and at the same time give us a most unusual and constant offensive threat. And so I devised the idea of the Lonely End as part of our offensive system for 1958.

"This would mean that our end, in this case Bill Carpenter, would line up on the line, but split fifteen yards away from the rest of team on offense. He would not have to huddle with the rest of the team, but would get his signals by the foot movements of our quarterback. I got the name, Lonely End, from that great sportswriter of the old *Herald Tribune* in New York, Stan Woodward. Before each offensive play, quarterback Joe Caldwell would take his position behind his huddled teammates, as if he were studying the opponents' defense. Then he would place either his left or his right foot extended, so that Carpenter from his Lonely End post would know the direction of the next play.

"We unveiled the Lonely End in our first game against South Carolina, September 27 at Michie Stadium, and before the game was over, the stands were buzzing with excitement and the Cadets were jumping up and down as we ran over, around, and passed South Carolina dizzy by a score of 45–8.

"In that game quarterback Joe Caldwell was outstanding, as was Pete Dawkins, who scored a record four touchdowns. Pete gained 113 yards on just nine carries. Bobby Anderson scored two touchdowns and the entire team carried off the new Lonely End offense to perfection. South Carolina had no idea what we were going to do, pass to Carpenter or run with the ball. As a result they had two and sometimes three of their defensive backs covering Bill, leaving our halfbacks and other flanker wide open. The result stunned South Carolina and startled and dazzled the many sportswriters covering the game.

"The next week we trounced Penn State in another dazzling offensive show. In the first half of the game we completed nine of eleven passes for 285 yards and 26 points.

"The following week it was Notre Dame with another very strong squad that included such stars as Bob Williams, Monte Stickles, George Izo, Red Mack, and Al Ecuyer. The Irish were pointing for us, but Notre Dame could not cope with our Lonely End and we beat them 14–2."

By the time Army had beaten Notre Dame,

the whole country was talking about the Lonely End. And Bill Carpenter filled the bill. A native of Springfield, Pennsylvania, Bill was tall, rangy, and fast as a streak. He was 6 feet 2½ inches, and at 225 pounds was strong enough to drive through any would-be tackler. A marvelous pass catcher and blocker, and smart as a whip, Bill became a darling of the nation's press.

The following week at Michie Stadium, the Cadets powered their way to another impressive victory as they defeated the strong Virginia Cavaliers by a 35–6 margin. Pete Dawkins and Harry Walters had been injured in the Notre Dame game and were out of the lineup, but the

Army's Lonely End, team captain, and All-American in 1959, Bill Carpenter became a national war hero in Vietnam when he called for bombing raids on his own troops to save them from annihilation by North Vietnamese overrunning his command. For his heroism, Captain Carpenter was presented with the Silver Star by General William Westmoreland.

Cadets by this time were clicking like a well-oiled machine and could not be stopped.

Pittsburgh, however, provided a tougher assignment, and on a cold, wet, miserable day, after Army easily scored 14 points and led 14–0 at the half, Pitt rallied to score two touchdowns and came away with a 14–14 tie.

With President Dwight D. Eisenhower in the stands at Michie Stadium the following week, the Cadets showed their most devastating offense as they moved over, around, and in the air against hapless Colgate and defeated the Red Raiders by a whopping 68–6 score.

Traveling to Houston for the first game ever against a well-drilled Rice University squad, Army eked out a last-minute 65-yard pass play, Caldwell to Pete Dawkins, with Pete catching the pass on the Rice 35-yard line, then zigzagging his way 65 yards for a touchdown that gave the Cadets a thrilling, last-minute 14–7 victory over a very rugged team.

In the final game before the Navy battle, Pete Dawkins simply could not be stopped and ran through and around a bedazzled Villanova squad for three touchdowns. Writing about that game, sports editor Stan Woodward wrote: "Pete Dawkins in scoring 3 magnificent touchdowns should be known from today on as 'The Royal Oak, Michigan, Warlock.' "

Navy had been a spoiler in the past years and could be again. Yet Blaik knew one thing about the Lonely End team. They would not let anybody down. For the first time in eight years, for the first time since 1951, since before the Cadets were expelled, Army was going down to the Navy game undefeated.

The Navy team also had a very fine record, 6–2. The Middies had been upset by a strong Tulane, 14–6, and had been soundly beaten by tough Notre Dame, 40–20. But they had been hampered by an injury to one of their key defensive men, big Bob Reifsnyder, Navy's All-American tackle. But with his return and the seasoned Joe Tranchini at quarterback, also a budding star in Joe Bellino, the Middies had won the rest of their games and loomed as a dangerous opponent for Army.

The night before the big game, Philadelphia was hit by a torrential downpour. The winds howled down from the mountains, swirling water into huge puddles, which soon began to freeze on the edges of the playing field, making playing conditions quite miserable. But a tarpaulin had been thrown over much of the center of the field, and when the tarp was removed before the start of the game the sun broke through and most of the field looked playable.

Army won the toss of the coin and Navy kicked off.

The kick went directly to Pete Dawkins, and he began to speed upfield. As Pete reached the 20-yard line, he cut sharply away from two Navy tacklers and headed directly for the right sidelines. As he turned upfield again, he sensed daylight to his left and cut in that direction. At that moment, a Navy man moved in from his right front. Bill Rowe, Army's big center, cut in to block the Navy player, and as Rowe moved over, he hit Dawkins. The ball popped out of Pete's hands and Navy fell on the ball on the 40-yard line.

On first down, Navy surprised Army as Tranchini passed to Bellino for a short again, then Bellino raced for 10 yards, and suddenly Navy was on the move and threatening undefeated Army. Tranchini faked a pass and slipped through the Army right side for 10 yards, and now it was first down on the Army 25-yard stripe. A Navy pass, Tranchini to end Johnny Kanuch, gained 15 yards. Then it was Bellino and fullback Dick Dagampat blasting the Army line for short gains of 2 and 3 yards. With the ball on the Army 6-yard line, Bellino took the handoff from Tranchini, cut off tackle, and darted in for a Navy touchdown. Ray Welborn missed the conversion, but Navy had a 6–0 lead.

Navy soon had the ball again; raging with desire, the Middies threatened to turn the game into a rout as they drove 74 yards on six plays with Tranchini mixing his passes, then handing off to Bellino and Dagampat for successive first downs to the Army 13-yard line. Navy was completely befuddling the Army defense with their double-wing T formation and double and triple flankers. Army had not been able to scout the Navy practice sessions, as Erdelatz held secret practice sessions for ten days prior to the Army game.

Suddenly, Army's defense stiffened. Carpenter, on a critical play, tossed Bellino for a 4-yard loss back to the 17-yard line and then finally Army took over the ball on the 17-yard line.

After that one big play by the Lonely End, the caissons started rolling to victory. Instead of Joe Bellino and Joe Tranchini with his rifle-shot arm, now it was another Joe—Army's great quarterback, Joe Caldwell, was doing the rifle shooting, tossing beautiful short, flat passes to Carpenter and Captain Pete Dawkins.

Bob Anderson, who had had a futile day against Navy a year ago, now began slashing and cutting through for the precious yards that meant first downs.

"On that first drive," said Coach Blaik, "Anderson was the dominant figure, for he did the blocking for Pete Dawkins and it was his effective blocking that paved the way for Pete as Army moved sixty-eight yards in a march that consumed thirteen plays, with Anderson smashing in from the three-yard line. Walters kicked the extra point and Army had a 7–6 lead at the half."

In the third period, Army began a determined drive and marched deep into Navy territory, but just when it seemed as though Army would score, Navy Captain Jim Dunn leaped high into the air to intercept a Caldwell pass on the Navy 14-yard line. But then, after Navy had made some headway of their own, Dunn fumbled the ball when hit hard by an Army tackler, and guard Bobby Novogratz recovered for Army.

Army then began a determined drive. Once more it was Joe Caldwell doing the pitching to Anderson and Dawkins. One of the passes produced a 28-yard gain, and now the ball rested on the Navy 2-yard line. On the next play, Anderson blasted off tackle for the touchdown, Walters neatly made the conversion, and it was Army 12, Navy 6 as the third quarter came to an end.

Near the end of the final period, Navy uncorked a drive that almost succeeded. But Tranchini, eager to score, hurriedly tossed a pass that Army's end, Don Usry, picked off and then dashed 38 yards for another Army touchdown. Then as the Cadets in the stands screamed their heads off, Captain Pete Dawkins took the pass from center, faked a run, and tossed a 2-point conversion to Bob Anderson to make the final score 22–6.

In the dressing room after the game, with a host of colonels and four-star generals present, Dawkins said to a sportswriter: "We sure got off to a great start, didn't I?"

Anderson, Dawkins, and Novogratz made the All-American team.

After the Navy defeat, General MacArthur wired Coach Earl Blaik:

IN THE LONG HISTORY OF WEST POINT ATHLETICS THERE HAS NEVER BEEN A GREATER TRIUMPH. IT HAS BROUGHT PRIDE AND HAPPINESS AND ADMIRATION TO MILLIONS OF ARMY ROOTERS THROUGHOUT THE WORLD. TELL CAPTAIN DAWKINS AND HIS INDOMITABLE TEAM THAT THEY HAVE WRITTEN THEIR NAMES IN GOLDEN LETTERS ON THE TABLETS OF FOOTBALL FAME. FOR YOU, MY DEAR OLD FRIEND, IT MARKS ONE OF THE MOST GLORIOUS MOMENTS OF YOUR PEERLESS CAREER. . . . THERE IS NO SUBSTITUTE FOR VICTORY.

One month later, January 13, 1959, Earl Blaik resigned as West Point's football coach.

21

The Unhappy Succession of Dale Hall: 1959-61

It was snowing hard and the winds howled down from the Hudson River as Colonel Red Blaik looked back on his eighteen-year career as football coach at West Point on January 14, 1959. That career would end February 15, on Blaik's sixty-second birthday.

"I didn't really decide to resign until last weekend," he told this writer. "My son Bob was home for the weekend and he, my wife, and myself discussed the situation. We've always been a close family and I wanted to talk this over with them before I acted.

"After the discussion with the family," said Blaik, "I informed the officials at West Point, and I talked it over with General MacArthur, my closest friend.

"My wife and I will hate leaving here," said Blaik. "We've been very happy here at West Point. Last night I had quite a time looking over some of my trinkets and trophies in my den and it brought back memories of some marvelous football games."

Asked if he would have a hand in selecting his successor, Blaik replied, "Oh, no. I don't think it is my prerogative or my affair. Of course I'm interested in the future of West Point athletics, football in particular. But I shall make no suggestion as to my successor unless I'm asked."

While Blaik was talking to this writer, Lieutenant General Gar Davidson, the Academy superintendent, announced that he would entertain applications from all interested coaches. He said the Academy was "rocked and shocked by the resignation of Blaik," who had been accepted as a fixture at West Point for eighteen years.

Blaik was relaxed through most of the interview. At times, especially when he talked of his decision to retire, he fingered his spectacles, removing and returning them to his forehead. When he reminisced about Army's great football tradition, his brown eyes sparkled and he laughed freely.

"The Blanchard-Davis team was the best I ever coached," said Blaik. "And if they had used the Lonely End formation, I can't imagine how many points we would have rolled up. Glenn Davis was the best halfback I ever coached and Doc Blanchard was the best fullback."

At the National Press Club luncheon in Washington to honor Earl Blaik, President Eisenhower praised Blaik as a "very, very great man, whose retirement as football coach at West Point would have happened a long time ago, had Blaik been thinking only of himself.

"I am delighted at this chance to say publicly that I have never known a man in the ath-

164

letic world who has been a greater inspiration for the men he is teaching, for the athletes under his control, for a whole Corps of Cadets and, indeed, for everybody that has known him.

"I think he has done a remarkable job, a very dedicated one and I am quite sure that if he had been thinking only of Earl Blaik he would have been long gone."

The President went on to say that he had written to Blaik this day, "trying to express my feeling of admiration and gratitude for a man, who for all these long years—I think it is now about twenty-five years—has been coaching young men at Dartmouth and West Point and doing a most remarkable job for all of us."

There was prolonged applause by the more than 1,500 members of the Press Club, and shouts of "Blaik, Blaik, Blaik" rent the air as the members rose to their feet.

Shortly after Colonel Blaik resigned as head football coach, General Gar Davidson, superintendent of the Academy at West Point, announced that thirty-six-year-old Dale Hall, one of the stars of the championship 1944 Army team and the defensive coach under Blaik since 1956, would be the new head football coach.

Now, on February 15, 1959, the press was gathered at Leone's restaurant in New York City. It was where Army usually held important press conferences, and Hall was making his first public appearance as head coach at West Point.

Tall, wide-shouldered, and good-looking, Dale Hall had been overshadowed as a halfback by Glenn Davis. But so had every other halfback in the nation at the time.

Questioned by reporters, Hall said: "I'll continue the great running tradition established by Colonel Blaik. We do have some excellent players returning, but not too many of them. I'd like to point out that Bill Carpenter will be back. So will Don Usry, our fine quarterback Joe Caldwell, and All-American Bob Anderson. I hope to continue the Lonely End formation. It has unlimited possibilities and we intend to exploit them."

Shortly after Colonel Blaik announced his departure and Hall was picked as the new head coach, the Naval Academy was shocked to learn of Eddie Erdelatz's resignation because of "a widening breach and misunderstanding in conducting the Navy's football program." Erdelatz, who had beaten Army in five of nine games with one tie, including three victories in a row, victories over some of Army's most glamorous teams, had had constant problems with the Annapolis administration. He left to take a post with the Oakland Raiders of the newly formed American Football League.

Erdelatz's successor was Wayne Hardin, described as "a man who knows and can solve the problems at the Academy, and sympathizes with them." At thirty-two, he was the second youngest coach ever to guide the Middies football team. Tom Hamilton, the Pitt athletic director in 1959, had been only twenty-seven when he first became the head coach at Navy in 1934.

In 1959, as Army and Navy approached their sixtieth football meeting since 1890, both teams appeared to be on a parity.

If there was a shade of difference either way, it had to favor the Cadets. While the Middies were having a rugged time beating George Washington University, 16–8, Army almost pulled off the upset of the year as they lost a last-minute heartbreaker to an outstanding Oklahoma eleven, 28–20.

Before that game, Army had destroyed Boston College, 44–8; lost to Illinois, 20–14; lost to Penn State, 17–11; beat Duke, 21–6; beat Colorado State, 25–6; tied Air Force, 13–13; and defeated Villanova, 14–0.

Navy opened the season with a strong win over Boston College, 24–3; defeated William and Mary, 29–2; lost to Southern Methodist, 20–7; lost to Syracuse, 32–6; lost to Miami, 23–3; tied a strong Penn State team, 22–22; lost to Notre Dame in a wild squeaker by 25–22; then finished the season before meeting Army by beating Maryland, 22–14; and defeating George Washington.

There were no championship implications as the Army team, hampered and battered all sea-

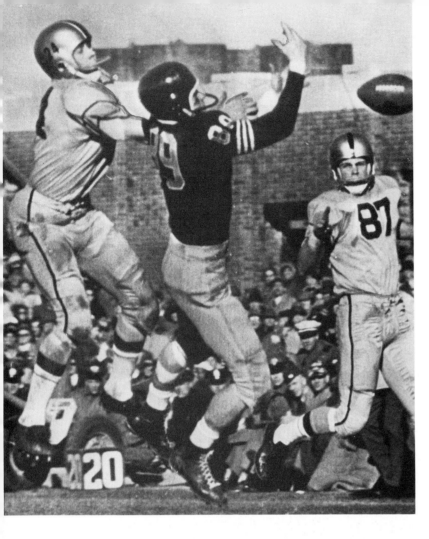

The four games from 1956 through 1959 were notable for their spectacular play and stellar performances on both sides. Opposite page, top: In the 1956 classic, Navy's Dick Dagampat flings himself at a solid wall of Army linesmen for the Middies' sole touchdown in a 7–7 standoff. Opposite page, lower left: In 1957, Navy captain Ned Oldham returns a fourth-quarter punt 44 yards for a touchdown as his teammates jump for joy; Oldham scored all of Navy's points in a 14–0 victory over a strong Cadet eleven. Opposite page, right: In the 1958 annual renewal, Bob Anderson, Army's All-American halfback, hurdles the Navy line to score Army's second touchdown on the way to a 22–6 revenge victory. Left: In the same game, Pete Dawkins (24) bats down a pass intended for Navy end George Bezek a Army's Bill Carpenter (87) moves in. Below: In the 1959 game, Navy halfback Joe Bellino outraces a diving Bob Anderson and Joe Caldwell on a 45-yard touchdown scamper, one of his three scoring runs of the day; the combined 43–12 score was the greatest point total in the long series of Army-Navy grid classics.

son long by injuries, prepared to take the opening kickoff before more than 102,000 spectators at Philadelphia's Municipal Stadium.

As quickly as you can say Joe Bellino, Navy had scored two touchdowns in the first period and left Army stunned and shocked by the swiftness and savagery of their running attack.

Army had taken the opening kickoff and failed to move the ball, and then the Middies took over and started to roll upfield.

Two beautiful trap plays with halfback Ronnie Brandquist going right up the middle brought the ball to the Cadets' 15-yard line. Then swifty, shifty Joe Bellino took a handoff

and cut inside his right end and was over and across the goal line for Navy's first score of the day. The extra point was blocked and it was 6–0, Navy.

Army received the kickoff but couldn't advance the ball, and Caldwell kicked to Bellino on the 37-yard line.

From here, Tranchini passed to Bellino for a short gain, then hit end Tommy Hyde with another pass to the Army 40-yard line.

On the next play, Tranchini called for a trap play once again. Bellino took the ball and sprinted up the middle through a huge hole in the Army line and simply outran the Army defenders to cross the goal line without a hand

Navy's Ronnie Brandquist slashes deep into Army territory in first-period action in the 1959 service classic.

touching him. Greg Mather made good on the conversion, and it was 13–0, Navy.

Army couldn't gain a first down until well into the second period, when Al Rushatz, the Army fullback, picked it up on the Navy 49-yard line. A couple of Army first downs placed the ball on the Navy 28, and Joe Caldwell, the Army quarterback, flipped a short pass to Lonely End Bill Carpenter, who outran three Navy defenders in a race for the end zone. Army had its first score of the day, and after Tommy Blanda, whose brother George had been a great pro star, failed in his try for the extra point and it was 13–6, Navy, the crowd began to whoop and holler for another Army touchdown that would tie the game.

But on the next kickoff, Navy continued to prevail, charging straight on up the field in a dozen plays, 67 yards to the Army 5. Then it was quarterback Joe Tranchini who cracked the Army line for another touchdown.

Now the Middies gambled . . . for two points.

Quarterback Joe Tranchini took the pass from center and shot a bullet pass to end George Bezek, who clutched the ball to his chest, fell over the line, and Navy had 2 more points.

Now it was Army's turn to attack, and they did with a vengeance that surprised the Middies and the huge crowd.

With the ball on the Navy 24-yard line, the Middies had a personal foul called and the penalty was for half the distance to the goal line.

This put the ball on the Navy 12-yard line and now Bobby Anderson, Army's great halfback, put on a show of his own as he zigged and zagged the 12 yards for an Army score. Caldwell's pass to Anderson for a two-point conversion was too high and Bob could not hold on to the ball, and the score now stood 21–12 Navy.

Late in the third period, Bellino intercepted an Army pass and sprinted 18 additional yards to Army's 18-yard line. In a series of five plays, all into the Army line, the Middies advanced the ball to the 5-yard line and then Bellino, his chunky legs churning the turf, smacked over for another Navy touchdown.

Once more Navy gambled. This time, Tranchini tossed a pass to Hyde on the conversion for two additional points, and Navy was out in front by a 29–12 score.

Just before the third period ended, Brandquist, Navy's fine fullback, broke through for a 23-yard dash to bring the ball to the Army 5-yard line as the quarter ended.

On the second play of the final period, Tranchini ran in from the 3-yard stripe for another Navy score, and then the Tranchini-Bezek passing combination was good for another 2-point conversion. Navy was now comfortably out in front by 37–12.

With time ebbing fast for the Cadets, Army went desperately to the air for a quick score. A pass from Joe Caldwell to Anderson was intercepted by Navy halfback Dick Pariseau, and he ran the ball to the Army 25-yard line.

Then it was Tranchini to Bezek for 5 yards. Then another pass play for 11 yards, bringing the ball to the 11-yard line. Three smashes by Bellino brought the ball to the 1-yard line, and Brandquist bulled his way over for Navy's sixth and final touchdown. Final score, Navy 43, Army 12.

In the clubhouse after the game, an assistant coach told Bellino that one more touchdown would have made him the only player in Army-Navy history to score four TDs. But only Joe Tranchini knew that Bellino's own selflessness had kept him out of the all-time record books.

"When we lined up for the last touchdown, I called Bellino's number," said the Navy quarterback, "but Joe said, 'No, give the ball to Ronnie Brandquist,' so I called Ronnie's number and he scored the TD."

Three touchdowns were enough, thanks to Bellino, who said he hadn't slept well for three weeks, worrying about this game.

"We put in that new halfback pass play just for the Army," said Joe, "and when I threw it to Dick Pariseau the first time and he missed it, I thought, Oh, we're going to have another one of those terrible days."

It was terrible all right, but only for Dale Hall and Army. Long after the dazed Cadets slumped off the field, Joe Bellino stood in the

Navy coach Wayne Hardin hugs three of his star players after the Middies' 1959 trouncing of the Cadets in the sixtieth game of the service rivalry. Around Hardin (left to right): end Tommy Hyde; halfback Joe Bellino, who scored three Navy touchdowns in the game; and quarterback Joe Tranchini, who directed the Middies' powerhouse offense.

center of a swirling mob in the dressing room, signing his name for strangers. His brother, Mike, a high-school star at Winchester, Massachusetts, was yelling, "Joe, you were great, great, great." Flashbulbs popped all around him, and teammates pummeled him while Navy admirals by the score lined up to shake the hand that beat Army.

For that moment, Joe Bellino was All Navy.

They were just three of the football fans seated on the Army side—up in the twenty-sixth row: three among a total of 98,616 who had paid as much as $250 each to witness the 1960 service classic.

If any of the three felt reasons to complain, he kept manfully silent, for like the 98,613 others he received full value for his six bucks.

The trio in the twenty-sixth row actually saw two football games. Navy won the first, 17–0. Army won the second, 12–0. Overall, to the dismay of the Army fans, including the three in the twenty-sixth row, the first half out-

weighed the second, and Navy scored its twenty-sixth victory against thirty Army triumphs (with five ties) in this storied series by a score of 17–12.

It was Joe Bellino, a Navy hero to compare with John Paul Jones, who fractured the egos and hearts of an embattled Army team in two ways at Philadelphia on this November 26, 1960.

Jumping Joe skewered the Cadets with a brilliant ball-carrying effort in a 17-point first half, then completed the job by killing a rally in the closing seconds of play with a startling pass interception on the Navy goal line.

Bellino's contributions, All-American all the way, paid off handsomely for a band of tough, fast, scrappy Middies who had just enough at the end to hang on to the considerable dividends they had reaped in the first half. They won the game, then accepted a bid to play Missouri in the Orange Bowl on New Year's day.

This was a game in the great tradition. The tacklers hit so hard that bones seemed to rattle high up in the press box, and the blocking just about jarred Philadelphia's Municipal Stadium to its foundations as Army fought its heart out to bring back a victory to West Point.

"Our boys were a little too keyed up, too eager to do the job," said Dale Hall, the Army coach. "I'm not trying to take anything away from Navy, and I think that Joe Bellino is the greatest back in the country, but we had too many passes batted down, too many fumbles, and too many missed tackles in the first half. That made the big difference."

"I thought Army played a helluva game," said Joseph Michael Bellino, "especially their line. I'd say the lines made the difference. I thought our line played a helluva game, too. We haven't played a better team all season long."

Like Caesar's Gaul, the football game was divided into three parts. Navy won the first part, and you have to give fullback Joe Matalavage some credit for that. He called the turn of the coin and elected to receive.

Bellino carefully plucked the ball out of the sky, tucked it under his arm, and with those short, churning steps, cut sharply to his left, avoiding two huge tacklers. Then picking up his blockers, he threaded his way, carefully but confidently, to the Navy 36-yard line before he was brought down, as the three thousand Middies rose as one and shouted his name. Three line plays by Navy failed to gain, and Greg Mather dropped back to kick. His punt, a high, booming, arching kick dropped into the hands of the Army fullback, Joe Blackgrove. Joe started upfield, lost the ball, and Ron Erchul, the big, aggressive Navy tackle, recovered.

But once again Army's stubborn defense held the Navy attack. Three Navy tries did not produce anything of substance, and Mather had to punt once more.

With the ball in their possession in Navy territory, Army drove to the Navy 31, and it appeared that they might have the upper hand. But on three plays, Army's drive stalled, and Paul Stanley of Army had to kick. His punt was a thing of beauty—out of bounds on the Navy 1-yard line.

With Navy virtually in its own end zone, it was Army's turn to cheer, and the 98,616 up in the stands sat on the edge of their seats in anticipation.

The moment the ball was snapped, Army's charged-up ends shot into the Navy backfield and ran past Bellino, who then slanted off to his right on an offtackle play and burst through the Army line as if it were Swiss cheese. Once out in the clear, Bellino veered to the right sideline, blowing right by a couple of tacklers. Now running with high-knee action and strides that covered the ground quickly, chunky Joe was a difficult target to tackle. Only one cadet was in pursuit.

"I think I could have gotten by that last man if he hadn't had a good angle to hit me," Bellino said later.

Bellino slowed down slightly, trying to lure Cadet George Kirchenbauer with a tricky hip-movement, but the Army halfback ignored the swivel hips and brought Bellino down with a clean, hard tackle.

Bellino had sped 58 yards on his great run, and now the ball was in Army territory. Navy picked up long yardage on two plays to get to the 12-yard line but here Army held, forcing Navy to attempt a field goal.

Greg Mather dropped back to the 25-yard line on fourth down and booted the ball hard, but the ball sailed low and wide and Army took possession on the 20.

But once again fate smiled on Navy.

On the first play from scrimmage, Army's halfback, Al Rushatz, fumbled as he was tackled and Vern Von Sydow, Navy's huge guard, fell on the ball.

Two Navy passes, from quarterback Hal Spooner to Jim Hughes and to Gary Kellner, brought the ball to the Army 5-yard line, and on the next play Bellino drove in for the first score of the game. Mather's conversion attempt failed and it was 6–0, Navy.

The second quarter was all Navy. They made it 9–0 after starting a drive from the Army 42-yard line. Bellino, with his elusive cutbacks over the right side of the Army line, and Spooner's accurate, pinpoint passing, moved the ball to the Army 9-yard line. At this

Second-quarter action in the 1960 game: Army quarterback Dick Eckert is down but not out, passing from his knees just before being hit by Navy's Ron McKeown (36); but the pass was ruled illegal, with Army penalized 15 yards.

point Army's forward wall broke through the Navy line and dropped Spooner for a 15-yard loss, and the Army contingent broke out into a loud cheer.

But Joe Bellino could not be stopped. He drove his team back to the Army 9-yard line, and then once again Mather attempted a field goal. This time Greg dropped back to the 27-yard line and calmly booted the ball right through the uprights for three more Navy points, raising the score to 9–0.

There was but one minute left to play in the first half when Army's halfback Jim Connors picked up 12 yards, but Army was then penalized for intentionally grounding a pass, forcing them to kick to Navy on the 46-yard line.

With thirty-five seconds left to play, Navy began to move. A 9-yard pass, Spooner to Prichard, gained 10 yards. Halfback Ron McKeown and Bellino alternated in drives that picked up additional yards.

The next play came like a flash of lightning, another beautiful pass, Spooner end to Jim Luper, and Luper was over for a Navy touchdown. Just seventeen seconds remained in the half, as Bellino, trapped in the backfield, tossed

a pass to Spooner, who raced over the goal line for the 2-point conversion that increased the Navy lead to 17–0 as the half ended.

Army received the second-half kickoff and immediately proceeded to stumble as Kirchenbauer bobbled the ball, then recovered it before dashing 13 yards to the Army 22.

Army's coach Dale Hall had evidently tongue-lashed his players in his talk between halves, for now the Cadets roared back with everything they had in their attacking arsenal. They held the ball for twelve successive plays, and every one of them gained ground except one incomplete pass. Tommy Blanda pitched perfect strikes to John Ellerson and Paul Zmuida, his ends. The two plays picked up 32 yards. Then Al Rushatz broke through Navy's left tackle for 18 yards before he was brought down. Then it was Rushatz, breaking through Navy's tough defense for the first Army touchdown. Blanda attempted a 2-point pass for the conversion, but Prichard broke up the play. Now it was Navy 17, Army 6.

Army's sudden turnaround sent the Cadets up in the stands into a roaring frenzy as they shouted and pleaded for Army to keep the caissons rolling along. This would be no easy Navy victory if Army continued such inspired play.

The third period ended with Army in possession of the ball on its 39-yard line. As the fourth and final quarter began, Army picked up the momentum. Dick Eckert, Kirchenbauer, and Al Rushatz pounded the line and moved the ball to the Navy 34-yard stripe. Eckert passed to Blanda for 8 yards. Another snappy pass to Kirchenbauer put the ball on Navy's 17-yard line. From there, Eckert and Rushatz alternated carrying the ball, until Al Rushatz smashed over Navy's left guard from the 3-yard line and Army had another touchdown. Vern Von Sydow then picked off an Army pass for the 2-point conversion attempt and Navy still held on to a 17–12 lead, with just ten minutes left to play in the game.

Now the battle intensified as Army battled the Middies in a toe-to-toe clash of strength. Like two heavyweight champions, the two teams slugged it out—up and down the field the play surged, with first Army picking up ground, then Navy, then Army.

Now it was Army driving, driving, busting through to Navy's 8-yard line. But here an opportunity, the biggest of the game for the Cadets, went glimmering as Blanda attempted a lateral pass to Rushatz, who fumbled the ball all the way back to the 20-yard line and Navy took over.

But there was one more opportunity for the Cadets.

They got possession of the ball after Mather punted. Blanda began to fire the ball, moving his team deep into Navy territory. A pass to end Roger Zailskas netted 16 yards, but then just when it looked as if Army might be headed for another score, Bellino leaped high into the air to snatch a pass right out of the hands of Rushatz. As he came down, Joe dodged one tackler, hurdled another, and quickly shot into the open. He managed to reach the 45-yard stripe before he was dragged down from behind as the game ended.

No sooner had Bellino been brought down than he was hauled back to his feet and onto the shoulders of his delirious teammates. You couldn't blame them, for Joe had carried the ball twenty times for a net rushing yardage of 85 yards. He had also contributed several dazzling runs, one of them for 65 yards that had brought those three spectators in the twenty-sixth row to their feet . . . cheering like the rest of the crowd.

And as the smoke of battle cleared, and the captains and the colonels left the stadium, the three fans in the twenty-sixth row could now be identified—the vice president of the United States, Richard M. Nixon; Attorney General William P. Rogers; and the former West Point football coach, Earl "Red" Blaik.

History contains no record of what the new President, John F. Kennedy, said to the governor of Pennsylvania during the first half of the 1961 Army-Navy game, nor what he said to the governor of Ohio during the second half, but on his return to the White House, the wartime PT-boat skipper declared that he had "thoroughly enjoyed every minute of the game."

And no wonder. President Kennedy had just seen his own former branch of service literally kick hell out of the Army team. Greg Mather, Navy's 212-pound end, who had received national attention in 1960 for a last-second field goal that gave Navy a 15–14 victory over a highly rated University of Washington eleven, booted a 32-yard field goal in the second period of the '61 service classic to put the Middies ahead; then after fleet Bill Ulrich had matched Army's third-period touchdown, Mather converted the extra point and finally booted a fourth-period 3-pointer from the 36-yard line to give Navy a 13–7 victory in the sixty-second game between these two rivals.

It was the third consecutive Navy win over Army, and it set off a demonstration that lasted until the three thousand Midshipmen were back on the campus at Annapolis. Then the celebration continued for another twenty-four hours, with the entire city of Annapolis pitching in and adding their zeal to the Middies' happiness.

Mather, a talented, multifaceted player from

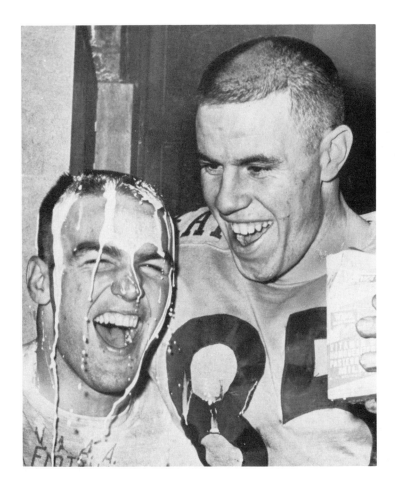

California, had an almost perfect kicking record in 1961, booting 21 extra points in a row and all 9 field goals attempted, before missing an extra point in Navy's 13–3 conquest of Virginia.

So it was only just that Mather's toe spelled the final difference against Army. Indeed, it was the first time that 2 field goals had resolved the annual Army-Navy classic.

President Kennedy, the first Chief Executive to attend the classic since Harry Truman saw Navy roll to a 7–0 win in 1952, witnessed a hard-hitting, no-nonsense, clean-fought battle as the two elevens cracked each other without abandon. The Middies had to come from behind to win this one, but they actually dominated most of the game. Army did not ring up a first down until the latter stages of the second period. Navy simply packed too much speed and flair for the Cadets, and if it hadn't been for the West Pointers' fighting spirit and gutty determination the score could have been much more decisive.

President Kennedy's silver DC-6B plane did not arrive at the Philadelphia Navy Yard until 12:55 P.M., and by that time the Corps of Cadets and Brigade of Middies had marched to their seats. At precisely 1:30 P.M., the two team captains entered the stand where the President was sitting and asked him to toss up the coin. Kennedy had come well prepared with two silver dollars.

He tossed the first into the air, and Mike Casp, the Army captain, correctly called the turn of the coin. Mr. Kennedy immediately gave him the silver dollar, minted in Philadelphia, 1935. As consolation, Navy's captain, John F. Hewitt, also received a silver dollar minted in 1935, the last year the United States turned out such coinage.

Army received the kickoff but could not get anywhere. Navy, thanks principally to a pass from Ron Klemick to Mather, made a first down, but then had to kick. Mather's punt bounced dead on the 1-yard line.

An exchange of punts followed, then Army

wound up in possession as a result of an interception by Harry McMillan on the Navy's 28.

Piling on cost Navy 15 yards on the next punt, and from their own 34, the Middies marched to Army's 11 before the first period closed.

On third down, with 7 to go, Klemick lost 8 yards on an attempted pass, and Mather had to drop back for a field goal. With 1:46 of the second period gone he made the kick and the score became 3–0.

Army received the ensuing kickoff with Tom Gulver returning Mather's boot 29 yards, but Steve Hoy intercepted a pass by Dick Eckert two plays later, and Navy was on the prowl again. From Army's 41, Navy moved to Army's 19 with the help of two passes. From there, Greg Mather dropped back to the 27 and tried another field goal.

He missed wide and to the left and Army took over on its 20. Now the Cadets made their initial first down. Halfback Jim Beierschmitt sparked this drive. He and Army's fastest back, Ken Waldrop, carried out to the 47. Then Cammy Lewis, son of the old West Virginia coach, came in as Army quarterback. With the help of an offside penalty, the Cadets moved to the Middies' 19. Here Dick Heydt dropped back to the 29 and attempted a field goal, which fell short.

During the intermission, the President went down to the mayor's private clubhouse and had a bowl of Philadelphia's famous pepperpot soup.

As a result, the second half was somewhat late in starting. As the second half began, Navy pounded out a first down but finally surrendered possession of the ball on its 37 after an incomplete pass by quarterback Ron Klemick. Mather kicked, and after Lloyd Asbury's return, Army was in possession on its own 31. Beierschmitt ran one play, then gave way to Dick Eckert. Throwing to his left, Eckert arched a pass over John Sai's head and Culver caught the ball. Down the field he dashed, until Sai caught him from behind and pulled him down on the Navy's 13-yard stripe.

Rushes by Al Rushatz and Eckert produced a first down on the 3. Rushatz plunged for another yard and a half, then dove over for an Army touchdown, Heydt's conversion made the score 7–3, Army.

But the Middies came roaring back.

There was an exchange of punts following the Army TD and Navy found itself in possession of the ball on its own 49-yard line. Then sub quarterback Bobby Hecht took the pass from center, faked an off-tackle sprint, and stopping dead in his tracks, fired a long, arching pass to Jim Stewart, who caught the ball over his shoulder and wasn't brought down until he reached Army's 13-yard line. The pass and run were good for 38 yards. Then Bill Ulrich followed three Navy blockers, and raced off tackle for 13 yards and a Navy touchdown. In two quick, savage thrusts, Navy had shattered the Army line, and now the score was 10–7, Navy.

In the fourth period an Army fumble crushed a possible score, and later in the period Army drove for two consecutive first downs to just inside Navy's 45-yard line.

Army's coach Dale Hall then sent in a tricky pass play, but the quick-thinking Navy defense batted the ball down and took the ball over on downs. Here Navy relied on sheer power and drove to the Army 19-yard line. Then Greg Mather came in and split the uprights with his second 3-pointer of the game, and Navy had a 13–7 lead.

Army received the Navy kickoff and tried several desperate pass plays. But once again Navy's defense knocked down each attempt and the game ended with Army still battling, still trying desperately to complete a long pass that might bring them across the Navy goal line.

Final score Navy 13, Army 7.

In Army's dressing room after the game, Dale Hall, the thirty-seven-year-old Army coach, faced reporters who wanted to know if he would be fired after three straight losses to Navy.

With frankness and candor Hall pointed out that he had another year left on his contract, that he had no wish to leave and had had no indication of displeasure from West Point officials, which was "all I care to say about the situation."

This year great things had been expected of Army. Navy had lost its superstar Joe Bellino and sixteen other starters, and Army looked like a sure winner. . . . But injuries and the lack of a consistent attack had hampered the Cadets all season long.

Three weeks after the Navy game, Dale Hall was fired. He was replaced by one of the nation's leading coaches, Paul Dietzel, former assistant to Earl Blaik and head coach at Louisana State University.

The Years of Jolly Roger: 1962-64

Seated high up in the grandstand at mammoth Municipal Stadium in 1960, the slim, boyish youngster kept rising to his feet, cheering and shouting as the Navy football team rolled over Army to its third straight victory by a 13–7 margin.

"It was a great game," that youngster recalled years later, "but I had a lot of trouble concentrating. I kept imagining that it was me down there on the field at quarterback and I was running the team against Army. I'd dreamed of just such a day since my first year on our high school football team. That's when a scout for the Navy came up to me after a game, congratulated me on a very good game, and said, 'Son, keep up the good work, concentrate on your studies, and keep throwing that ball.' Then he winked at me. 'And don't forget, Navy might be able to use you.'

"I never forgot that scout," said Roger Staubach, "though at the time I couldn't believe it would actually turn out that I would be able to attend the Academy."

In 1962, before 100,000 wildly screaming fans at Philadelphia, Roger Staubach's boyhood dream came true like a 3-D, stereophonic-soundtrack movie. It was one of the most complete and startling naval conquests in history.

Against Paul Dietzel's Army team, the highly publicized "Chinese Bandits," Roger Staubach, a nineteen-year-old sophomore, passed 34 yards to end Neil Henderson for Navy's first touchdown and then, a few plays later, sprinted 35 yards for another Navy score and a 15–0 Navy lead. Before he was taken out of the game in the last period—near collapse from exhaustion—Roger Staubach had knifed through a tough Army line for a third score, then completed a 65-yard pass play for a fourth touchdown to rout a tough Army eleven coached for the first time by Paul Dietzel.

Seemingly unmindful that he was performing before his idol, President John F. Kennedy, and playing the biggest game of his young life, Roger ended up passing for 188 yards; he was also the leading Navy ground-gainer. In all, he had turned in the finest performance in the history of the Army-Navy game, overshadowing those of Doc Blanchard and Glenn Davis of Army, and Joe Bellino and George Welsh of Navy. And he did it as a sophomore, playing in his first game against Army.

"Sure I was nervous," said Staubach in the dressing room. "With your parents, a hundred thousand people, and the President of the United States in the stands, who wouldn't be nervous?"

To everyone else, Staubach, nicknamed

"Jolly Roger" by Annapolis publicity, was the coolest man on the field. "He was great," said Dietzel. "When he's in there, he's in charge. All day long he turned potential losses into gains with those passes and his runs. He's a real football player. Navy's not the same without him."

Navy coach Wayne Hardin was even more enthusiastic about his hero. "Roger's fantastic," said Hardin, wiping sweat off his face in the now steaming, teeming dressing room. "But I've been saying that all year and nobody believed me."

Staubach had been making believers out of football coaches and scouts since his senior year at Cincinnati's Purcell High School, when he started playing offensive quarterback for the first time. Tall and rawboned at 6 feet 2 and 193 pounds, he attracted scholarship offers from most of the Big Ten schools and midwestern independents. At first, Staubach couldn't make up his mind. "Ohio State coach Woody Hayes spent five days out of eight with me for a couple of months," says Staubach with a grin, "but Ohio State seemed a little too worldly for me." The fact that Hayes frowned on a passing offense didn't help his sales pitch.

At one point during his senior year, Staubach, who had once thought about becoming a priest, decided he wanted to go to Notre Dame. "They told him they didn't have any quarterback scholarships left," says Hardin. "Then a Notre Dame coach saw him play in the Ohio All-Star Game and they told him a scholarship had opened up. Having been turned down once by them, he refused it. That's the kind of kid he is."

By rejecting Notre Dame, Staubach had merely narrowed the field. Finally, he signed a letter of intent with Purdue, but at the last moment he changed his mind, settling this time on the Naval Academy. There was only one drawback: though his grades were better than average, his math marks were low, so he had to go to junior college for one year before entering the Academy. At New Mexico Military Institute, a favorite finishing school for Naval Academy athletic prospects, Staubach learned enough math and considerable football. He was

an all-around athlete—averaging 13 points a game in basketball and hitting .320 in baseball—but it was on the football field that he made the greatest impression. Developing quickly as a T-formation quarterback, he completed more than 60 percent of his passes at New Mexico, sparked the school to a 9–1 season, and earned first-string Junior College All-American honors. "He's a tremendous prospect," said his coach Bob Shaw, who as an assistant coach with the Baltimore Colts had worked with Johnny Unitas for two seasons. "If he keeps improving, there's no telling how great the boy's going to be."

Though he was outstanding as a plebe in 1961, starring in basketball and baseball as well as football, he was still a third-string quarterback when he joined the varsity for the 1962 season. "It wasn't that we didn't think he was good," said Hardin. "We knew he was a real good one, but we didn't think he was ready." In Navy's first three games that year, the team was no more ready than its young quarterback. The Middies lost to Penn State, 41–7, staggered past William and Mary, 20–16, and then collapsed against Minnesota, 20–0. In those first three games, Staubach played a total of six minutes, threw four incompleted passes, and lost 14 yards rushing. A nervous youngster who occasionally tore away at his fingernails to relieve the tension, he rarely had enough time to warm up before entering the fray. "I feel a little sick before every game, but after the first play I'm all right," he has admitted. "I still thought that if I had the right chance, I could move in."

Staubach got the right chance in Navy's fourth game against Cornell. The starting backfield couldn't move the ball, so Hardin called his lanky sophomore to his side, told him the first few plays he wanted him to call, and sent him into the game. By the end of that afternoon, Staubach had completed nine of eleven passes for 99 yards, raced 68 yards on one option play, and scored two touchdowns in a stunning 41–0 Navy victory. "We knew all along that he'd take over eventually," explains Hardin. "It took him awhile to work himself

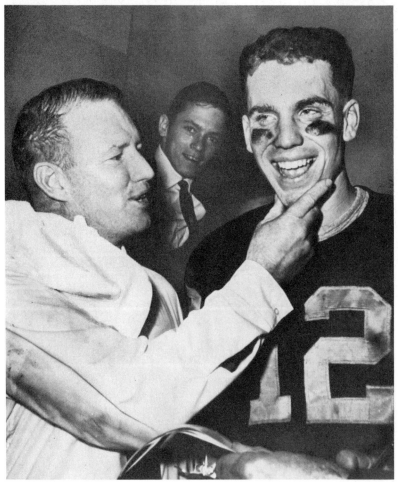

Top, left: *In 1962 it was all Staubach, Navy's brilliant sophomore quarterback.* Top, right: *Jolly Roger is shown getting off a 30-yard scoring strike despite being hemmed in by a trio of Army rushers, then connecting with back Jim Campbell for the Middies' fourth touchdown; Staubach also scored twice himself as Navy won 34–14.* Left: *After the game, the hero is congratulated by his coach, Wayne Hardin.*

in. Once he got in, he was in to stay."

Cornell was only the beginning. The next week, against Boston College, he completed fourteen of twenty passes for 165 yards and two touchdowns, and his combined statistics outgained the Eagles 186 yards to 184. Against Pittsburgh, with the defenses now stacked against him, he rolled up 230 yards on the ground and in the air for a 32–9 Navy victory. In three games as a regular, he had completed thirty-one of thirty-nine passes. Suddenly everybody in the East was talking about the young red-haired quarterback from Cincinnati. "If we lose, we don't hear from anybody," said Hardin. "We win, so everybody is all over the kid. Some players can take it and some players can't. Joe Bellino could turn it off or on. He had great powers of concentration, but usually this comes with experience. I didn't know if Roger had it yet. A sophomore at the Academy has a lot of things on his mind."

Hardin had little to worry about. With the poise of a senior and an endless drive to improve himself, Staubach was bothered by nothing but a few minor failings, which for the most part existed only in his mind. "Sometimes I turn my wrist when I throw the ball," said the right-handed passer. "The ball wobbles. I like to throw a spiral every time."

When Staubach wasn't within hearing distance, Hardin and his assistants often paid glowing tribute to the youngster. "Roger not only can throw the ball, but when a team puts a big rush on us he has the speed and agility to move with the ball," Hardin said to this writer. "He also has the rare gift of looking over his receivers in only a second and picking out the one most open. I've been around for a while and I've seen very few with this sixth sense. Heck, he's already proven himself under fire more than any sophomore I ever coached."

The Army-Navy game was still the premier event of the college football season, attracting more fans, more publicity, and more second-guessing than even the Rose Bowl. For any coach, victory in the Army-Navy game could turn a dismal season into a glowing one. At Army, Paul Dietzel had done a spectacular

job with unspectacular material, picking up the pieces left by his predecessor, Dale Hall. Up to the big game, the Cadets in 1962 had compiled a record of 6 and 3. For Dietzel, one of the highly publicized bright young men of coaching, a loss to Navy would erase almost everything he had accomplished. A defensive specialist, Dietzel figured the youngster would suffer from nervousness at least in the beginning, possibly making a mistake or two before regaining his poise. Any sophomore is a serious liability in an Army-Navy game, and a soph quarterback usually courts disaster.

Navy scored the first points of the game on a safety that followed a quick kick. Dick Peterson, Army's punter, could not field the pass from center and the ball rolled over his head into the end zone.

But the Cadets came back fighting mad. They drove to the Navy 20-yard line where Dick Heydt attempted a field goal. The kick was wide and Navy took over.

With Jolly Roger leading the way, the Middies drove downfield. The big play was a marvelous 40-yard one that brought Navy within range. Surrounded by a sea of Army tacklers, Staubach broke loose and tossed the ball to his end, Neil Henderson. Henderson, guarded by two Army backs, jumped high in the air to snatch the ball for a touchdown.

Navy did not waste time in scoring again. The next time they had the ball the Middies drove 65 yards for a score as Staubach guided his team with the precision of a veteran drillmaster. Roger completed two pinpoint passes good for 26 yards. Then he faked a pass before dodging, twisting, and turning for another 23 yards through nearly every member of Army's defensive unit for a touchdown. Vern Von Sydow added the extra point and it was 15–0, Navy.

But Army was far from through. Cammy Lewis, the Cadets' fine quarterback, passed to end Bobby Wright for 25 yards, and Wright sped 27 additional yards after pulling in the ball. The play brought the ball to the Navy 3-yard line, and in two line-battering crashes, halfback Donny Parcells scored. Army missed the conversion and the score at halftime was 15–6.

Army tried a fake kick after a drive to open the second half, but the play boomeranged and Navy recovered the ball on their 35-yard line. On the very next play the Middies' fine fullback, Nick Markoff, took off for the far sidelines, outran a couple of Army defenders, then jumped high into the air for a Staubach pass that easily was thrown at least 60 yards. Once Nick had the ball safely tucked under his arm, he had to run only 10 more yards for another Navy score. The play covered some 65 yards and brought the three thousand Middies and the crowd of more than 100,000 to their feet with a roar that could be heard back at Annapolis. Now Navy had a 22–6 lead.

In the fourth period, Navy drove downfield for 90 yards and another score. Two Staubach passes, one to end Dave Sjuggernud for 50 yards, another to halfback Johnny Sai for 10 yards, brought the ball to the Army 2-yard line. Then Staubach knifed through tackle for the touchdown.

Army wasn't ready to throw in the towel just yet. With Lewis directing their attack, the Cadets drove downfield, completing five straight passes. The fifth pass, to halfback Johnny Seymour, was good for an Army touchdown. Then Army scored on a 2-point conversion, and the score was 28–14 with less than five minutes remaining to play in the game.

Army continued their passing attack and reached the Navy 10-yard line, but just when it seemed the Cadets would mount another drive, Navy intercepted a pass. Then Ron Klemick, who had come in for an exhausted Staubach, passed to end Jim Campbell for another touchdown. Navy missed the conversion, but by that time it was Navy 34, Army 14.

In the dressing room after the game, Terry Shore, a reporter for the *Minneapolis Star*, asked Wayne Hardin if he felt there was a turning point in the game. Hardin looked at Staubach, grinned, and said, "Yep. When he showed up on the field."

Staubach laughed easily. "It's still really hard for me to believe all this has happened," he said, wiping the burnt cork from under his eyes. "It will take awhile for me to get used to all this."

Although pro football scouts traditionally have ignored players on the service teams because of their military commitments, several of them were already vitally interested in Roger Staubach.

With Hardin having announced he would switch over to a more wide-open passing offense in 1963, Staubach, who had the height and potential to play pro football, figured to attract even more interest in his next two seasons at the Academy.

"Right now, it looks like I'm going to be in the Navy for quite a while," he said. "But who knows: I kind of like the idea of playing professionally, the challenge of proving I'm as good as some quarterback from Miami or Michigan. It's certainly something I'm going to think about."

But if the Army and Paul Dietzel had had their way, Staubach shouldn't waste time thinking. He should turn pro immediately. And Army and Dietzel would be willing to give him a thirty-two-gun salute and best wishes on his way.

President John F. Kennedy was assassinated on November 22, 1963, and the Army-Navy game, scheduled to be played the next weekend, was postponed. It was then rescheduled for December 7 at the request of the President's widow.

The pregame ceremonies of this sixty-fourth meeting of the two service rivals were appropriately simple and dignified. An honor guard of two hundred Cadets and Midshipmen in alternate rows marched to the center of the field after the two teams had warmed up. The National Anthem was played, and a minute of silence was asked for by Cadet Richard Chilcoat, first captain of the Corps, and first captain of the Middies, Walter Kesler. Then the honor guard marched off the field. There were no floats, no signs, no taunting skits as were usually part of the game's anticipation. Just two traditional features were in evidence: the impressive parade into the field by the two student bodies, and the hat-waving roaring produced by both rooting sections.

The year before, President Kennedy had tossed the coin at midfield. This time, no dignitary took part in the tradition. The two captains, Tom Lynch of Navy and Dick Nowak of Army, were brought together by Barney Finn, the referee. The starting lineups were then announced and the game began.

For the want of a time-out, the game was lost by Army. On their way to what could have been a tying or winning touchdown, the gallant Cadets, slowpokey and confused, used up fifty-six seconds to get off one play and were two frustrating yards from glory when the gun ended this playing of the annual service classic. With a trip to the Cotton Bowl hinging on the outcome, Navy came off with a 21–15 victory as fullback Pat Donnelly scored three touchdowns to tie a record and Roger Staubach never stopped acting like the most exciting quarterback in the country.

It was Navy's fifth consecutive triumph in this end-of-season spectacular, and it equaled a record set by the Midshipmen from 1939 through 1943.

At the same time, Wayne Hardin extended his own victorious coaching streak over Army to five in a row, and there were many, including his players, who hailed him as the "Coach of the Year."

Said team captain Tom Lynch: "If he isn't, there is something funny."

The Middies also accepted, by acclamation, an invitation to play the national champion, Texas, at the Cotton Bowl in Dallas on New Year's Day.

A 12-point underdog, the Cadets scored the first time they got hold of the ball. From their own 35, a possession team strictly, Army kept pounding up the field. First Ray Paske, then Ken Waldrop, and then a masterful running quarterback named Carl Stichweh.

When Stichweh, on a third and 9 countdown, went around his own left end 10 yards for the score, carrying Johnny Sai with him,

things looked good for the blue-and-gold Cadets. Dick Heydt placekicked the extra point, and many of the 100,000 onlookers were saying, "Maybe we're going to see a ball game after all."

The same watchers knew for sure a few minutes later. After Navy took the ensuing kickoff they moved quickly to the Army 3, with first down and goal to go. And then . . . Sai made a yard off tackle. Sai lost 2 around end. Staubach went to the 1-foot line on a keeper. Roger was stopped for no gain off tackle. Army had stopped the Middies on four thrusts from within their 5-yard line!

Taking over on downs, the Cadets immediately added insult to injury. After two power plays gained 3 yards, Dietzel's offense got uncharacteristically tricky. After going into their regular T formation, the West Pointer backfield started to shift for a punt. But as kicker Ray Hawkins was moving into position, Stichweh took the snap from center and barreled off tackle for 8 yards and a first down.

"A well-educated play," Hardin admitted.

But then Army had to kick, and it became a question of coping with Staubach.

With the ball slightly in Army territory, Jolly Roger took over. Twice he ran for big gains after being forced out of the pocket. He also hit Sai for a 26-yard gain. Finally, with the ball on the four, Donnelly went off tackle to score. Marlin kicked the point and the teams went into the dressing room at halftime with a 7–7 stalemate.

"That's when we changed around," said Hardin afterward. "We went back to our basic stuff after wasting a lot of time on special plays we put in for Army."

What he meant was—they gave the ball to Roger.

The third period was well on its way when the future All-American and Heisman Trophy winner asserted himself. He made it look easy, too. He connected on passes to Neil Henderson and Orr, and there were a couple of runs up the middle after apparently being trapped. And once, about to be tackled, Roger threw a lateral to Donnelly.

THE WHITE HOUSE

WASHINGTON

December 2, 1961

TO THE CORPS OF CADETS AND THE BRIGADE OF MIDSHIPMEN

It is easy to pick the real winner of the annual
Army-Navy football game: the people of the United
States. For the outcome is certain from the great
spirit of competition, the lessons of good sportsmanship, and the skill and perfection with which
the players of both teams perform, all of which
bring to the Officer Corps of our Armed Forces
lasting benefit in terms of leadership. From this
leadership, our nation is stronger, and the cause
of freedom in the world is safer from encroachment.

A less serious benefit, of course, is what the
Army-Navy football game brings to intercollegiate
football, and to the world of sports. The game
sets a fine example of hardhitting fair play that I
hope will inspire Americans, young and old, in
the world of sports.

My greetings and warm good wishes go to all of
you who support the West Point and Annapolis teams
today.

A president who loved the game. Opposite page: In 1961, President John F. Kennedy expressed the meaning of the Army-Navy game, both for himself and for the nation, in a letter to the "Corps of Cadets and the Brigade of Midshipmen." Above: A year later, prior to the start of the sixty-third contest, President Kennedy flipped the coin at midfield; watching are Army captain John Ellerson, an end, and Navy captain Steve Hoy, a guard. Below: In 1963, barely a week after the President's assassination, the sixty-fourth game was played at the request of his widow. The only pregame ceremony was the observance of a moment of silence in tribute to the slain commander in chief. Shown standing before the array of flags with heads bowed are Midshipman Boyd Knowles and Cadet William Cesarski. The following year, Philadelphia's Municipal Stadium, which had become the traditional site of the annual service classic, was renamed John F. Kennedy Stadium.

Right: General of the Army Douglas MacArthur (who had been superintendent of the U.S. Military Academy from 1919 to 1922) acts as intermediary between Army coach Paul Dietzel and Navy coach Wayne Hardin at the 1963 Hall of Fame dinner. Opposite page, top: A few weeks earlier, the Midshipmen had beaten the Cadets 21–15. Some of the action in that scintillating contest. Opposite page, bottom: After Army had drawn first blood, Navy fullback Pat Donnelly takes a handoff from quarterback Roger Staubach and heads for a second-period touchdown. And late in the fourth quarter, Army quarterback Carl Stichweh scores on a rollout just as Navy's Skip Orr (23) and Johnny Sai (48) meet him at the goal line. Stichweh was spectacular all afternoon as he led the Cadets to a pulsating close-but-not-quite finish against the highly favored Middies.

"What can you do with a guy like that?" the soldiers seemed to be saying.

From the Army nine, Sai made 4, and Staubach then took it to the 1. Sai was stopped for no gain, and it looked as if Army was making another stand. But Donnelly went off left tackle for the 6 pointer, Marlin's kick was good, and Navy was ahead, 14–7.

It stayed that way until the start of the final period, when the Cadets made a wrong call that may well have decided the game. It went like this:

With the ball on the Navy 17, Army sent Waldrop off tackle for a 7-yard gain. But Navy was offside on the play.

Official: "You Army fellows can keep the ball where it is and have a second down and three to go—or you can take the penalty and have a first down and five to go. What'll it be?"

Dietzel on the sideline: "We decline the penalty."

This is what followed: Ray Paske went up the middle for no gain. Paske went off right tackle for 2 yards, inches short of a first down. Ken Waldrop was thrown for a yard loss on fourth down. Navy took the ball at the 8.

With the Middies given a new lease on life, Donnelly scooted for 13 yards, then made 4 more. And when somebody was detected piling on, a 15-yard penalty was added. Then an Army player hit a Navy player on the chin (out in the open, too), which brought 15 more yards. This put the ball on Army's 28, and three plays later Donnelly went off tackle, hightailed it for the sideline, and eluded Stichweh to score.

Now it was 21–7, and Army sounded the famous cavalry charge. And on the field, the Cadets charged back. Nothing fancy, simply power football. Slam-bang stuff. Stichweh and Waldrop took turns bruising the Navy line. The leather was really cracking.

Stichweh ended a 52-yard drive by rounding his own right end for a touchdown after faking to Waldrop. Quarterback Carl then stormed into the end zone for the 2 extra points. It was Navy 21, Army 15.

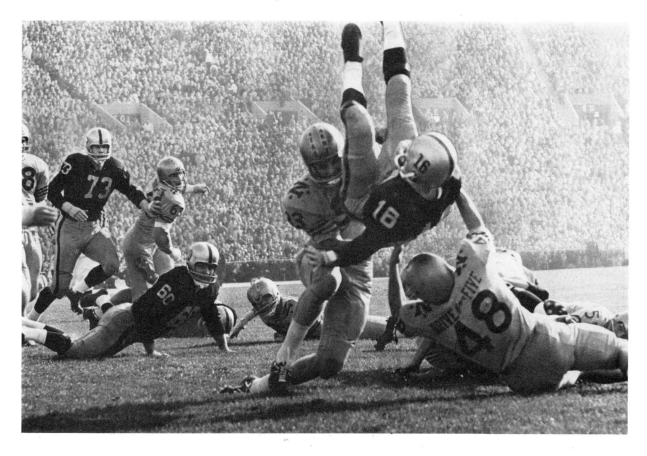

Dietzel again reached into his bag of grid-iron tricks. On the kickoff, Army lined up as usual, only Heydt was turned sideways near the ball as though he was going to give the "go" sign to his teammates. As Hawkins took his steps toward the ball, Heydt eased over and gave the ball a cross-field boot—and Stichweh grabbed the slick onside kick to give Army the ball on Navy's 49.

Six minutes and thirteen seconds remained in the game.

But it wasn't quite enough.

With Ken Waldrop and Ray Paske hammering away at off-tackle plays, the Cadets kept grinding out the yardage, twice barely making the necessary inches on fourth-down situations.

There was one point at the 23 when Dietzel sent in a replacement to use up Army's last time-out. Stichweh obliged the West Point cheering section with a pass in the flat to Don Parcells at the 7 for a first down with one minute and thirty-eight seconds to play.

It seemed ample. For Hardin it seemed forever.

Now the audience was in a standup bedlam. Stichweh couldn't hear his own signals.

Parcells made 2 hard yards over left guard. Navy was digging in and everyone was watching the clock. Only 1:22 to go.

Waldrop pounded off tackle and was hit hard and stopped at the 4. There were fifty-eight seconds left as he picked himself off the ground.

Army went into a huddle, then came out and took formation. But Stichweh backed away. Too much spectator noise. The referee, Barney Finn, stopped the clock. And that's when Navy got a break.

Not knowing that the clock was started again as soon as order was restored, the Army players went into another huddle, which used up twelve more seconds.

So, only twenty-four seconds remained when Waldrop finally took a handoff from Stichweh and went off tackle again—to the 2.

Now it was fourth and goal for the Cadets. Only they never came close to running off an-

other play. The Middies took their time getting up from the ground, and there were a lot of blue-shirted soldiers running around trying to get in formation just as the game ended.

The jubilant Middies jumped and danced in glee. The crestfallen Cadets trudged off the field. Some of them went into the clubhouse and cried—unashamedly.

Dietzel said: "Our boys couldn't hear the signals. There was too much racket and the clock ran out as we tried to get a little quiet."

Some of the Army players said they were not aware that the clock was restarted when they went back into that second—and useless—huddle.

But as a local football official pointed out: "It took some guts for Ray Barbutti [field judge] to stop the clock in that kind of a situation—in an Army-Navy game."

Stichweh said he couldn't believe the game was over. "We tried to yell out a play but our ends and tackles couldn't hear because of the noise. We tried to go to the referee, but either he didn't hear me or see me."

At least the slender 185-pounder from Williston Park, New York, had the satisfaction of stealing some of the individual thunder from the heralded Staubach.

Dietzel praised Stichweh as "the outstanding player on the field, bar none."

While Stichweh was pounding out 103 yards for the Cadets, mostly on rollouts and keeper plays, Staubach handled Navy's pro-type attack like an artist. Roger not only completed six of eleven passes but he caught one from Ed Orr and himself picked up 20 running yards.

Donnelly's three touchdowns tied a Navy modern service game record set by Joe Bellino in 1959. He went over twice on short bursts and once from 20 yards out.

The motif set by Navy after 1963 was, "Even the Score in 64," and even though the Middies did not reach their goal in the sixty-fifth game with Army at newly named John F. Kennedy Stadium, Philadelphia, they did achieve a wide edge in the extra-game activities that make the Army-Navy game the most colorful of college football extravaganzas.

The Middies provided all of the color, both before the game and between the halves. And for the first time in years, Army seemed to disdain such activities as immaterial. Once seated, the Corps of Cadets did not even bother to form the traditional lane through which its football team runs out onto the field.

Navy, on the other hand, was busy with cute tricks and gimmicks, electrically and manually. First, they put up two huge electric signs on two buildings outside the stadium reading, GO NAVY, and BEAT ARMY. Inside the stadium, they erected another electric display that would have done credit to Times Square. It blinked SIX AND EVEN, wishful thinking that their team would even the series at thirty victories each (five have been ties) and take the sixth in a row over the Cadets.

Then, among other lavish displays, there was a group of Middies clad in the national cos-

tumes of several foreign countries. And each Middie carried a colorful banner which read, BEAT ARMY, NEIGHBORS, inscribed in the native language of the country, including one printed in Russian.

Among the high-ranking officials who enjoyed the antics were Deputy Secretary of Defense Cyrus Vance, Secretary of the Army Stephen Ailes, Navy Secretary Paul Nitze, and Secretary of Labor Willard Wirtz, along with dozens of high-ranking Navy and Army officers, who took their seats just as Navy kicked off to Army and the game began.

With the wholehearted cooperation of an old-fashioned Army football team, a team that disdained cute gimmicks, platoons, and free substitutions, "Rollie's Redemption" played a smashing one-stand performance before a crowd of 100,000 at John F. Kennedy Stadium that November 29.

Army's Captain Rollie Stichweh, its indefatigable running-and-passing quarterback and top all-around performer, finally caught up

Army coach Paul Dietzel gives some final pre-Navy instructions to his 1964 backfield: John Johnson, Don Parcells, John Seymour, and Carl Stichweh. It apparently worked because Stichweh, Johnson, and Parcells stood out in a thrilling 11–8 Army win.

with Navy and its great star, Roger Staubach, and beat them as decisively as any team could in an 11–8 contest. It was Army's first victory over Navy since the 1958 battle, when the Cadets triumphed by a 22–6 margin.

Thus the grim and resolute underdog Cadets got even with their tormentor Staubach in his final varsity game. The Cadet defenders harried, harassed, and tackled Roger from the opening moment of the game to the final whistle.

In the first fifty-three seconds of play Army charged and battered Roger to wrench a safety and 2 points from Navy with a gang-tackle of Staubach 13 yards behind the goal line. For most of the first half they dominated the fierce action of the game. They marched 54 yards for a touchdown on Johnny Seymour's two smashing runs and Stichweh's 5-yard pass to Sam Champi. Navy came back on a drive featuring the indomitable Pat Donnelly, before the injured fullback had to leave the game. Donnelly's inspired running was the key to Navy's tying the game just before halftime, helped by a holding penalty. And so the game stood until Army marched 77 yards in the fourth period to set up Barry Nickerson's 20-yard field goal to wrap up the win.

Roger Staubach, penned and cornered and hit hard as he never had been in his three varsity years, wound up with minus 22 yards for the day, but he was always a dangerous threat passing, completing twelve of twenty-one for 110 yards. And he did make a 2-point play for Navy to tie the score 8–8 at halftime.

"And if you can't run the ball, you can't win the game," said Rip Miller as he sadly made his way out of the field after the game.

Rip should know. He was one of the Seven Mules on the legendary Four Horsemen team at Notre Dame back in the 1920s and had been serving Navy in a number of capacities, including a stretch of three years as head coach.

Perhaps the Old Ripper was merely pinpointing the obvious and there was no need to look further for an explanation of Army's upset of Navy. The Cadets had hammered out 215 yards on the ground, the Middies a mere 31. That was the big difference.

Except for one stretch in the second quarter when Navy drove for a touchdown and its 8 points, the pressure on the Navy wonder-worker never eased.

Yet Navy dreamers of the might-have-been could not help but imagine the difference if the injured Pat Donnelly had been healthy. Only for a brief time was this ripsnorting fullback in the offensive lineup, and only on that late-first-half drive could the Middies move. Once he limped to the sidelines, the Annapolis attack lost its flow.

Navy was balked at every turn, although Army almost let its traditional foe wriggle off the hook in the last quarter by the most stupid of all mistakes. When the frustrated Middies were forced to punt, an overeager West Pointer poleaxed the kicker. Reprieved, Navy regained possession and went down to the 27-yard line. That's when Army, scenting victory, rose in all its might and blitzed Staubach with a controlled fury. They handed him a fourth down and 45 yards to go, an impossible situation even for the brilliant Jolly Roger.

And so Coach Paul Dietzel produced his first success over the Midshipmen. He had planned well and deserved it fully.

The Remarkable Succession of
Tom Cahill: 1965-67

*T*here were a couple of odd twists to the annual North-South college All-Star football game in January 1965. At quarterback for the losers in that wingding game was Roger Staubach, and filling one of the two coaching posts for the same North team was Wayne Hardin.

Everyone knew then that the remarkable Staubach had played his final football game at Annapolis, and that this phenomenal young athlete would shortly be commissioned and his college football days be a thing of the past.

But few suspected then that Hardin was also on the verge of pulling up his Annapolis anchor. About a month before, after the Navy coach had lost to the Cadets for the first time in six years, he had been given clearance to head out for the open sea. Technically, Hardin had resigned, despite a four-year holdover clause in his contract. But that device fooled no one when his resignation was revealed after the North-South game. He didn't fall, he was pushed.

Except in his final injury-laden season, Hardin was a winning coach at Annapolis, and five years in a row, up to 1964, he had come through with the sine qua non of any successful Navy coach, victory over Army. But Hardin had a personality that did not endear him to

the Navy brass. His outspokenness had antagonized many of those close to him at Annapolis and had especially irritated gruff admirals scattered around the globe. And so Hardin was gone as well as Staubach.

Late in January, Captain Bill Busik, director of athletics at the Navy, announced that Bill Elias, the football coach at the University of Virginia for the past four seasons, had been named to replace Hardin.

The new Navy coach, handsome and personable at thirty-nine, and with a mild manner of speaking, immediately showed that he was already well indoctrinated in the Navy way of thinking.

The first thing Elias said was, "I think you can say that Navy will put continuous emphasis on the Army game." He added, however, that he saw little reason to employ gimmicks to fire up the Middies for their annual contest with Army.

Wayne Hardin, Elias's predecessor, had been strong on gimmickry. It was part of his gamesmanship—successful in five years out of six—to send Navy players against Army wearing jerseys or helmets emblazoned with BEAT ARMY or DRIVE FOR FIVE.

"There's no need to stoke Navy fires already

burning with the desire to win. There's such wonderful esprit de corps at Navy, I feel all I have to do is know how to spell one four-letter word—A-R-M-Y," said Elias, whose Virginia team had upset Army in 1964, 35–14. "Coaching at Navy has been my burning desire since I was seventeen years of age. As high school seniors at Martins Ferry in Ohio in 1941, my teammate Lou Groza and I were taken to our first college football game. It was between Navy and Notre Dame at Cleveland. Notre Dame won the game, but Navy won my heart with their spirited play. In fact, I turned to Groza during the game and said, 'Lou, I don't know how or even when, but someday I'm gonna coach that Navy team.' And so when Captain Busik called me and offered me the job some twenty-five years later . . . I think his call came in at one-thirty and at one-thirty-five I accepted."

As the day of the game approached both teams arrived at Philadelphia and went right to the John F. Kennedy Stadium for a brief final workout. Like two championship boxers entering the ring, the Army and Navy players got their first curious closeup of each other this day before the sixty-sixth game as both teams limbered up and ran through a few drills.

The Middies were unusually quiet in their own drill. Normally they came out the day before a game with a whoop and a holler, but today they were sober and all business.

"I hope this indicates the kids are feeling this game way down deep inside, because that's where it is going to be won," a Navy assistant coach said.

Army's demeanor was also sober and unruffled, but the Cadets were characteristically that way.

The day of the game a gray, leaden sky and a steady rain beat a tattoo on the city. By noon there were patches of blue, and the usual crowd of spectators at the stadium had to contend only with cold, gusty winds . . . and, unfortunately, a rather uneventful game. Army traveled by ground and Navy traveled through the air, with neither team showing much offense. They matched first-half touchdowns, then second-

half futility; neither team could gain the upper hand in a 7–7 tie. In fact, both had needed breaks to score at all.

Army's break came on the Middies' second series of offensive plays. Cadet end Tommy Schwartz drove into Navy's soph quarterback Johnny Cartwright just as he tried to flip a short pass to his halfback Al Roodhouse. Cartwright was hit so hard that the ball went flying back to the Navy 31-yard line, where Sam Champi, Army's outstanding end, made the recovery for the Cadets.

Three plays later, Sonny Stowers, the big, husky workhorse halfback, scored for Army on a 25-yard run to give the Cadets an advantage they held until well into the second quarter.

Navy's big break came on a Cartwright pass that could have been intercepted, but wasn't. Townsend Clarke, Army's powerful linebacker, had his hands on the ball but dropped it. Given another chance, Cartwright was more accurate and fired a perfect strike to Murray for the Middies to score with 63 seconds to go in the half.

That was the sum and substance of the day's offense. For the rest of the game both defensive teams did a fine job. Navy's pass receivers were well covered all afternoon; nevertheless, the Middies continued to pass, with Cartwright underthrowing most of his tosses. John missed on twelve consecutive passes in the second half, and the few that were on target were dropped by overanxious Navy receivers.

When flanker Fred Barofsky was hurt early in the game, Army's only offensive weapon became the 190-pound Sonny Stowers, who gained 92 yards in twenty-seven attempts but could only score once.

Defensively, the Cadets blitzed continuously, producing losses of 68 yards for the Middies and leaving them with a net rushing mark of 16 yards.

A somber-faced Bill Elias faced the press in the Navy locker room after the battle.

"I'm disappointed, of course," Elias said. "We came here to win, not play a tie. I'm not disappointed with the team, I'm very proud of

Army halfback Sonny Stowers scores in the first quarter of the 1965 game, despite efforts of Navy defensive halfback Duncan Ingraham.

them. But I am disappointed about not winning."

In the Army dressing room, a not-unhappy Paul Dietzel also spoke to reporters: "We didn't win and we didn't lose. A tie game is like kissing your sister. It's no fun. However, I was real proud of our defensive team. That's where our strength has been all year, and they really came through today."

Considering the players Navy had lost the previous year—Roger Staubach, Pat Donnelly, and Skip Orr—Bill Elias had a successful season in his first year at Navy with a won-lost record of .500 and a tie with his archrival. And Paul Dietzel agreed that with another break here or there, Army could have made it two in a row. "That would have been great, but we'll get them next year."

Dietzel had it right about Army "next year," but wrong about himself. Yet no one else that day could have guessed just who, other than Dietzel, would coach Army in 1966.

Paul Dietzel's tenure as the Army head coach was hardly a fabulous success story. In his first two years, 1962 and 1963, his Army teams went 6–4 and 7–3, and split the games with Navy. The next two years, 1964 and 1965, were plain disasters, and for the first time since the cribbing scandal of 1951, Army had losing records. Not only that, the Cadets lost to teams they had hardly ever lost to before. They were beaten by Duke and Virginia and Colgate, the last a team that had not beaten the Cadets in thirty years. Army even had to battle for its life against such normally easy victims as Rutgers and VMI.

After the 1965 Navy game, one of the dullest

in the long history of the service classic, Dietzel had had to admit, "We were so bad offensively, we could have played for a week and neither team would have scored again. It was kind of like the battle of the ants."

If the attitude of West Point officials toward Dietzel at this point was not exactly mutinous, it was certainly unhappy and noticeably sullen.

"One thing I never realized," Paul said later, "was how much the situation at West Point had changed since 1955. And it was obvious to me that the lack of blue-chip players at the Academy was catching up to us. It didn't look like we were gaining enough ground."

At the end of the 1965 season, Dietzel received several offers of jobs at other colleges but turned them down. Instead of quitting he prepared a paper that would suggest an improved policy in conducting the football program at West Point and turned the paper over to Colonel Ray Murphy, director of athletics. Then he sat back and waited. A month went by and there was no response. "And the longer I waited," said Dietzel, "the more I realized they just were not interested."

Then, just three weeks before spring practice, Dietzel received an offer of a ten-year contract from the University of South Carolina as head football coach and director of athletics.

Paul went to General Don Bennett, superintendent at the Academy, to discuss the situation. After listening to Dietzel explain the South Carolina offer, General Bennett replied: "Well, Paul, if you left us now it would work a hardship on us. But don't let that have anything to do with your decision. We'll get along."

A week later, April 6, 1966, the Athletic Board at West Point agreed to release Dietzel so that he could sign a ten-year pact with South Carolina. Within days, Dietzel had packed up and left West Point, taking with him five of Army's assistant coaches—George Terry, Jim Valek, Bill Rowe, Bill Shalosky, and Larry Jones. Dietzel left behind only Tom Cahill, who had coached the West Point plebes for seven years.

So with spring practice just around the corner, Army not only had lost its head coach but five of his top assistants. The Academy was clearly in a precarious position. Army not only had to find a head coach, they also had to move quickly to find someone to get spring practice started. The Athletic Board turned to Tom Cahill, the "quiet man," for its more immediate need and began a frantic search for a name coach. The Athletic Board wanted to select an Army graduate to handle the team, but the field was quite limited. Candidates did apply for the job, mostly assistant coaches at other schools, but Tom Cahill was not among them. Tom had never applied for a coaching job in his life, and he wasn't about to change his ways. Instead he calmly and efficiently went about the business of conducting spring practice.

During the next several weeks a number of candidates were interviewed—Bobby Dodds at Texas Western, John Green at Vanderbilt, Bill Yoeman at Houston, John Michelosen at Pitt, Pepper Rodgers at UCLA—but none was selected.

Meanwhile, Cahill and a staff of assistants continued to run the players through spring practice. The sessions were spirited, well organized, and, according to Army watchers, the best practice sessions Army had had in years. The players were enthusiastic, hitting hard and generally responding to Cahill's coaching. Tom switched several players to different positions and made some adjustments in the dull Cadet offense. He installed two plebes, Steve Lindell and Jim O'Toole, at the quarterback position, and since both Lindell and O'Toole could run as well as pass the ball, the offense began to open up for the first time in four years.

One interested spectator at a practice session was General Bennett, who had dropped around because "I wanted to see who this Tom Cahill fellow was." Bennett, who had been superintendent of West Point for just a short while, said, "I liked the way Tom handled things. The Cadets seemed to play with real spirit out there."

Cahill, who had had only several years experience as a prep- and high-school coach in addition to his years as the plebe coach, was such a plain and modest man it was several weeks before he moved from a tiny cubicle office into Red Blaik's plush, carpeted office. And then came the announcement. Tom Cahill was Army's new head coach for the season.

"I was absolutely thrilled," said Tom. "You can imagine how long it took me to accept the deal. I didn't talk salary or contract or anything, I just took the job, I was so happy. However, I did ask Colonel Murphy how long the appointment was for."

Murphy had answered, "Well, if you have a good season we'll talk about it later in the year."

"What constitutes a good season," asked Cahill, "10–0, 5–5, beating Navy?"

Murphy refused to be pinned down, but then told a sportswriter, "No matter what happens, Tom Cahill is a part of the West Point family. We expect he'll be around here for a long, long time."

The official announcement that Tom Cahill was West Point's new head coach was made in a low-key manner, without the usual hype the event called for. But the next day at practice, when Colonel Murphy announced the selection to the football squad, the players let out a roar that is normally reserved for the Navy game. It was clear that the choice was a most popular one. And when the roar subsided, Cahill, nervously gripping a bullhorn in one hand, a clipboard in the other, addressed his team. The talk lasted all of thirty seconds.

"I'm happy that the situation has been resolved," Tom told his players. "There are a lot of obstacles ahead of us and the best way to overcome them is to get after them right now. So let's get to work."

What had been an impossible dream just two weeks ago had become a reality. Tom Cahill, plebe coach for seven years, just happened to be in the right place at the right time. To everyone's surprise, not least of all his own, he was now the head football coach at West Point.

There probably never was a head coach who went into his first year the way Tom Cahill did.

He kept telling people to pinch him. "I'm dreaming," he would say.

Cahill did not think of himself as a great coach. "What is a great coach? A great coach is somebody who has outstanding assistants and is smart enough to let them coach."

So Cahill hired the best assistants he could get on such short notice and prepared a time schedule that would ready the Cadets for what was expected to be the roughest year in their football history. He had a one-year contract and the vague promise of a future at Army.

Cahill had resisted moving into Blaik's plush office until just before the announcement, and he did not move his family into Blaik's great mansion overlooking Michie Stadium until late in August.

"Each game we won that fall," said Bonnie Cahill, "we opened another crate of dishes and unpacked a bit more of our furniture and linens.

"When we opened the season beating Kansas State, 21–6, I unpacked more dishes. Then the following week we beat Holy Cross, more unpacking. It really wasn't until we beat a very strong Penn State team, 11–0, in a big upset,

Army's fine quarterback, Steve Lindell (right), has a warm-up session with his talented receivers, ends Terry Young (center) and 6 foot 5½ inch Gary Steele, prior to the 1966 Navy game.

that I really felt we were home to stay for a while."

Tom Cahill has his own memories. "After we beat Rutgers, we were set up at the Waldorf-Astoria Hotel," he recalls. "I told Bonnie to get us some cheese and crackers and we'd have a little celebration. Suddenly there was a knock on the door, a bellhop entered pushing a cart full of fancy bottles and great things to eat. I told the bellhop he had the wrong room, but he insisted this was the right room. I told Bonnie to throw out the cheese and crackers and we went to work on the delicious stuff.

"Following the Rutgers game, we beat Pittsburgh, 28–0, lost our second game to Tennessee, 38–7, then came back to beat George Washington and California before getting ready for the game against Navy."

So far, Cahill's 1966 season had been a totally unexpected smash success. But Army still had to play Navy, and despite Cahill's remarkable record that first season, not everyone was yet a believer. There were still many who would measure the coach just on what his team would do against Navy.

Even the bookies showed their lack of confidence in Tom Cahill and his Army football team as they installed Navy as a 5-point favorite.

There was no argument that the game would be a battle of tough defenses. Certainly Army's defense, which had given up only 25 points to the seven teams it had beaten, was at least as good as Navy's defense. And on offense, Cahill had his two outstanding quarterbacks, Steve Lindell and Jim O'Toole, who as plebes had somehow been buried in Dietzel's system. Lindell was poised, moved the team well, could run like a deer, and was a capable passer; O'Toole was an outstanding passer. Cahill had alternated the two quarterbacks in every game and was satisfied with both players.

Other players had also blossomed under the new coach and showed star qualities: Townsend Clarke was a real All-American candidate; Tom Schwartz and Dave Rivers had matured into outstanding ends; tackle Bohdan "Bud" Neswiacheny was an almost immovable

object in the center of the line; guard Pat Mente and cornerback Jim Bevans were solid; and Gary Steele, a 6-foot-5 end with great speed and marvelous hands, and the first black ever to play on an Army varsity, was an incredible find. In the Cadets' backfield, Chuck Jarvis, a big, hard-hitting fullback who could block, tackle, and run like a locomotive, was the key man. When Jarvis had the ball, it took two or three opponents to bring him down.

With all of this football history taking place at West Point, Coach Bill Elias, in his second season at Navy, promised a few surprises for the Cadets. A solid coach, easygoing and an eternal optimist, Elias insisted that the Middies weren't going to Philadelphia to play another tie game and had no compunctions about picking his team to rout the Cadets. "I feel as confident about this game against Army as any I've ever had to play," he said.

As the teams trotted onto the field, the crowd of 102,000 spectators stood and roared their shouts of encouragement to both. Navy won the toss of the coin, elected to kick off, and the game began.

Army took the kickoff and didn't give up possession of the ball until they'd scored a touchdown in just nine plays.

With Chuck Jarvis carrying, Army reached midfield. Then came a quick flip, Lindell to Jarvis. Chuck swung to his left, got a great block from Terry Young, then bolted 49 yards for Army's first score of the afternoon. The run came so quickly and suddenly—within two minutes and twenty-nine seconds of the opening kickoff—that it took the huge, stunned crowd awhile to erupt in a roar that could be heard all the way to Annapolis.

Navy, entering the game a 5-point favorite, now had to play catch-up ball, and proceeded to do just that by taking to the air. Cartwright, the Middies' fine passer, just barely missed his receivers on several occasions in the first period, but he was magnificent in the second period as he led his team on a 70-yard drive that took Navy across the goal line. The kick for the extra point was good and it was a 7–7 game.

The Middies stopped Army cold on the subsequent kickoff, and now Navy appeared to be in command of the game as they began a drive to the Army goal line. But then Cartwright attempted a long pass to Clark—a pass that if caught would have meant another Navy score—and Army's defensive halfback, Jim Toczylowski, intercepted the ball on Army's 19-yard line.

Unable to move the ball, Army kicked, and again Navy began an immediate attack. Cartwright passed to Taylor for a short gain. Another pass, Cartwright to Taylor for 25 yards, brought the ball to the Army 29-yard line with but five seconds to go in the half.

Desperately trying to beat the gun that would signal the end of the half, Navy tried a 46-yard field goal by Johnny Church, but the kick fell woefully short.

As the third period began, Navy penetrated

to the Cadets' 18-yard line, where Murray lost 2 yards trying to buck into the Army line. Then Cartwright, attempting to pass, was chased by three Army defenders, and threw the ball wildly. It was picked off by linebacker Jim Bevans and returned to the 10-yard line.

Here Army's offense stalled, and on fourth down they had to kick. Navy brought the ball back to the Army 35-yard line. Three line smashes got Navy just 3 yards, and then Clark of Navy attempted a 47-yard field goal. The kick was blocked by Townsend Clarke, and Bob Gora recovered the ball for the Cadets on the Army 42-yard line.

Now the Cadets went to work with a vengeance. After two line smashes by Jarvis that gained very little, Lindell stayed in the pocket behind good blocking just long enough for his receiver Terry Young to speed past Navy's de-

John Wayne, former USC tackle, joins Army coach Tom Cahill at the 1966 National Coaches' Association dinner, where Cahill was named Coach of the Year.

fensive back, Joe Bayer, then shot a marvelous pass right onto Young's fingertips and Terry was over the goal line on a beautiful 42-yard scoring play.

Navy, appearing stunned by the touchdown strike, lost the ball after taking the kickoff.

Once more Lindell began to pass to his favorite targets, Young and Jarvis, and on three pass plays Army moved the ball to the Navy 23-yard line. Then Lindell faded back and, behind some marvelous blocking, spotted fullback Carl Woessner in the clear and tossed another great pass, which Woessner took 23 yards for another Army touchdown. Lindell missed the conversion, but now the score was Army 20, Navy 7.

After Navy took the ensuing kickoff, it seemed that their attack simply couldn't move against Army's tough defense. But suddenly two quick passes clicked, and just when it seemed as if Navy might score a touchdown, having finally reached Army's 28-yard line, the game ended.

Army heroes were plentiful: Steve Lindell, who completed twelve of seventeen passes for 164 yards and two touchdowns; Terry Young and Carl Woessner, who had caught the scoring passes; Jarvis, whose 49-yard run had given the Cadets the first touchdown; Clarke, the All-American linebacker, whose block of a Navy field goal had ignited Army's impetus to win.

Following the game, the Army locker room was bedlam. Generals, colonels, majors, captains, and even a few lieutenants stormed the barricades to congratulate Cahill and his team. And Cahill, outwardly calm despite the tremendous excitement that must have gripped him, accepted the kudos with a wide grin. How did it feel? He spread his arms out and answered, "I'm at peace with the world!"

And why not? His first year as a head coach had been a tremendous success. Army had finished the season with an 8–2 record, its best mark since 1958 when Colonel Red Blaik's last team finished with an 8–0–1 season.

Army expressed its gratitude to Cahill by giving him a new contract as head coach. And several weeks later, the National Coaches Association voted Tom Cahill "Coach of the Year."

"You don't realize how big this game is until you lose it and have to live with that loss 365 days a year," Coach Bill Elias said after Navy's 19–14 upset victory over a heavily favored Army team in 1967.

Elias was not merely paying lip service to the "bigness" of the game he had just won. On that Saturday, December 2, 1967, he was demonstrating how the supreme importance of the Army-Navy game had motivated him from the day a year ago when the tables had been turned and his Middies had suffered a startling upset at the hands of Tom Cahill's Cadets.

"Although we were under pressure to change our game pattern early this season, especially in the span when we were losing four games, we decided to take a beating and keep our surprises for the Army game."

Last spring he had put BEAT ARMY signs on everything in his office that did not move. His assistant coach, Lee Orso, had started keeping a "Days-to-Army" calendar.

"It's just 'another game' if you win," said Elias, quoting Tom Cahill from the year before. "It's not just another game if you lose."

With a 4–4–1 season in 1967, Navy had allowed more points (253) than any team in Academy history, so during the entire month of November, Elias had devoted almost all of his time to mending the defense. He even announced that he would start three raw rookies in the Army game—Shelly Butrill, Gerry Moil, and Jim Sheppard.

Corso, meanwhile, was allowed to concentrate on the offense, resurrecting a formation from his own quarterbacking days at Florida State some fourteen years before. He had been itching all year to use it for Navy. It was what has come to be known as "a straight I formation," as originated by Corso's coach at FSU, Tommy Nugent. All four of the backs line up behind the center, single file, one behind the other.

The I formation would give the Navy offense

Bohdan Neswiacheny, newly elected captain of the 1967 Army football team, gets the traditional "water bath" from teammates Townsend Clarke (left) and Hank Toczylowski.

an extra blocker in the backfield—which meant more power to attack Army's tackles and to kick out on Army's ends.

But in the final analysis it was quarterback John Cartwright's great passing, and his selection of passes, that made the difference.

The game began with the usual jam-packed crowd of 102,000 spectators at John F. Kennedy Stadium, with more cabinet officials, high-ranking politicos, and Army and Navy brass than had attended since the 1941 game just before Pearl Harbor. They saw one of the most spectacular, spine-tingling service games ever as Navy completely outplayed the Cadets in the first half of the game to take a 17–0 lead, seemingly ready to turn the game into a rout.

Navy received the opening kick and began

to hit the Army tackles for short gains. Suddenly Cartwright, Navy's marvelous quarterback, rolled out to his left and tossed a perfect pass 36 yards to end Rob Taylor, who then dashed to the Army 13-yard line. Two smashes at the now tightened Army defense picked up a couple of yards. Then Church kicked a 29-yard field goal and Navy had a 3–0 lead.

Moments later an intercepted pass gave Navy the ball in midfield, and Cartwright, mixing up his passing attack with three smashes off tackle, advanced to the Army 2-yard line. There Dan Pike drove the ball in for a touchdown. The kick was good and Navy was out in front by a 10–0 lead, and the Midshipmen were going crazy in the stands.

Cartwright, running the team like a field

The coaches and their stars before the 1967 game. Opposite page, top: Army's Tom Cahill with quarterback Steve Lindell and end Terry Young. Opposite page, bottom: Navy's Bill Elias with halfback Terry Murray and quarterback Johnny Cartwright. Navy scored a major upset by beating the Cadets 19–14, as Cartwright completed nineteen of twenty-nine passes for 240 yards, thus bettering Roger Staubach's three-year pass-completion record.

marshal with shoulder pads, was calling all the plays and had not made one poor-judgment call. In the second period, he completed four passes out of four, two of them to tight end Mike Clark, who was open so often it looked as if he were popping right out of the ground. Now Navy had a first down on the 13-yard line. Cartwright took the pass from his center, looked right, faked a pass, and handed the ball off to halfback Balsly, who crashed through for another Navy score. The extra point was good and now Navy had a 17–0 lead. It looked like a Navy blowout.

If there was one thing you could be sure of since calm-and-collected Tom Cahill came to be West Point's head coach, it was that at moments like this—even after a safety had added two more points for a 19–0 Navy lead—Army would not fold. The Cadets had come from behind seven times in past Army-Navy games to win over insurmountable odds. This was going to be number 8, almost.

With only thirteen minutes left to play in the game, Cahill called on his second-string quarterback, Jim O'Toole, to replace an ineffective Steve Lindell, and suddenly Army caught fire. The change was nothing short of miraculous.

Soon after the free kick following the safety, Army took over the ball and O'Toole proceeded to drive the Cadets 51 yards to a touchdown. He passed to Hank Andrzejczak, a substitute, for 10 yards. O'Toole and Chuck Jarvis, Army's fullback and last year's hero, drove to the Navy 2-yard line, and then Moore, another sub, smashed in for the score.

Now the Army defense caught fire, too,

stopping Navy dead in midfield. The Middies punted and Army had the ball with less than seven minutes to play.

On their first play from scrimmage, O'Toole dropped back and fired a long pass to Gary Steele. Steele had been dropping passes all day long, and he dropped this one, too. Undaunted, O'Toole called the same play again. Later, when asked why he did it, with Steele's fumbling performance up to then, Jim shrugged and said, "I had a hunch." This time, with two Navy tacklers on him, Gary Steele jumped into the air for O'Toole's even longer pass, plucked the ball out of the sky, and sped over the goal line. Now the Cadets in the stands went nutty, and there was an even louder noise as O'Toole passed into the end zone for the 2 points.

The score was Navy 19, Army 14, and there still remained seven minutes to play.

Nick Kurilko kicked off for Army, and Pike was smothered by Cadet tacklers at the 9-yard line. Army was now raging to make up for its earlier derelictions, and the Middies seemed unable to hold them off.

A poor Navy punt, only 11 yards, gave the ball to Army on the Navy 23-yard line.

The place was a madhouse. Army's crazed fans were all standing and screaming for a score. Nothing, it seemed, could stop their team now. Nothing could save Navy.

But in an instant, Army's miraculous comeback was shattered by a blow of misfortune, its last chance gone. Army fumbled the ball and Ray De Cario, Navy's sophomore guard, fell on it just before time ran out.

Navy had pulled the season's biggest upset. It finished the year with a 5–4–1 record for its first winning season in three under Bill Elias, who remarked after the game, "Winning is good for the soul."

He could also have said it is good for the future, because his job, in doubt before the game, was secured with a new one-year contract shortly afterward. Army finished 8–2 for the second straight year under its remarkable coach Tom Cahill, who took the loss in stride. "We'll get 'em next year," he said with a wry smile.

24

Cahill Holds His Edge: 1968-72

The U.S. Military Academy, which had supplied officers for the strongest air arm in history, the U.S. Air Force of World War II, on November 19, 1968, hired a four-seat civilian plane to bomb the U.S. Naval Academy at Annapolis.

The bombardment consisted of 71,130 surrender leaflets weighing a total of 169 pounds. The drop was made at 12:50 P.M., just about the time the Midshipmen were filing out from lunch in Farragut Hall, the Academy's huge dining room.

The surrender leaflets, which posed a cleanup problem for the Academy's maintenance crew, read:

Attention, all Midshipmen—

Surrender! Your situation is hopeless! You support a losing cause. Your football team couldn't even beat Boston College. [Boston beat Navy, 40–15; Army had defeated Boston, 58–25].

Your losses are many . . . your victories are few. We recognize that you are a determined enemy. Your 1-point romp over a tough Pitt team is testimony enough. But, we wish to spare you from a humiliating defeat in Philadelphia, tomorrow. Your only chance is to take this leaflet and with your

hands over your head, surrender. Otherwise the Army football team will show no mercy. If you refuse we can only hope and offer you this good advice: HANG IT UP, NAVY . . . YOU'RE GONE.

The 1968 Army football team was the best that coach Tom Cahill produced in his first three seasons; the team had the poorest won-lost record, however. In 1968, Army had compiled a 7 and 3 record, as opposed to the 8–2 record for each of the first two years Cahill was in charge of the football program.

The 1968 team had a more functional offense—it ran better, passed better, and after losing the second and third games, it blocked and tackled with such intensity that opponents were being knocked out of the line of action before a play got under way.

In a sense Tom Cahill was sad about this upcoming Navy game, for it would be the last for some of the finest players he had ever worked with, players who had seen him through the dark, uncertain days when he was Army's "interim coach."

Gary Steele was a typical example. He would be graduating and moving on to an Army career. The tall, speedy end was the only member of the squad starting his thirtieth consecutive game for Army—the maximum starts in a three-year career. Then there were Steve Lindell, the fine quarterback, and Charlie Jarvis—as sophomores, both had started the 1966 opening game against Kansas and helped Cahill begin his career as Army's head coach on a winning note. At that time it had been generally believed that Lindell, Jarvis, and Steele would be around a lot longer than Tom Cahill. There were other players who had started playing for Cahill in 1966 and who were ready for this, their last game. Several were defensive stars: Ken Johnson, Steve Yarnell, and Jim McCall. All had played against Navy the two previous years and now were ready for their finale against the Middies.

At Annapolis, Coach Bill Elias was searching for the right "pebble" with which to beat Army. He used the word by way of comparing his team's chances to those of David in the biblical clash with Goliath. "A year ago," said Elias, "the same situation existed that exists today. We are like David. I asked Admiral Tom Moorer [Chief of Naval Operations] if he thought we could win. He said 'It can be done if Navy finds the right pebble.' "

As the game got under way Army seemed unable to dent an inspired Navy line, outcharging and outfighting the Cadets as both teams took turns trying to move the ball.

Then late in the first period, Army started to move. They took over a Navy punt on the 34-yard line, and led by Chuck Jarvis and Hank Andrzejczak went 66 yards in nine plays, all on the ground. On successive power sweeps, Jarvis smashed off-tackle for 14 yards. On the very next play, Jarvis slashed through a big hole in the Middies' line for 22 yards and a first down on the Navy 30-yard line. Two more line smashes, then Andrzejczak took a handoff from Lindell, swept to his left, and broke out into the open for a 14-yard sprint to the 8-yard line. On the next play, Jarvis twisted and turned and battered his way across the goal line, dragging two Navy tacklers with him for the touchdown. The extra point was kicked by Arden Jensen and it was 7-0, Army.

Two minutes before the end of the first

quarter, Army again took over the ball from Navy and began to drive upfield.

Andrzejczak spurted around the Navy's left end behind marvelous blocking and streaked for a 36-yard gain before he was tackled from behind. Army was pounding the Navy line, opening wide holes for their backs. Six running plays picked up additional yardage, then Jarvis just took the ball under his arm, drove up and over the Navy defenders from the 1-yard line, and Army had another touchdown.

With Army comfortably out in front by 14-0, the raw, overcast skies must have looked like West Point gray to Navy eyes.

Then, suddenly, a surprising fumble of a routine punt by Army turned the complexion of the game into at least a blend of Navy blue.

Mike Clark, Navy's fine captain, fell on the ball at the Army 33-yard line, and the Middies, fired up by this sudden break, roared right back into the game. Six ground plays—the big one a 24-yard scramble by Dan Pike—gave Navy the ball on Army's 8-yard line. Navy quarterback Mike McNallen tried two successive line smashes, but Army did not give way. On third down, however, Pike cut to his right, then slashed through two Army tacklers and drove in for Navy's first score. The kick was good and it was 14-7, Army.

Now the momentum swung over to Navy, while Army faltered and the game became a wild battle of fierce line play, gang tackling, and a seemingly endless barrage of punts (nine by Navy, eight by Army) as both teams fought up and down the field.

Late in the third period, Steve Lindell, who had been having problems all afternoon with his passing, set up a pass play to Steele, his big end. As Steve brought back his arm to throw the pass, a hard-charging McNallen deflected the ball. It was picked off by LaForce, who promptly took off like a streak of lightning and was across the Army goal line without a hand touching him. Ed Cocozza kicked the extra point, and it was a 14-14 battle.

On Army's next series, Lindell attempted two straight passes that were not completed, and Coach Tom Cahill decided to switch quarterbacks. He brought in Jim O'Toole with instructions to "be careful, but throw a couple of good ones."

On his very first play, O'Toole took the pass from his center, faked to his right, then faked left to his big end Steele. His faking was so good that the Navy's defensive backs were pulled out of position and no one was covering end Joe Albano. So O'Toole promptly shot a perfect strike to Albano, who caught the ball on his fingertips and raced to the Navy 18-yard line before being tackled from behind. The play covered 63 yards and sent the Corps of Cadets into a delirious frenzy of shouting for their team.

On the next play, Charlie Jarvis cracked through a big hole in the Navy line and streaked over for his third score of the day to give Army a thrilling 21–14 victory.

Back in the dressing room after the win, Ken Johnson, captain of the Army team, concealed a grimace of pain as the two team physicians prodded his lower left leg to confirm their diagnosis that the leg was broken and that Johnson had played at least two full periods with a broken leg. While Lieutenant Colonels Joe Rokous and John Feagin searched for the exact spot of the break, Johnson smiled broadly and said, "It was unbelievable. This team, these guys are the greatest." He even hopped up and around to greet former teammates such as Bud Newieascheny, last year's football captain, on hand to congratulate the team.

Coach Tom Cahill was his usual quiet self.

"I thought maybe we'd blow them out. But it was very tough at the end. But that's as great as winning big. A win is a win."

Dan Pike, star tailback on the 1969 Navy football team, was born in the tiny town of El Reno, Oklahoma. Lynn Moore, Army's All-American star that same year, lived a block away. They played and grew up together in El Reno, went to high school and were teammates on the same football team.

Pike had wanted to go to Army, while his pal Moore wanted to attend Annapolis. But the first choice of each showed no interest in them as football players. So both boys switched schools.

On November 29, 1969, Dan Pike and Lynn Moore met face-to-face for the toss of the coin in the center of the gridiron at John F. Kennedy Stadium as captains of their respective teams.

As if to vindicate himself for his dismal showing in the 1968 game against Navy, when he carried the ball only six times, Moore was nothing short of sensational. He carried the ball forty times, scored one touchdown, and bore the brunt of an attack that led to three additional tallies, as the Cadets pounded out a decisive 27–0 win over the Middies. Moore's record total of forty carries broke an Army rushing record set twelve years previously by All-American Bob Anderson.

The 6 foot 3 inch, 200-pound speedster scored Army's first touchdown after a sustained Army drive of 65 yards early in the second period had brought the ball to the Navy 5-yard line. Then, on a spin and drive off tackle, Moore pounded in for the first Army touchdown.

Army's second touchdown came in the third period on a 6-yard pass from Bernie Wall, the Cadets' junior quarterback, to end Mike Masciello. Army's third score followed another drive, led by Moore, who scored from the 1-yard line to give the Cadets a 20–0 margin. Then, a 5-yard off-tackle dash by Hank Andrzejczak late in the final period resulted in yet another Army touchdown. Jensen kicked the extra point, and Army had a resounding 27–0 lead at game's end.

With his third victory over Navy in four attempts, Army coach Tim Cahill said that Army's success at running the ball was the result of a power I formation installed just for the Navy game. "And it worked to perfection," he said. Cahill had taken a page from Tom Corso's playbook of 1967, when the Navy offensive coach had resurrected the I formation from his days at Florida State.

Most disturbing for Coach Rick Forzano, who replaced Bill Elias in 1969 as Navy's head coach, was Navy's inability to maintain any momentum. On seven third-down situations, Navy had managed to convert only twice. In the second half, before mounting a drive that reached the Army 1-yard line, the Middies had given up the ball four more times.

Only once had Navy come close to scoring. After reaching the Army 23-yard line with eighty-five seconds to play in the first half, Navy quarterback Mike McNallen faked, rolled to his left, and threw the ball into the end zone. But Johnny Brenner, an Army defensive back playing in his hometown, stepped between a Navy receiver and the flag and took the ball right out of the Navy player's hands for his seventh and most important interception of the year.

Had Navy scored that touchdown, and kicked the extra point, it would have given the Middies a 7–6 lead and perhaps the impetus to forestall Army's bid for another win.

Coach Forzano was asked how it felt to lose the game. "It was like my legs went out from under me," he said flatly, "like I was dead."

What did he have to look forward to?

"With a one-and-eight record this year, I guess you can only go up. But then there is the freshman team. They're eight and zero and they're a hell of a lot bigger than this team."

In 1969 the Army had been accused of playing "soft" football schedules, that year and over the

Arden Jensen, Army's outstanding kicking specialist in 1970.

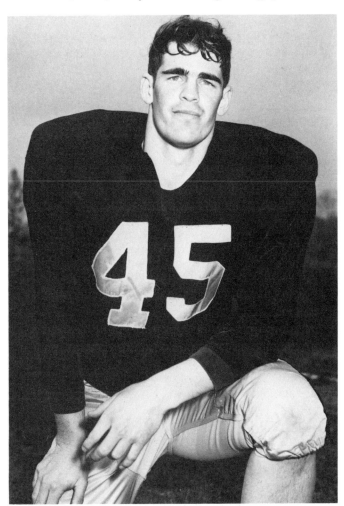

THE FOOT IN ARMY FOOTBALL

Arden JENSEN

ARMY'S KICKING SPECIALIST CONTINUED HIS ASSAULT ON THE ARMY RECORD BOOK WITH A BOOMING **47**-YARD FIELD GOAL AGAINST THE CAVALIERS OF VIRGINIA. THE KICK, BETTERED BY ONE YARD, THE PREVIOUS RECORD SET BY JENSEN AND NICK KURILKO. JENSEN ALSO KEEPS ADDING TO HIS RECORD CAREER TOTAL WHICH NOW STANDS AT **26**.

recent past. This bothered the Army brass so much that a change was made in the 1970 schedule—a change that hurt the Cadets throughout the season.

The Black Knights, rating well down the list of the nation's better teams, had to face four of the previous year's bowl competitors— Nebraska, Tennessee, Notre Dame, and Penn State—also Holy Cross, Baylor, Virginia, Boston College, Syracuse, and Oregon, before the season's finale against Navy.

The result was one of the poorest season records in the history of West Point. After opening with a solid win over Holy Cross, 26–0, the Cadets dropped games to every opponent on the schedule.

The season ended for Army with Navy coming from behind in a thrilling second-half battle to score 11 points, defeating the Cadets by a score of 11–7 in a game that saw neither team muster a winning offense.

Navy cornerback Mark Schickner, hero of this Navy win, said he had seen a way to success in the eyes of Army's quarterback Dick Atha. "I noticed that Atha would look at his receiver each time he faded back with the ball, then he would throw right at the player he was looking at. So from then on whenever he faded back, I just went for the guy he looked at and I was lucky to intercept the ball on four different occasions."

Schickner, a junior, had not played football in 1969, concentrating instead on basketball. He ended up as Navy's leading scorer in 1970. Schickner also received the game ball for "best player" in the service classic.

In the Army dressing room, Dick Atha said, "I'm most unhappy for the seniors who won't get another chance to play against Navy. But I know that we can win with this team next year."

Atha, a sophomore, then blamed himself for Arden Jensen's missed field-goal attempt in the final period. "I just fumbled that pass from center."

Navy had just moved ahead of Army, 8–7, on a touchdown and a gambling 2-point con-

version pass, Mike McNallen to end Karl Scheim.

After Jensen's missed field goal, another fumble by Atha at the Army 27-yard line put Navy in position for a 33-yard field-goal attempt by Lanning, which was right on the money and put Navy out in front 11–7 with less than five minutes to play. Army could make very little headway after the ensuing kickoff, and the game ended with the Middies out in front.

In 1971, the Army and Navy football elevens wrote a once-in-a-lifetime, a storybook thriller as raindrops kept falling on the heads of the second largest crowd to attend a football game all year long.

Some 97,047 rain-drenched spectators saw the fortunes of the Cadets and the Middies rise and fall like the proverbial seesaw before Coach Tom Cahill's gritty Cadets prevailed by a 24–23 margin in a game that had the crowd screaming, yelling, and pounding each other throughout the final two periods.

Incredibly, it was the first one-point margin in the seventy-two-game history of the series, and it took all of the stubbornness of an Army mule to hold off a driving Navy team, not once but twice, at the roaring finish.

Prior to the kickoff, the heavily favored Cadets were supposed to have both the stronger defense and the more explosive offense, but as so often happens in these traditional battles, form went out the window.

Early in the game, the Middies looked as dreary as the day, as they fumbled three times to enable Army to pile up a 16-point lead within seven minutes.

Then, when Navy's top receiver, Larry Van Loan, went out of the game with a broken clavicle after making his first and only reception at the Army 39, Navy hopes seemed to fade.

But George Berry, an unsung Navy halfback who had gained a total of only 81 yards in three years, and soph quarterback Freddy Stuvek,

In 1971 and 1972, Army was led by two fine quarterbacks—Dick Atha and King Fink.

just out of sickbay, sparked the Sailors to a re-markable comeback.

Working the power I formation to perfection, Stuvek either kept the ball or pitched to Berry as the Middies drove 52 and 69 yards to score and narrow the gap to 16–14 at the half.

Following intermission, the Navy sailed down the field 69 yards in thirteen plays. Half-back Steve Ogden made a miraculous over-the-shoulder catch of Stuvek's high, arching pass, then outjumped those Cadet defenders to catch the ball before falling into the end zone for the touchdown that gave Navy a 21–16 lead.

Now Navy seemed to have all the momentum.

But a fine Army punt by Ron Danhof pinned the Middies deep in their own territory, and after a short return punt the ball was taken by Army to the Navy 31 in six smashing plays.

Then Kingsley "King" Fink, Army's quarterback, tossed a 5-yard touchdown pass to tight end Ed Frances, and another pass to Frances for the 2-point conversion, and Army had the edge, 24–21.

But Navy was still alive.

They drove and smashed at the Army line, some 61 yards to the Army 8-yard line, before cornerback Steve Bogosian threw Stuvek for a loss. Then Randy Stein intercepted the next pass. But a fumble by Army was recovered by Navy to give the Middies new life.

Quickly they were knocking at the Cadets' door, 5 yards from pay dirt.

Now Stuvek and Berry tried to work their option play, but two attempts failed, and Army took over the ball.

Army's punter, Danhoff, instead of attempting a kick from his end zone, touched the ball down and intentionally gave Navy a 2-point safety just as the gun sounded to end the game. Tom Cahill's gritty Cadets had a magnificent 24–23 victory in a game that is still a topic of conversation among sportswriters discussing great Army-Navy battles.

The win, the fourth of six over Navy under Army coach Tom Cahill, gave the Cadets a record of 6 and 4 for the year.

— ★ —

The 1972 Army football team, having trailed in nine of its previous games, and tying five of them, attempted to pull one out against a highly favored Navy eleven. But the high-riding Middies came out from the opening kickoff, battered and bruised the Army line, quickly scored 12 points, and had the Cadets reeling like a punch-drunk fighter as the first half ended with the Middies taking a 12–0 lead.

Army and Navy actually played two different ball games this day before a crowd of more than 95,000 spectators at John F. Kennedy Stadium, Philadelphia. The Middies took the first one 12–0, but the scrappy, gutsy Cadets remembered that football games have a second half and scored 23 points for a stunning 23–15 comeback victory in a game that had to be one of the sweetest in the seven-year reign of Army coach Tom Cahill.

Many a Cadet played the hero in that brilliant second-half surge, but Bobby Hines, a recent convert to tailback, was outstanding as he dashed for 172 yards on forty-three carries, including Army's first touchdown on a 43-yard gallop around right end.

Early in the fourth period, Bruce Simpson, filling in at tailback whenever Hines tired, scored on a 21-yard dash.

A host of Army defenders played like demons all afternoon—Steve Bogosian, Joe Furloni, Tim Pfister, Jim Bryan, and Scott Beaty—and were particularly effective in the blazing second half against a favored Navy eleven.

Key man for Navy during the first half was a little sophomore from Rochester, New York, Cleveland Cooper, who picked up 135 yards rushing on twenty-six carries. Cooper became the first Navy runner in history to rush for more than 1,000 yards in a season, as he raised his total to 1,046.

Four minutes after Hines had scored, Beaty, the right cornerback, recovered a blocked Navy field-goal attempt and ran 84 yards for the touchdown that put Army in front 13–12. They were never again behind.

Army's strong corps of linebackers on the 1972 team (left to right): Skip Wjitman, Tim Pfister, Dave Molten, and Gary Topping.

Jim Barclay kicked the extra point after Army's first score, but a 2-point conversion attempt after the second score failed.

With time running out for the Middies in the fourth period, Army's Barclay and Navy's Roger Lanning exchanged field goals of 23 and 37 yards, respectively.

Navy's failure to move the ball when it got inside the Army 25-yard line on three different occasions in the second half proved to be the chief reason for their downfall.

Army's strongest defense paid off in the third period as Navy drove to the 5-yard line. On fourth down and 2 yards to go, Al Glenny was swarmed under by a horde of Army tacklers as he tried to run around his own right end.

Army then took over, failed to gain on three plays, and punted. But Navy could not move the ball and kicked back to the Cadets. This time Army mounted an attack that hit the Middies with everything in the Cadets' offensive arsenal, finally reaching the 25-yard line. There Simpson faked a buck through the line, suddenly stopped, pivoted, and dashing around his

own left end streaked across the goal line for the Army touchdown.

Navy received the Army kickoff and began their strongest offensive march of the day. On successive first downs, the Middies drove to the Army 30-yard line, where Lanning booted a 37-yard field goal to cut the Army lead to 20–15.

Army then took over and quickly moved into position for Barclay to kick a field goal, and it was Army 23, Navy 15 with one minute left to play.

The Middies fought back desperately, but try as they might they could not mount another tally, and the game ended with the Cadets out in front by a 23–15 margin.

As the whistle signaled the end of the game, Navy was disconsolate with its seventh and, of course, most important loss of the season. The Middies had won just four games.

The Army win plus an earlier victory over a strong Air Force team gave the Cadets the first Inter-Service Trophy as winner of the Army, Navy, Air Force round-robin series.

George Welsh Burns the Cadets: 1973-77

December 1, 1973.

This was a big day for George Welsh, the biggest day of his life, for it marked the end of his first season as head coach of the Naval Academy football team with a magnificent win over Army by the widest margin of victory that ever separated the two teams—a 51–0 annihilation of the once-mighty Cadets.

Welsh, a star quarterback for the Middies in 1954 and the spearhead of Navy's 27–20 win over Army that year with his marvelous pin-point passing, must have thought he was still at Penn State, where he'd been an assistant coach for eleven years and such lopsided victories came often.

Never had a service team so dominated this rivalry, even back in 1890 when Navy first challenged Army and defeated them 24–0. Never before had an Army team had such a poor record as the 1973 Cadets, who lost all 10 of their games this season.

The Middies had not had a successful season either, having lost seven of eleven games. But the win over Army and the manner in which they defeated the Cadets did much to erase the memory of those seven losses.

The Navy success came on the strength of a powerful running game led by Cleveland Coo-

per, the junior tailback. Cooper ran for 102 yards on eighteen carries and tied an Army-Navy record by scoring three touchdowns. Cooper thereby joined the great Joe Bellino (1959) and Pat Donnelly (1963) in scoring three touchdowns in one service classic.

Cooper, Ed Gilmore, Bob Jackson, and Al Glenny ran through, around, and over Army's defensive units for a total of 368 yards as the Middies completely dominated Army in every area of play.

The 91,926 attendance established this gathering as the smallest since the series moved back to Philadelphia in 1946.

A bright, warm sun kept the fans happy despite a strong northwest wind, and most of the throng was seated for the magnificent opening ritual of the Brigade of Middies and the Cadet Corps as they marched up and down the field and into their seats. It was the last time the Army fans had anything to cheer about, for as soon as the game began the Navy took command.

Navy received the kickoff and promptly marched 70 yards to the Army 15-yard line, where fullback Bobby Jackson streaked off tackle for a Navy score. The kick was missed.

In the second period, after Army had failed

to gain on virtually every possession, Navy turned the game into a rout by scoring four touchdowns in rapid-fire order.

Al Glenny, directing a fine offensive attack that combined several running plays plus a forward pass, advanced the ball to the Army 40-yard line. Then on a fake linebuck, Glenny faded back and tossed a short shovel pass to Larry Van Loan, who sprinted 39 yards for the second Navy touchdown.

Once again after receiving the kickoff, Army advanced the ball to midfield but had to relinquish the ball and Navy took over. Five plays and some 55 yards later, Glenny skirted left end for 5 yards and another Navy score.

With the score 34–0, and a minute and a half remaining in the first half, Steve Dykes booted a magnificent 44-yard field goal, after Army had offered stubborn resistance, to make the score 37–0 as the half ended.

In the second half, Coach Welsh inserted every Navy player in uniform to try to make the game more of a contest, but even the substitutes ran up 14 additional points in the third period for a final 51–0 victory.

Navy's victory was the Middies' thirty-second in the series. Army had won thirty-six times, and there had been six ties.

Just after the game ended, Lieutenant Colonel Pete Dawkins, who won the Heisman Trophy as Army's star halfback in 1958, said: "I really believe that there is great resiliency in the Cadets and Army football. I honestly think they will come back strongly." But for once Dawkins was wrong.

For Army's head coach Tom Cahill, it was the saddest of afternoons. His three-year contract with Army was to expire at the end of the season, and Army officials had thus far refused to say whether Cahill would be asked to stay on again, although one official had said, "Tell me when we last fired an Army coach."

After the game, Cahill allowed, "They [Army officials] don't take kindly to a loss to Navy, especially by this kind of score. If you don't win here, you're gone."

Early in January 1974, Tom Cahill was notified that he would not be Army's coach that year.

Starting where they left off a year before at the John F. Kennedy Stadium, when they trounced Army 51–0, a flashy Navy football team hitting on all "eleven cylinders" beat Army in 1974, shutting the Cadets out for the second year in a row as they romped to a 19–0 victory before a still-smaller crowd of 86,246, that at least included the former University of Michigan star center, President Gerald Ford.

The Middies began the game as if they wanted to drive Army into the sea, piling up 10 points in the first period. Then they added a second-period touchdown and a third-period safety to complete the scoring for this seventy-fifth Army-Navy battle.

Navy's thirty-third victory in the series was not as close as the score would indicate. Coach George Welsh's eleven so dominated the action that Army was never a real threat after the end of the first quarter.

This was largely the result of Army's wishbone offense, not an attack capable of producing a come-from-behind victory. Once behind, wishbone teams are in more serious trouble than teams utilizing more pass-oriented offenses.

Also, Army's choice of plays for the wishbone seemed unusual at times, to put it mildly. One included a rollout play that Army used from its own 1-yard line, which resulted in the Army quarterback, Scott Gillogly, being brought down behind his own goal line for Navy's final two points. Most teams in such a situation call for a quick-opening, straight-ahead play to try to get more room to maneuver.

Navy, on the other hand, utilized a versatile running attack, organized by frosh quarterback Mike Roban, the first Navy plebe quarterback ever to start a modern Army-Navy game. Just a year before, the 6 foot 2 inch youngster had been calling signals for the Great Falls, Montana, high school.

Roban kept the Cadets continuously off balance and got the Middies to strike and score quickly from early opportunities.

Over the first nine minutes, the Cadets never advanced beyond their own 20-yard line. During that time Navy scored 10 points, more than enough to win the game. The first 3 points came when Steve Dykes booted a 45-yard field goal, equaling the longest kick in an Army-Navy game. Shortly after Dykes's placement, John Stuffleben got off a 36-yard punt that was fumbled by Army's Gary Smithey and recovered by Navy's Carl Sherperson at the Army 13-yard line.

It took Roban just three plays to move his team to the Army 3-yard line and a first down. On the next play, Bobby Jackson drove over left tackle for the touchdown. Dykes added the extra point.

Jackson scored again after nine minutes into the second period as Roban directed a dazzling drive that had Army completely baffled and off balance. On one play Roban faked a pass, then ran the ball himself. On the next play he feinted a run and tossed a short shovel pass. And so it went—the plays alternating to the right, to the left, right again, left again—over a magnificent series that advanced the ball 67 yards in just seven plays, with Jackson slamming through from the 6-yard line for the touchdown.

Navy opened another drive in the third period after Jeff Scott, a big linebacker, intercepted a pass by Army's Leamon Hall, Army's own plebe quarterback.

Scott took the ball at the Army 8-yard line, and in twelve plays, once again led by Roban, Navy reached Army's 1-yard line. But here the Cadets' Dave Duncavage batted down a fourth-down pass, and Army took over, just a yard out from its own goal line. On their first play from scrimmage, Army suffered the indignity of a safety when Gillogly was tackled in his end zone.

It was the final insult added to all the injury Navy inflicted that afternoon upon the Army wishbone offense installed at West Point by Homer Smith when he took over as coach from Tom Cahill. Smith did manage to win three games this fall, an improvement over Cahill's

final, all-losing season, but his team failed to win the "big game" against Navy.

Coach George Welsh's team finished the year just as it did the previous one, with a 4–7 record. And "the big game" vs Army was another very big win, and again by a shutout. Two in a row for Welsh.

President Gerald Ford said after the game that the players today seemed to be better than when he played back in 1930 with the University of Michigan. "But we had to be tougher than these boys are. You see we had to play both on offense and defense, and that isn't easy, especially when you're playing on a losing team."

November 29, 1975. The day started badly for the Cadets of the United States Military Academy. They had spent more than $10,000 for a 65-foot balloon-replica of the Army mule, and just prior to the beginning of the Army-Navy game, try as they might, they were unable to get this mammoth Macy's-parade-type balloon into the air above the four thousand Midshipmen at Municipal Stadium, Philadelphia. There was a defect in the rubber mule, it turned out, and they never even got it off the ground. So there it sat atop the north stands throughout the game, its huge head drooping and sadder-looking by the minute as the Middies ran up the score.

The Army mule perfectly mimicked the hangdog expression of the four thousand Cadets sitting in the stands as they watched their football team try to penetrate the Navy line.

Perhaps Coach Homer Smith, who had altered the Army offense several times this year, could be excused for sending his team reeling and staggering into a rough, tough Navy line. Army had virtually no passing offense. What else could they do?

So Army kept trying, and in the final quarter, with the Middies far ahead by 30–0, the Cadets actually had the ball on the Navy 2-yard line. Three times the Army backs powered into the Navy line, and three times the Navy forwards hurled them back. But on fourth down, Navy cracked just a mite, enough for Army's quarterback Leamon Hall, all 6 feet 5 of him, to eke through the Navy wall and stretch himself across the goal line. Army had finally hit pay dirt. It was the only time during the entire game that the Cadets had something to cheer about.

Having been shut out by Navy in 1973 and 1974, the Cadets, who had never stopped fighting, at least had broken that ignominious string, while Navy had to settle for its third straight decisive win in a game that was witnessed by the smallest crowd to see the big game in thirty-seven years. The attendance this year was 81,576, 2,000 less than the low mark set the year before.

From the very beginning it was apparent that Navy had the better team. The Middies blocked with a ferocity that could be heard high up in the stands. And every time a Navy back started to run, there were two and three blockers in front of him, clearing the way for long gains.

On Navy's first possession Bob Jackson scampered off tackle for a first down on the Army 45-yard line. Then it was Jackson and halfback Bob DeStetney for another first down. On the fifth play of the series, the Army line stiffened, holding Navy on the 27-yard line. Two more times Navy's attack was stopped, and on fourth down, the Middies' outstanding guard, Larry Muczynski, a strong left-footed kicker, booted the first of three field goals, from the 27-yard line, and Navy had a 3-0 lead.

Early in the second period, after Army had failed to move the ball, Navy took over and marched straight down the field with Jackson leading the way to the 2-yard line. Here Army held again, but this time just for two downs. On the third try, Jackson smashed in for a touchdown. Muczynski kicked the extra point, and the score was Navy 10, Army 0.

Following the touchdown and another failure to gain ground, Army attempted a punt from their 45-yard line. The kick was blocked by Jeff Hoobler and picked up at the 42-yard line by Navy's Bob DeStefney, who raced in for another Navy touchdown. Muczynski again

kicked the extra point and Navy had a 17-0 lead.

With just two minutes before the end of the half, Navy worked the ball to the Army 22-yard line. Three plays failed to gain ground for the Middies, and once again Muczynski booted a 31-yarder. So it was 20-0 as the half ended.

In the third period Muczynski kicked his third field goal of the afternoon, this time from the 28-yard line, to give the Middies a comfortable 23-0 lead and start the crowd's exodus from the stadium.

Early in the fourth period, Bobby Jackson pounded over left tackle for Navy's third touchdown, and it was 30-0.

At this point Coach George Welsh took out his first-string defense and inserted all of the substitutes he could find. Navy had rushed for a total of 322 yards, and although Army did manage that one score, it was only a matter of time before Army's misery would mercifully end.

After the game some of the Navy players expressed disappointment over their failure to shut out Army, but Coach Welsh said, "We haven't had a winning season since 1967, and these guys did it. That's what counts—winning, not shutouts."

The Navy football team, which had lost two games this season by a single point, narrowly missed a bid for a big bowl game.

It was the fifth time that the Middies had won three consecutive victories over Army since the series began in 1890.

Navy coach George Welsh just couldn't resist needling an old teammate, just a little. So when someone asked him the inevitable question about comparing his 1976 halfback Joe Gattuso, Jr., with his father, Joe Gattuso, Sr., who had starred for Navy along with Welsh in 1952-53, George unloaded like the slick quarterback he once was.

"I don't think the older Gattuso could carry his shoes," said Welsh with a big smile. "And you can tell him I said it."

With his father in the stands wearing a fa-

Leamon Hall, Army's 6 foot 5 inch quarterback, was one of the nation's top passers in 1976. But against Navy that year, Hall completed only thirteen passes out of thirty-one attempts. Here he is throwing to Greg King, good for a 20-yard gain. But it was Navy's game all the way as the Middies prevailed 38–10 for their fourth straight win over the Cadets.

miliar Navy cap, Joe, Jr., scored three stunning touchdowns as the Middies trounced Army, 38–10, for the fourth year in a row.

"I've never scored three touchdowns in a game even in high school," the twenty-year-old junior tailback said after the game.

Navy's fourth consecutive triumph over Army meant more than extending the Middies' recent dominance in the series. It capped a turnabout that saw Navy win their last three games after staggering through six losses in their first seven games of the 1976 season.

"It was in the middle of the season when I told the team, 'We're not gonna win one game, and furthermore Army's gonna beat the pants

off us, unless you pick it up,' " Welsh said. "And it worked. The team got real mad at me and they did pick it up and they did begin to win."

It was a cloudy and threatening day that November 27 when Navy began the proceedings by kicking off to Army. The kick put the Cadets in immediate trouble as they mishandled the ball and Navy got possession on the Army 9. A Navy fumble and now it was Army's turn as they picked themselves off the ground and slowly began to move upfield. Leamon Hall began to fake a pass, then ran up the middle for 5 yards. Another try off tackle gained 3 more.

Then switching his offense, Hall decided to pass the ball, and on the next play, finding no one out in the open, he tossed a lateral pass to halfback Tony Payne. But Payne, all alone and caught by surprise, fumbled the ball and Navy recovered on the 14-yard line. On the very first play, Navy's Joe Gattuso sprinted around his right end for a touchdown.

Army came right back, fighting through the Navy line and picking up two first downs. Then Army got a break as the field judge ruled interference on a 37-yard pass play, and the Cadets had a first down on the Middies' 11.

On the first play from scrimmage, Greg King, behind marvelous interference, sprinted around his left end for the Army touchdown. It was only the second Army score against Navy in four games.

Army might have a chance after all, it seemed, but then came the play that appeared to completely change the momentum of the battle.

With the score tied at 7–7, Navy was faced with a fourth down and 1 yard to go on the Army 31-yard line. As the Army defense massed to stop a power play, or quarterback sneak, Bob Leszczynski faked a handoff to his right, kept the ball, and broke around his left end for a 16-yard gain. It was a naked reverse that seemed to destroy the fight and confidence of the big Army line. Two plays later, Leszczynski threw a bulletlike pass over the middle of the line to a diving Phil McConkey, and Phil was over the goal line for a Navy score. It was a bang-bang play that again caught Army totally by surprise and brought a roar from the Middies in the stands. The kick for the extra point was good and it was 14–7, Navy.

After the kickoff, Army tried to shake off the effects of the Navy score and did move upfield behind a couple of fine running plays by Hall. A pass by Hall then brought the ball to the Army 30-yard line. Here Navy stiffened and held Army on three running plays. Then, on fourth down, Mike Castelli, Army's fine field-goal kicker, booted a 37-yarder just as the half ended to bring the score to 14–10, Navy.

Navy received the kickoff at the start of the second half and just marched right up the field. Leszczynski connected on two pass plays to spark the 75-yard drive. Then Joe Gattuso took a pitchout from quarterback Leszczynski and slanted off right tackle for 20 yards and a Navy touchdown. Now it was 21–10.

In the third period, Gattuso banged across the Army goal line from the 2-yard line after Navy had again marched the length of the field practically unopposed. Then, after Army gave up the ball on downs, Navy resumed banging away, picking up first downs until their attack stalled on the Army 28-yard line. On fourth down, Bob Tata calmly dropped back and kicked a perfect 33-yard field goal to give Navy a 24–10 lead.

In the fourth period, after an Army attack petered out, Navy took charge of the ball and once again proved they were unstoppable. The Middies marched to the Army 15-yard line, then Leszczynski tossed a beautiful pass to Dave King, who staggered across the Army goal line with two Cadet tacklers on his back, and a successful conversion raised the score to 31–10.

In the final period Army, determined to score at least one more touchdown and make the game closer, mounted a furious passing attack, masterminded by the nineteen-year-old Army quarterback Leamon Hall. Hall tossed several successful passes midway in the period, then, after being chased by two Navy tacklers, Leamon threw a hurried pass that defensive back Greg Milo intercepted for Navy.

Then Leszczynski tossed a shovel pass to

Dave King, and King drove in from the 16-yard line for the final touchdown; the kick was good, making the score 38–10.

Joe Gattuso's three touchdowns equaled the exploits of Joe Bellino, Pat Donnelly, and Cleveland Cooper, each former Navy backs who scored three times against Army. Four Army players have scored three times against Navy, but Charles Emerich of Navy still holds the single game record of four touchdowns, scored in the very first game of the series in 1890.

The Army football team ended a four-year famine against Navy with an exciting, nail-biting 17–14 victory over Navy, November 26, 1977, at John F. Kennedy Stadium, Philadelphia, before a frostbitten, numbed crowd of 81,091, nearly all of whom sat through the entire game as the wind and sleet howled through the stadium.

In a battle that pitted a driven Army team against a bunch of Middies who wouldn't be beaten, the Cadets came through with a memorable finish that barely squeezed out the win.

It was a ball game that rekindled the great spirit and spark in this ancient series. The Middies refused to attempt a field goal from the 26-yard line in the final minute of the game, a field goal that would have tied the score. Instead the Middies went for broke with fourth down and 2 yards to go and the ball on Army's 9-yard line.

Navy coach George Welsh, who had not lost to Army in his four previous years at Navy, turned to his best runner, halfback Joe Gattuso, for the crucial 2 yards that would spell victory or defeat. Gattuso, who had scored three touchdowns in 1976 and two in 1975, took a pitchout and stepped off to his left. But seeing that there was no room to run, Joe lofted a high arching pass into the end zone, hoping that one of his eligible receivers could handle the ball. There was no Navy player in the immediate vicinity, and the ball fell for an incomplete pass. Army took over the ball and just ran out the clock.

The game began with Army kicking off to Navy.

On the second play from scrimmage, Gattuso darted laterally as if he were going to go around his own right end, but then cut sharply and sliced through tackle well into the Army secondary. The play picked up 38 yards and brought the ball inside the Navy 30-yard line.

The Cadets in the stands rose as one man and shouted, "DEFENSE, DEFENSE," while the Middies roared "TOUCHDOWN, TOUCHDOWN."

Three plays into the line failed to gain any ground, and then Navy's field-goal kicker, Bob Tata, dropped back for a 47-yard attempt. A low snap from center disrupted Tata's rhythm, and the kick went to the left of the goal posts.

The Cadets also misfired on their first scoring opportunity. Army drove down to Navy's 10-yard line, then lost a couple of yards on two running plays. On third down, Mike Castelli also attempted a field goal, from the 26-yard line, but his kick misfired and was wide to the left.

The Middies never were in the lead in this game. Continually they were thwarted by an aggressive Army line led by middle guard George Mayes, an Orange, New Jersey, sophomore who fired up the Cadets with his aggressive tackles.

But the Middies did repeatedly convert on crucial fourth-down plays to sustain their drives. The first of these came with Army out in front by 10–0. Navy scored and made the kick and it was 10–7.

After Army scored another touchdown in the third period, Navy worked the ball downfield and had a fourth down and 2 yards to go on the Army 22-ard line. Then halfback John Kurowski took a handoff from Gattuso and sped 18 yards before Army could bring him down. Three plays later, Gattuso smashed across the goal line, and the score was Army 17, Navy 14.

Now as the game began to wind down—there were only four and a half minutes left in the game—the Middies began their last heroic move upfield.

Quarterback Bob Leszczynski tossed a sharp, flat pass to end Phil McConkey, and Phil blasted for 18 yards before he was tackled on the Navy 39-yard line. On the very next play McConkey took an over-the-shoulder pass from Leszczynski and raced to the Army 1-yard line.

Now the entire crowd of 81,000 fans were up on their feet screaming and cheering over this most exciting finish in years. After three running plays failed, Gattuso attempted to pass the ball. The pass fell incomplete, and Navy's hopes went glimmering. Army took over the ball and ran out the clock, maintaining their 17–14 lead.

After the game Coach George Welsh said: "I couldn't have lived with myself if I'd tried to tie the game with a field goal. I made the choice to pass and I still think it was a good play to call. It was a tough thing to ask Gattuso to do, but I felt that play was going to win the game for us. We don't play for ties at Navy."

Leamon Hall, Army's 6 foot 5 inch senior quarterback, glowing over the first victory of his career against Navy, said he was not surprised by the play. "You just don't try for a tie in an Army-Navy game," said Hall, who had scored Army's first touchdown and directed an 80-yard drive for their second score. "In this service game you play to WIN."

26

Army's Famine Resumes: 1978-83

With Bob Leszczynski, a twenty-one-year-old Milwaukee senior directing a magnificent offense, Navy made a shambles of Army's resistance in 1978 and swept to an unexpectedly easy 28–0 shutout win at Philadelphia's John F. Kennedy Stadium.

The win was Navy's fifth in six years over Army, all under Coach George Welsh, a former star Navy quarterback in the mid-1950s. Navy triumphed before a crowd of 79,026 and a national television audience. It was its thirty-sixth in the series, putting them one game behind Army, and there have been six ties.

It was a strong finish to Navy's regular season, in which the Middies, having won 8 games and lost 3, were invited to the first Holiday Bowl, in San Diego, to play Brigham Young University.

Navy's record this year was its best since 1963, when Roger Staubach was the Navy quarterback and the Middies posted a 9–1 record, but lost to Texas in the Cotton Bowl. That had been the last Navy trip to a bowl game.

For Army the game was just the opposite: an unhappy finish to a losing season. The Cadets' record that year ended up 4 wins, 6 losses, and a tie.

Army received the kickoff, but Navy's stiff defense stopped the Cadets cold and forced them to punt.

Navy took over on the Army 48-yard line, from where Leszczynski led his team to the Army 3-yard line. It took but nine plays, with Navy hammering the Army line almost at will for huge gains and piling up four consecutive first downs.

It was fourth down. On an option play, Leszczynski faded left, found he had no receivers, tucked the ball under his arm, and spotting a big hole to his right smashed in for the touchdown to make the score 7–0, Navy.

Again Navy kicked off, and again Army was held by Navy's tough line play. Once more Army was forced to punt, and Navy got the ball on their own 48-yard line.

Now, feeling certain he had Army on the run, Leszczynski hit them with his big guns. He picked Army apart with pinpoint passes, and when the Army defense fell back to stop the passes, the canny Leszczynski had his big backs smash through the line. It took Navy just three minutes to drive the 52 yards for a second Navy touchdown, as Steve Callahan, a big sophomore tailback, smashed in from the 1-yard line. Bob Tata kicked the second of four extra points, and now Navy was under full sail and Army in retreat.

In the second period the Navy quarterback began another drive upfield on a series of running plays and two short passes that brought the ball to the Army 1-yard line. Again on the option play, Leszczynski went left, held on to the ball, and dove in for Navy's third touchdown.

In the third period, Army rallied to stop yet another Navy drive, holding the Middies to fourth down on the 1-yard line. At this point Coach Welsh sent in his field-goal kicker Tata, who dropped back to the 24-yard line. The pass from center flew over Tata's head, but Leszczynski ran for the ball, picked it up, and dodged several tacklers until he was at the Army 40-yard line. From there, still on the same wild play, he fired a pass to Callahan at the 10-yard line, and Callahan went in to score Navy's fourth touchdown of the day.

The defeat cost Coach Homer Smith his job as the Army coach. Smith, a former star at Princeton back in the 1950s, had taken over at Army in 1974 and had enjoyed only one winning year—1977.

"The victory was a tribute to our players," said Coach Welsh. "They were down after three straight losses and we just had to get together and beat the Army. It was a marvelous performance and I'm proud of them."

Eddie Meyers, an Army brat who decided as a youngster that he preferred the Navy, destroyed the Army football team single-handedly in the eightieth annual football classic, December 1, 1979, in John F. Kennedy Stadium, Philadelphia.

The Navy's great tailback, son of a retired Army chief warrant officer, set a new Navy rushing record of 279 yards and scored three touchdowns as the Middies easily romped over Army, 31–7, before a crowd of 77,052. Meyers's forty-three carries were also a record in the service classic.

Eddie and his teammates had very little trouble on this day in evening the series at thirty-seven victories each.

After the game, Coach Lou Saban, the much traveled first-year Army coach, who finished the season with a woeful 2–8–1 record, said, "The Navy played exceptionally well and that

Meyers is absolutely a sensation. Our situation here at West Point is the same as it has been all year long. Our men try hard, but they come up far short. As a matter of fact," said Saban, "we had so many injuries to key personnel that I had to utilize T. D. Decker, a junior, as our starting quarterback, even though he never had played a single minute of varsity football. That should speak for itself."

Navy finished the season with a fine 7–4 record, giving the Middies a two-season record of 16 wins against 7 losses.

Eddie Meyers began the season as the fourth-string Navy tailback, but when injuries cut deeply into the list of Navy running backs, Meyers jumped into the starting post against Notre Dame, in the eighth game of the season, and did well against the Irish.

From then on, the 5 foot 9, 210-pound back had no trouble keeping his starting job, and if there remained any doubts about the wisdom of Welsh's trust in Eddie, they were erased that great day against Army as he drove through and around the Cadet defense for almost 300 yards.

If any college football coach in the nation in 1980 had found a successful answer to balancing classroom needs with those of the football field, it was the forty-seven-year-old Navy coach, George Welsh, about to complete his eighth season at Annapolis.

An outstanding quarterback for the Navy teams in 1953, 1954, and 1955, Welsh left the Navy after graduation to take a post as an assistant coach at Penn State under Joe Paterno. He came back to Annapolis in 1972 as head coach, and within three years had developed Navy into one of the nation's leading football powers. By 1980, Welsh had led the Middies to two bowl games, three consecutive winning seasons, and, most importantly, his teams had beaten Army in six of eight contests. Suddenly every school wanted to hire Welsh away from Navy.

"It used to get me uptight and worried when all those football guys called to talk with George about a new job," said J. O. Coppedge, Navy's athletic director. "But I don't worry anymore. Not because he might take another job, but because . . . well, what else can I do?"

It was not always so.

Until 1978, which Welsh has described as "the turning point" in the renaissance of Navy's football fortunes, he had managed only one winning season.

"I made a conscious personal decision then," Welsh recalls. "If I couldn't get things going that year, I figured why stay? I thought we were doing a good job, but some problems were too difficult to solve."

One persistent problem, as always, was the strenuous Academy workload. After years of comparing game results and injury patterns against Middie class and exam schedules, he came to the conclusion that his players could not reach a maximum peak for a game every week. There would be hills and valleys. The secret was to find and develop consistent habits.

For example, Welsh knew that Tuesday nights were traditionally heavy book nights; Wednesday practices would always be poor, with players tired and easily injured.

"So we adjusted and tried to make it so practice was not so tough. I also eased up on workout and team meetings during the midterm exams. I wanted to set a system to fit the player instead of forcing the players into the system. An early lunch and a forty-minute midday meeting were set on Mondays, Tuesdays, and Wednesdays during the season so that players could be ready to start practice later in the day with films, game plans, and other mental preparations already completed."

Welsh's new methods and practices resulted in developing some of Navy's most successful football teams. The Middies' 1980 win over Army by a 33–6 margin marked the seventh time a Welsh team had beaten Army in eight games.

Navy's newfound football fortunes could also be traced to a group of seniors recruited by Welsh and his staff, many of whom had spent five years together, starting at the Naval Academy Prep school in Newport, Rhode Island.

About twenty of Navy's sixty varsity players came from that prep-school background. The schools (West Point has one, too) are a sensitive issue with the service academies, because they suggest a modified farm system; but without the additional year for the boys to mature, develop friendships, and resolve any insecurities about life in the military, many of the finest prospects might not go to either of the two service schools.

This season Welsh's methods had produced some of Navy's finest players. There was Eddie Meyers, the chunky halfback from New Jersey who rushed in 1980 for 957 yards on 204 carries; Fred Reitzel, a 6-foot-3, 210-pound quarterback with a great arm, who completed thirteen of eighteen passes in the Army game; Ted Dumbauld, senior linebacker; Terry Huxel, a middle guard; and Steve Callahan, a wide receiver who caught passes for touchdowns in every game this year.

The 1980 game at Philadelphia's Veterans Stadium was the first Army-Navy game ever played on artificial turf, and both teams wore sneakerlike shoes with small rubber "grabbers" on the soles.

Whatever the shoes worn, Navy seemed to have all the advantage, on the ground and in the air, as they pulverized Army's defense in scoring a smashing 33–6 victory.

This was the eighty-first game played between the two schools.

The Middies took immediate command in the first half with a touchdown and field goal in each quarter to take a 20–0 lead at halftime.

In the third period, after Army had driven the length of the field to score its only touchdown with six minutes left, Navy added another touchdown and extra point and two field goals to go ahead 33–6.

Both of Navy's first two touchdowns were scored following aerial attacks deep into Army territory spearheaded by quarterback Fred Reitzel. Then, on short line bucks, Reitzel carried the ball across the goal line for both touchdowns.

Navy scored their third touchdown when Reitzel, after sparking a Navy attack to the Army 10-yard line, started an off-tackle run, but instead lobbed a short pass into the end zone to split end Dave Dent. Navy's kicker, Steve Fehr, kicked his fourth extra point, tying the Army-Navy game record for conversions.

Gerry Walker, Army's sophomore halfback, scored the lone Army touchdown in the third period when he took a lateral pass and pounded his way through several Navy tacklers for a 30-yard gain into the end zone.

In 1976, Gerry Walker had been an enlisted soldier on duty in South Korea. One of his officers, seeing him play football one wintry day, arranged for Gerry to take some academic tests, which he passed with flying colors. Then came more tests, more studying day and night, until finally Walker passed the entrance exams to West Point and was admitted into the class of 1981. At the Academy, although he had not played football in high school in Greenville, South Carolina, the Army coaches turned him into a running back.

After today's game, Gerry Walker had run for 917 yards for the 1980 season, a record that placed him ahead of Chris Cagle and Doc Blanchard, two Army immortals, for first-season yardage.

As he left the game this day, Gerry Walker said he was not thinking about any records he might set.

"Next Monday," he said, "I have a physics test, a test in calculus, and a final in chemistry."

The loud blast of cannon fire that traditionally signals victory in the annual Army-Navy football game exploded from both sides of the stadium at Philadelphia, late this sunny and warmish December day after the eighty-second Army-Navy game ended in a 3–3 tie.

Appropriately, Army's salvo was the last and the loudest. For Navy had been so much a favorite that the West Pointers could be very happy with anything less than a beating.

Over land and sea the game was followed on worldwide television and radio—from far-off sentry posts in South Korea, to stations in West Germany, to the American embassy in

Moscow; wherever an American soldier, sailor, marine, or Coast Guard unit was stationed, it was possible to hear this game play-by-play. All over the globe men of the armed forces had an ear cocked toward Veterans Stadium, Philadelphia.

Promptly at 1:30 P.M., with the sun high in a clear sky, the Cadets and Midshipmen marched into the stadium. Led by a band dressed in blue-and-gold uniforms with capes of bright yellow, the Middies stepped off smartly in columns of squads, then cut across the field, did an about-face and marched back across the field once more before nimbly hopping into the grandstand seats. They numbered about 4,500 men, and their march was so minutely timed—every man in perfect harmony with the man in front of him—that the crowd burst into cheer after cheer as they swept by.

A few minutes later the Corps of Cadets came into sight, marching in perfect cadence in a column of squads. Here was that flawless rhythm, that perfect swing of the finest drilled body of Cadets in the world. They came on across the field in a straight, unwavering line, stopped in front of the Middies, lifted their caps in salute, then stepped off smartly and marched to the opposite side of the stadium and their seats.

Then the game began.

It was a game marked by long drives by both teams, drives that ended unsuccessfully when both Army and Navy backs fumbled the ball within reach of the opponents' goal line.

Army lost at least four scoring opportunities, while Navy's quarterback Marco Pagnanelli had two chances snatched away from him as the alert Army defense intercepted touchdown-bound forward passes deep in Army territory.

Navy scored first when Steve Fehr kicked a perfect 35-yard field goal with just one second left in the first half.

In the third period, Army drove from its 19-yard line to the Navy 27 before the Middies held on three successive thrusts into the line. On fourth down, Dave Aucoin kicked a 27-yard field goal to tie the game at 3–3. And so it ended, with the Army defense stopping

Joe Gattuso, Jr., running wild in 1976, scoring 3 touchdowns to help Navy beat Army 38–10, while his father, Joe Gattuso, Sr. (right, during his own playing days as a Navy back, 1953), watches from the stands.

the Navy attack time after time, as it had throughout the game.

In the locker room afterward, Army's second-year coach Ed Cavanaugh said, "Somebody, some general, said it was a moral victory for us. But I don't like that. Way I look at it, Navy didn't win the game."

"Tomorrow it'll feel like a win," said Gerry Walker, Army's star halfback, who had had to leave the game in the second quarter because of an injury to his leg. "A tie never feels like a win when the game is over. We should have won this game."

Walker's absence and the benching of Army's quarterback Bryan Allem after a poor first quarter made Army's performance, especially their defense, all the more remarkable.

The tie game, the first since the 7–7 standoff in 1965, was the seventh in the series, which Navy now led 38–37. This was also the first game without a touchdown since Navy won 3–0 in 1934.

The eighty-third meeting between Army and Navy in 1982 was played in some of the most

delightful weather conditions in the history of the series. It was the warmest, sunniest day for an Army-Navy game since World War II, with the temperature reaching 70 degrees late the first half.

By that time Army had already given up 10 points on several errors. It was a poor start for the Cadets against a great Middie defensive team that took every advantage.

The first big break of the game came on the fourth play, when the Middies, after receiving the Army kickoff, failed to net a first down. Navy's kicker, Mark Colby, punted and the ball zoomed high into the air. Army's punt returner, Dee Brant, watched as the ball soared over his head. But instead of letting the ball go, he spun around and tried to catch the high-flying pigskin while racing into the end zone. The ball hit his hand, flew off, and Rick Pagel of Navy recovered it on the 8-yard line. Pagel, a fine defensive end, would go on to make several extraordinary plays, including eight tackles in the game, three of which knocked Army backs for a total loss of 17 yards.

On third down, Navy's flash back, Napoleon McCallum, smashed off tackle for the touch-

Navy's two-time All-American, Napoleon McCallum, about to be brought down after a 22-yard gain in the 1985 game, won by Navy 17–7. McCallum carried the ball forty-one times for 217 yards to end his glorious career as the NCAA's leading all-purpose runner with a total of 7,172 yards.

down. Billy Solomon kicked the extra point, and it was Navy 7, Army 0.

Army had not yet run a play. On the third play after the ensuing kickoff, the Cadets' quarterback Dick Laughlin tried a high floating pass to his end. But the ball was intercepted by Navy's roving back, Brian Cianella, who ran it back 15 yards to the Army 15.

Now the Army defense rose up and stopped Navy in its tracks. Three times Navy backs pounded at the Army line, but every time the Cadets turned them back without giving up any ground. Then on fourth down, Solomon dropped back to the 25-yard line and kicked a 3-pointer to give Navy a 10–0 lead.

Late in the second period, Army recovered a Navy fumble on the Navy 15-yard line, and on the third play of the series, Laughlin smacked across the goal line from the 4-yard line to give Army its only score of the day.

McCallum keyed two fine Navy drives in the third period, as halfbacks Rick Williamson and then Jim Scannell scored touchdowns to give the Middies a 24–7 triumph. But it was Napoleon who pounded the guards and tackles for 3, 4, or 5 needed yards.

Even before the final whistle, Army's coach Ed Cavanaugh walked slowly and all alone to the Army dressing room, to be followed fully five minutes later by his team coming in from the field. It was the third losing Army season under Cavanaugh, and the game marked three years without a victory over Navy. For a West Point coach, it was unforgivable.

Cavanaugh, whose contract expired at the end of the season, said he was realistic about his future. In three years under his direction, the Army football team had won but ten games, but the sorest spot was no victories over Navy.

On the other hand, Navy was thrilled with their easy victory before a crowd of more than 67,000 spectators at Veterans Stadium, particularly so since the Middies were under a new coach, Gary Tranquil, and had completed a winning season by virtue of their win over Army. Their record stood at 6 and 5.

Three weeks after the football season ended,

Coach Ed Cavanaugh was informed that his contract was not going to be renewed.

December is usually the month when football coaches are plotting and planning their annual recruiting visits. At West Point, Army officials were looking not for players but for a new football coach—a big-time coach, they thought, who would have the patience and knowledge and background to reverse the fortunes of the Army football program, so dismally moribund since 1966, when Tom Cahill took over and gave the Cadets several winning seasons.

Along came Jim Young, forty-seven years of age and with a fine record at Purdue, where he had guided the Boilermakers to a five-year, 38–19–1 record, played in three bowl games, and always had his team in contention for Big Ten honors.

So Jim Young succeeded Ed Cavanaugh and promised at a press conference in New York: "We have some plebes here who look very good. They're not quite ready to start games, but they'll play and Army will win again. This place has a tradition of winning football games, and I'm here and I'm going to do my level best to carry on that great tradition."

However, 1983 was to be a year of frustration, of tears and hopes and struggle. It was a year which saw the Cadets under their new coach win but 2 of 10 games, including 5 losses in a row just prior to the Navy game.

It took all of Coach Young's ability and experience to rebuild and instill the confidence needed for the big battle against Navy, a team with a similar losing season.

Arrangements had been made between Army and Navy officials and the city of Pasadena and its Chamber of Commerce to have the 1983 Army-Navy game played at the site of the Rose Bowl, and when all financial arrangements were at last finalized, and plans for housing and transporting the players and some ten thousand Cadets and Middies to the game site were resolved, the game was set for November 25.

It was the first Army-Navy game to be played west of Chicago since the series started in 1890. It was also the eighty-fourth game in the celebrated rivalry, with Navy leading with 40 wins to 37 for Army, and 7 ties. Since 1972, Navy had won 8, lost 2, and tied 1 game.

By game time, with all of the usual pageantry that is part of the annual game over and done with, a crowd of more than 81,000 West Coast aficionados sat back for the start of what promised to be a bitter contest. For both teams desperately wanted a victory to climax their season.

Army kicked off, and seventeen seconds later Navy led, 7–0. After two minutes, thirty seconds, Navy had a 14–0 lead. After three minutes, fifty-seven seconds, Navy was out in front by 21–0.

It was the most incredible game-opening three minutes in all of the eighty-four years of Army-Navy football, and the big crowd, up on their feet since the kickoff, cheered and cheered. Navy was magnificent.

The game did become competitive after that incredible opening assault, but Army had much too much ground to make up, and Navy easily won the game, 42–13. The score was a tribute more to the Middies' opportunism and to the explosiveness of a couple of Navy backs than to all-around team superiority.

Each team took the field for this final game of the season with a 2–8 record, but Navy was the favorite mainly because of its tailback Napoleon McCallum, the national leader in all-purpose rushing. On this day, McCallum had his greatest rushing performance of the season, as he carried the ball thirty times for 182 yards and one touchdown, even with Army keying two, often three, defenders to tail McCallum on every play.

On the opening play of the game, Army kicked off to McCallum on the 5-yard line. Just as he was hit by an Army tackler, McCallum flipped a lateral pass to halfback Eric Wallace. It was a play Navy coach Gary Tranquil had worked on and decided to use just before the kickoff.

Wallace took the ball, cut to the sidelines, outran the last Army defender on the 30-yard line, and sped 95 yards to a touchdown, with the Rose Bowl crowd up on their feet cheering his every yard.

It was the longest kickoff return in Navy history, and the only time that an opening kickoff had been run back for a touchdown.

Navy then kicked off to Army and halfback Elton Akins fumbled the ball. Andy Ponsiego recovered for Navy on the Army 17-yard line. Three plays picked up a couple of yards to the 15. Then McCallum swept around his own right end for another touchdown and it was 14–0, Navy.

Army took the kickoff once more and began to move upfield. Two plays failed to gain and then quarterback Rob Healy threw a pass intended for end Scott Spellmon. But cornerback Steve Brady of Navy intercepted on the Army 35 and dashed 65 yards, aided by marvelous interference, for the third Navy touchdown.

"Those first four minutes probably were the worst four minutes I have ever experienced in all my years of coaching," said Jim Young. "What happened then took us out of the game and took away a lot of our steam and momentum."

But Army was far from through. McCallum fumbled the ball on a line buck, and after Army recovered, Craig Stopa promptly kicked a field goal. An exchange of downs followed, and Army picked up the pace to move the ball to the Navy 25-yard line, where again Stopa booted a field goal. Now Navy's lead had been cut to 21–6.

Army punted to Navy, and when a Navy receiver fumbled the ball, Army recovered and promptly drove in for a touchdown. Now it was 21–13 and Army was right back in the game.

But in the fourth period Navy's quarterback Rick Williamson sparked two touchdown drives: the first on a 54-yard march, the second going 77 yards. And in the final two minutes, Ponsiego intercepted a pass and sprinted 30 yards for the final Navy score to give the Middies a 42–13 victory.

Coming Back: 1984-88

Carl Ullrich, Army's director of athletics, hadn't bid a normal good-bye to anyone for over a week. Instead, when visitors left his office at the Academy at West Point, Ullrich looked them right in the eye, gripped his visitor's hand, and slowly uttered two words: "BEAT NAVY."

Ullrich's enthusiasm in November of 1984 was reflected in the stickers pasted all around the campus imploring the Cadets to MOP UP THE SWABBIES, and in the assignment of two rugged military policemen to stand guard over Army's four mascot mules. But few people expected the Cadets to defeat Navy this year, for by now the Middies had won five of the last seven games between the two rivals.

Coach Jim Young had spent an entire year trying to solve Army's problems. In past seasons, those problems had been magnified against such Class A teams as Pittsburgh, Notre Dame, Syracuse, Boston College, and Michigan State, teams that had any number of huge players, many 6 feet 4 and 6 feet 5, and weighing as much as 260 and 270 pounds. It was impossible for the smaller and much lighter Army players to contend with such behemoth teams.

But this year the opponents would be more Army's size, and to take advantage of that, Young decided to scrap his pro-style offense and to copy the wishbone offense that the Air Force Academy had adopted and had been using successfully.

The wishbone depended on lightning reflexes, fast-moving, fast-thinking running backs, and quarterbacks who could think and act instinctively.

The result was Army's greatest season since 1966, when Tom Cahill won 8 and lost 2 games.

Utilizing the wishbone offense, Army won over Colgate, tied a strong Tennessee team, beat Duke, Harvard, Penn, Air Force, Boston College, and Montana. Games were lost to Rutgers and Syracuse.

Essentially, Young used two key players to make the wishbone work—Nate Sassaman at quarterback and Doug Black at fullback. The result was better than expected as Army actually led the nation in rushing offense.

Sassaman, who had played most of the season in the defensive backfield, faced Navy with three cracked ribs. "But that's okay," said Sassaman, "it only hurts me when I breathe a lot."

Black, a junior who had developed into the Cadets' leading ground gainer, had been dropped from the varsity two years ago, but in 1983 Young brought him back to be the pile driver in the wishbone.

In just the second game of the year, Navy

had suffered a mortal blow to its hopes when All-American Napoleon McCallum, leading rusher in the nation at the time, incurred a broken foot and was sidelined. Then Bill Byrne, a sophomore quarterback with a flame-throwing arm, was also sidelined because of a foot injury. Thus Army and Navy faced each other with both teams beset by injuries to star players.

The Army offense started to move after an initial exchange of downs. Navy punted and Army, after receiving the ball on their 20-yard line, began to move upfield.

In just eight plays the hyped-up Cadets—blocking and carrying out their offensive assignments perfectly—slammed to the Navy 40-yard line. Here, with fourth down and 1 yard to go for a first down, Coach Young ordered, "Go for it." Black did just that. The tough Army fullback plowed through the Navy

Navy halfback Clarence Jones starred in all three of his Army-Navy games—1984–86.

tackle for a 5-yard gain and the first down. Army seemed to be in command.

Then Sassaman faded to his left, pitched a pass to halfback Clarence Jones, and Jones caught the ball on his fingertips and sprinted in for the Army touchdown. The kick was good and Army had a 7–0 lead.

The next time they had the ball, Army came right back. Starting on their own 29-yard line and led by Sassaman, cracked ribs and all, the Cadets moved in sixteen plays to the Navy 3-yard line. Here Black tore through the center of the line and into the end zone for Army's second score. Now it was Army 14, Navy 0.

Near the end of the second period, Bob Misch, Navy's sophomore quarterback, who had engineered Navy's big upset win over South Carolina two weeks prior to the Army game, began to hit his targets with beautifully thrown passes. He moved Navy to the Cadets' 14-yard line. Then, on third down, Misch was tackled by Jim Gentile, and Navy was forced to settle for a field goal, a 40-yarder by Todd Solomon. The score was Army 14, Navy 3 as the half ended.

As the third period began, Navy battled back furiously, but on two occasions, deep in Army territory, the Cadets' stubborn defense halted a Navy drive.

Then another Navy drive was barely getting under way when Bob Misch completed a 35-yard pass to end Mark Stevens. Stevens was hit so hard by cornerback Kevin McKelvy that he fumbled the ball, which bounced far back into the end zone where Eric Griffin of Army fell on the ball for Army's third touchdown.

In the final quarter, Sassaman, once again bearing the brunt of the attack in the wishbone option, engineered another Army drive to the Navy 8-yard line in a series of running and pass plays. From there the resourceful Sassaman dashed into the end zone and Army had a 28–11 victory.

After the game, Coach Jim Young said: "What we've done this season wouldn't have meant a thing if we hadn't won this game. But after those first two drives gave us two touch-

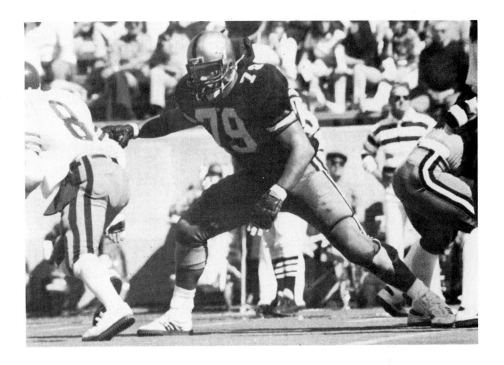

Don Smith, Army's All-American guard in 1986, in action against Navy in the 1985 game.

downs, we had the confidence and knew we could do it."

The victory over Navy gave Coach Jim Young and his Army team its first winning season in seven years (a 7–3–1 record), its first win over Navy since 1977, and its first bowl appearance ever, versus Michigan State in the Cherry Bowl. Army won that game too, 10–6, to end a most successful year.

It was in the Central Highlands of Vietnam that Rollie Stichweh came to realize just how important the Army-Navy football game could be to people from either of the two academies.

In 1964, Rollie had been the star quarterback of the Army team that had defeated Roger Staubach, after five straight losses to Navy. Three years later he was an officer in Vietnam, right on the border of Laos and Cambodia, in a terrible war getting worse every day.

As Stichweh recalls: "You were in a whole different world. Most of the time you were fighting boredom. Then all of a sudden it was life and death.

"When the Army-Navy game came around

in November, you became very cognizant of it. The game gave you an anchor, it focused your thinking, you felt like a participant."

Yet his memories of "the big game" operated as more than merely a diversion from the life-and-death reality around him in battle.

"When I was playing football at West Point, I sensed I was experiencing an important moment in my life. People were quite overt about it. I was the quarterback of the Army team, and the game naturally focused on the quarterback. People expected the quarterback to execute, and also provide leadership."

Yes, at West Point they take leadership seriously. People would come up to Rollie Stichweh and say, "We're counting on you . . . it's up to you, Rollie . . . this is our last chance."

Stichweh remembers the intensity of the big game for the Cadets, and not just in terms of the game itself.

"I hesitate to use the word 'hatred,' " he said, "but Navy dominates your thinking all year round as a member of the team. In the week prior to the game, it is a minute-by-minute event. Professors refer to it. Officers talk about it day and night. Physically, you are aware of the 'Beat Navy' banners, hanging everywhere. Every night for a week there is a pep rally, and they ask you to say a few words about the team and game.

"The feeling for Navy is very, very strong. It is a long eleven-plus months if you lose."

The 1985 game reminded Rollie of that feeling. In his junior year, Navy was ranked second in the nation, but was leading Army by only a 21–15 score as Stichweh moved Army to the 1-yard line in the closing seconds. But the game ended as he tried to ask an official to call time out because the players on his team could not hear his signals.

"I'll never, ever forget our captain, Dick Nowak, coming up to me," Stichweh said, "tears in his eyes, the whole melodrama, saying, 'Rollie, we never beat them the whole time I was here.' "

Although he has not attended a game in several years, Rollie said he has always arranged to watch the game on television, rooting as always for Army to beat Navy, just as he rooted in 1967 from a far-off place called Vietnam, and just as he rooted for them eighteen years

later in a game that so reminded him of his own great but losing battle in 1963.

And in 1985, Don Smith, Army's first All-American in seventeen years, knew exactly how Rollie Stichweh felt when Army lost to Navy that day twenty-two years ago, for in the biggest game of Smith's life against Army's bitterest rival, the Cadets lost to Navy by 17–7.

Smith had tasted the sweetness of victory the year before when Army pasted Navy, 28–11. That the Cadets would lose this day was a thought that had never entered his mind. And he didn't know it could hurt so much.

He sat all alone, in front of his locker, a few minutes after the final clock ticked off the seconds to end the game, his head buried in his hands. Occasionally he brushed away a tear from eyes that were red and swollen.

"This is the kind of loss where you don't want to hear anything from anybody. You just want to be left alone until it gets better . . . if it gets better. You just have to swallow it."

On paper, Navy wasn't supposed to win this game.

They had entered the game with a 3–7 rec-

Craig Stopa, one of the greatest kickers in Army's history. Stopa led the Cadets in scoring in each of his four years (1983–86), finishing with 250 career points and five field goals of 50 yards or more. He also holds the Army record of sixty-one straight points after touchdown.

ord, facing the reality that this would be another losing season for them.

It was a different scenario on the other side. Another winning season for the Cadets was guaranteed, with a marvelous week-long trip to Atlanta to face Illinois in the Peach Bowl at its end.

Each team scored on its first possession.

Navy had Napoleon McCallum driving over and around the Army line. In nine carries McCallum gained 45 yards, his final one taking the ball to the Army 13-yard line. Then Bob Misch, Navy's quarterback, tossed a pass to Troy Saunders and Saunders went in for the score. Solomon made the extra point and it was 7–0, Navy.

Navy's kickoff was taken by halfback Clarence Jones, who sprinted 61 yards, only to be brought down from behind by a Navy tackler. In the next eight plays, Army drove to the 10-yard line. Here it was up to Jones, and the big halfback cracked through the Navy line for 10 yards and a touchdown.

Craig Stopa booted his sixty-first consecutive extra point and it was a 7–7 game.

There were numerous scoring opportunities for both teams in the second and third quarters.

The first such drive started with Army's quarterback Rob Healy tossing a "perfect strike" to tight end Rob Dockeron. The play gained 35 yards and brought Army to the Navy 42. Eight plays later, Army was on the 2-yard line and might have had the game in their hands . . . if they could get the final 2 yards. They never got them as a tough Navy defense stopped Army's backs and forced the Cadets to give up the ball.

Again after an exchange of kicks, Army drove down the field and once again reached the 30-yard line. Then Stopa, who seldom missed a place kick, was short on a 37-yard field-goal attempt. It was the last time Army would be in position for a possible score.

In the fourth quarter Navy drove 77 yards with McCallum and fullback Chuck Smith churning out first downs to the Army 5-yard line. Then it was Smith bursting through right guard for the touchdown. Solomon kicked the

extra point and Navy had broken the tie. Now it was 14–7, Navy.

On their next possession, the Middies, with Napoleon leading the way, moved from their own 33 to the Army 23-yard line. Army stopped them on the next three plays, but on fourth down Solomon dropped back and kicked a 26-yard field goal to give Navy a hard-earned 17–7 victory.

Junior fullback Dave Marks—cut from Army's varsity roster a year ago, back on the varsity this year just in time for the Navy game—played the game of his life. In the second half of the game, Marks took the opening kickoff, eluded several Navy tacklers, and sprinted 44 yards to the Navy 44-yard line. Marks's run set the stage for the first Army touchdown.

Junior quarterback Tory Crawford also had his wish come true, as he became only the sixth player in the history of Army football to rush for 1,000 yards in a single season, with his 115 yards in the Navy game putting him over the mark.

Senior linebacker Dave Scheyer, who was playing his first game in two months against Navy, was the defensive star of the game with fifteen tackles.

And Army's sophomore place-kicking star, Keith Walker, getting his first chance to kick in a Navy game, booted two 24-yarders in the first half, giving the Cadets a 6–0 lead which they never relinquished.

These were but a few of the Army heroes who played key roles in making this December 6, 1986, a day to remember. For on this very sunny, warm afternoon in Philadelphia, the Cadets sank the Navy fleet, 27–7 before a crowd of more than 71,000 spectators at Veterans Stadium.

With this win, Army had a final 6–5 season, assuring the Cadets of their third winning season in a row for the first time since the Tom Cahill teams of 1966, 1967, and 1968, which rang up a 23–7 total.

The game opened with Army kicking off to Navy. On the very first play from scrimmage,

Left: *Army quarterback Tory Crawford on a rollout against Navy in 1986. Crawford led the Cadets to a 27–7 victory by rushing for 94 yards.* Above: *The head coach, Jim Young, is tired but jubilant after his first victory over the Middies in four tries.*

tailback Tony Hollinger, attempting to skirt his own right end, was hit hard by two Army tacklers and the ball popped out of his hands. Cornerback Bill Sanders and defensive back Bill Horton of Army pounced on the ball.

Quick to take advantage of the recovery, Army put together a series of fine running plays that advanced the ball to the Navy 10-yard line. Here the Middies held for three downs. On fourth down, Keith Walker kicked a field goal to give Army a 3–0 lead.

The next time Army got the ball, they advanced upfield on a series of cross bucks and off-tackle plays, mixed in with two short passes, to reach the Navy 7-yard line. Three times Army pounded the Navy forward wall, but the Middies fought back and held them.

Once again Keith Walker dropped back to the 27-yard line on fourth down and kicked a perfect field goal, and it was 6–0 Army.

Navy did advance the ball to midfield on two separate occasions, but Army fought them off and took over the ball on downs on each occasion.

In the third period, the Army offense shifted into high as Marks returned the Navy kickoff 35 yards to midfield. Then it was Clarence Jones, Andy Peterson, and Ben Wright smashing the Navy line for successive first downs. On a third-down play, Tory Crawford fumbled the ball, but Wright recovered for Army on the Navy 3-yard line, and Peterson bulled his way in for an Army touchdown. The kick was blocked and Army had a 13–0 lead.

But Navy responded with a drive of their own as halfback Don Hall led the Middies in a fourteen-play series that gained more than 71 yards and brought Navy to the Army 4-yard line. In a final burst, Hall broke through left guard and scored Navy's first touchdown. The

Dave Scheyer, who wound up his four-year career with Army in 1987 as one of its most outstanding linebackers of modern times. Scheyer was credited with fifteen tackles in the 1986 game against Navy.

conversion was good and it was 13–7, Army.

On the following kickoff, Army marched 79 yards, with Tory Crawford banging in from the 4-yard line to give Army a 19–7 lead. The kick was good and it was 20–7.

Navy failed to gain after receiving the kickoff, and Army took over on their 45-yard line. Then, at the end of a series of eight plays, halfback Clarence Jones smashed in from the Navy 5-yard line. Walker kicked his third extra point and it was 27–7 Army.

Late in the final period, with just three minutes to play, quarterback Bob Misch of Navy engineered a drive that had the Middies inside the 5-yard line. But Hollinger on two tries at the Army line was held to a 1-yard gain. Then Misch tried two successive passes, both failed, and Army took over the ball on downs as the game ended.

In the locker room after the game, Coach

Jim Young, looking back on his 6–5 season, said: "We weren't a very good team in the middle of the year, but we hung in there and improved as we had to. Today we were right on the ball."

The 1987 game was a classic case of conventional warfare, except that the battle fatigues and foxholes and ammunition were missing.

And for the Middies, so were the offensive weapons.

Army used a pair of second-half touchdowns and an airtight defense to march off with a 17–3 victory in the eighty-eighth renewal of the Army-Navy classic at Veterans Stadium before a crowd of 68,000 spectators.

The victory over Navy was the Cadets' second in a row for Jim Young, the Army coach in his third year. As for the beleaguered Middies, the game completed their first season under Coach Elliot Uzelac without defeating a single division 1-A team.

The game proved to be a case of brute Army strength, patience, and persistence, with each team giving ground begrudgingly.

Army simply had more of everything.

It was not the most exciting game in the long history of these two ancient rivals, but then both teams utilized the wishbone offense, which eschews the pass and rarely scores points for spectacular plays.

"When you use the wishbone," said Army's slippery, hipper-dipper quarterback Tory Crawford, "you've got to keep pounding the enemy until something gives. It takes an awful lot of patience, but if you stay with it and keep doing the right things, you'll get that ball across the line."

But it wasn't until the second half of the game, with Army out in front 3–0 as a result of Bit Rambusch's 40-yard field goal, that Army started to move the ball inside the tackles, rather than try to cut the corners as they had been doing.

The strategy paid off as freshman halfback Mike Mayweather bounced in and around and through the middle of the Navy line for 119 yards on twenty-five carries, while Ben Barnett picked up 78 yards and Peterson 71 yards.

"We just couldn't get started in the first half," said Mayweather, "and I don't know why. I was so darn nervous about playing in my first Army-Navy game that my head was actually spinning."

"There was nothing special, nothing fancy, about the Army offense," said Coach Jim Young. "Our ability to block on the inside in the second half was the key to the ball game."

The win was Army's third over the Middies in the last four games and narrowed Navy's winning margin in the series to 41–40.

As the game began, Army kicked to Navy, but the Middies failed to make a first down and had to punt. Army then took possession and drove upfield for 47 yards, with Tory Crawford and Mike Mayweather carrying the brunt of the action. Navy halted Army's drive on the 23-yard line, and Rambusch kicked a field goal from the 40.

Neither team scored until the fourth period, when Army pounded out one first down after another, to the Navy line in an 81-yard advance, and then Peterson took a pitch from Crawford to dash around left end for an Army touchdown. The kick by Rambusch was good, and Army was out in front by a 10–0 margin.

Navy received the kickoff after the Army touchdown and began their only and longest drive of the day. Starting at their 6-yard line, the Middies, with quarterback Alton Grizzard passing off to John Neuman and Bob Hughes, gained a first down on the Army 13-yard line. But the Middies were held by a stubborn Army defense at this point and had to settle for a field goal by Ted Fundoukos from the 30-yard line.

With just five minutes remaining in the game, and Army in the lead, 10–3, Navy kicked off to the Cadets and Johnny Barth brought the ball 13 yards upfield. Then it was Mayweather for 14 yards and Barnett cracking inside the Navy line on the option play for 14 yards. At this point, everyone in the Army backfield got a chance to carry the ball. Mayweather, then Barnett, then Peterson slammed into the Navy line for 3, 4, and 5 yards.

The ball was on the Navy 10-yard line and there were just forty-two seconds left to play.

Crawford, playing his final game for the Cadets, and on the final play of the game, took the snap, crossed to his right, and sped across the goal line for one of the greatest touchdowns of his career.

"I can't imagine a better way to end it than on a touchdown like this," said Crawford in the locker room. "I know I'll remember this day for the rest of my life. This is as sweet as it comes."

Opposite page: *The Commander-in-Chief's Trophy, presented to the winner of each year's service academy football games. Army received the trophy for both 1987 and 1988.*

— ★ —

The Notre Dame football team had Knute Rockne and the legendary George Gipp to inspire them, and Army has General Douglas MacArthur.

For the game against Navy on December 3, 1988, Army football coach Jim Young dredged up an old MacArthur fight talk to inspire his team. The general's speech had been recorded before a 1958 Army-Navy game, and the Cadets had come away from that meeting with the general "fighting mad" and defeated top-rated Navy, 22–6.

In the speech, MacArthur talked of difficult battles and how to "outsmart and outfight the enemy," and he talked of pleasant thoughts about his days at West Point.

Young used one more motivation idea, ordering the players to wear shoulder patches that represented the Army's eighteen fighting divisions.

"Coach wanted us to realize we were playing for the entire Army," said guard Bill Gebhards. "This always represents a last game for the seniors, even though we were going to the Sun Bowl this year. None of us around here are going to be professional football players. We're going to be professional soldiers."

But for Navy there would be defeat, tears, frustration, and pain, as the Middies came up just short against Army for the third straight year, losing a hard-fought battle 20–15. It was a well-played game, with no holds barred. The blocking and tackling were so sharp and savage that spectators up in the stands cringed when a player was knocked down, and in a few instances down and out. One player was carried off the field on the opening kickoff, another player wobbled off the field with some help; linebacker Mark Pimpo, who played almost an entire game despite a bruised knee, reinjured his knee and limped off, and quarterback Alton Grizzard staggered around in the backfield after being blindsided on a couple of plays. But it was good, clean, hard football.

Yet all of the grit wasn't enough. Navy scored the last touchdown of the game, but it was Army who came away with a brilliant 20–15 victory.

For Army, 9–2 in the season and bound for a date with Alabama in the Sun Bowl, these days may well be the best of times since the glory days of Doc Blanchard and Glenn Davis. The nine victories in a season are the most for the Cadets, who clinched the Commander-in-Chief's Trophy by defeating Navy.

Early in the game Navy showed that Army would have no picnic that day. The Middies put their trust in Alton Grizzard, the sophomore wishbone quarterback, and he proved worthy of that trust. In the first half Grizzard directed an offense that managed to get close enough to the goal line for Ted Foundoukos to boot a 44-yard field goal that gave the Middies a 3–0 lead.

But Navy seemed unable to handle the prosperity.

Army promptly drove downfield some 63 yards in sixteen plays, then fullback Ben Barnett smashed in for Army's first touchdown.

Navy then drove down to the Army 35-yard line on a series of well-executed rollouts, with Grizzard carrying the ball, and it was here that Army made its stand of the day. Navy could not move the ball in three attempts, so Foundoukos kicked his second field goal, this one for 35 yards. The score was now 7–6, Army.

With only three and a half minutes remaining in the half, Army began its big drive. Calvin Cass spun off on the option play and threaded his way for 30 yards before he was tackled. Then McWilliams blasted through the line for 11 more. Here Navy stiffened and held, and Army's Keith Walker kicked a 22-yard field goal. At the half Army led 10–6.

In the third period both teams traded field goals, and it seemed as though the Middies would be able to stop the Army attack, which had been so successful in the first half. The third period ended with Army still out in front, but only with a 13–9 lead and Navy on the move.

But then the Cadets held Navy on a fourth-and-two play and took possession of the ball.

With quarterback Bryan McWilliams carrying the brunt of the attack, the Cadets then drove 60 yards in twelve plays, the last a smash across the goal line from the 2-yard stripe. Now Army had widened its lead to 20–9.

With less than just two minutes to play, Navy came right back, driving upfield as Grizzard completed two consecutive passes for the first time in the game. Then Jim Bradley smashed across the Army line for a touchdown, and it began to have the feel of another Army-Navy thriller, down to the very last moment.

The score was Army 20, Navy 15.

Grizzard then tried for a 2-point play after the touchdown, but missed his target, and an attempted onside kick was recovered by Army. So the game ended with the ball in midfield and a stubborn, hard-driving Navy team just caught short.

"It was a real hard-fought game, but we weren't quite good enough," said Navy coach Elliot Uzelac. "But mark my words, we'll get 'em next year."

Appendix

Major Army-Navy Records

STATISTICS AND HIGHLIGHTS
(1890 to present)

INDIVIDUAL RECORDS
★

Single Game

TOTAL OFFENSE
Most rushing and passing plays
 N—50, John Cartwright, 1965
 A—44, Richard Atha, 1970
Most rushing and passing yards gained
 N—278, Eddie Meyers, 1979
 A—209, Richard Atha, 1970

RUSHING
Most carries
 N—42, Eddie Meyers, 1979
 A—40, Lynn Moore, 1969
Most yards gained
 N—278, Eddie Meyers, 1979
 A—206, Lynn Moore, 1969

FORWARD PASSING
Most passes attempted
 N—39, Bob Misch, 1984
 A—36, Earle Mulrane, 1978
Most passes completed
 N—22, Bob Misch, 1984
 A—16, Earle Mulrane, 1978

 A—16, Bill Turner, 1983
Most yards gained
 N—280, Bob Misch, 1984
 A—190, Earle Mulrane, 1978
Most touchdown passes
 N—3, George Welsh, 1954
 A—2 by 4 players (most recent, Kingsley
 Fink, 1971)
Most passes intercepted
 N—4, Tom Hamilton, 1924; Tom Forrestal,
 1957
 A—4, Bob Blaik, 1950; Richard Atha,
 1970

PASS RECEIVING
Most passes caught
 N—10, Mike Clark, 1967
 A—6 by 4 players (most recent, Rob
 Dickerson, 1983)
Most yards gained
 A—115, Lou Merillat, 1914
 N—113, Mike Clark, 1967
Most touchdown passes
 N—2, Earle Smith, 1954
 A—2, Lou Merillat, 1913

INTERCEPTION RETURNS
Most passes intercepted
  N—4, Mark Shickner, 1970
  A—2, by 7 players (most recent, John Hilliard, 1977)

Long Plays

RUSHING
  A—92, Rip Rowan, 1947
  A—92, Bobby Vinson, 1949
  N—60, Ralph Strassburger, 1902

PASSING
  N—65, Roger Staubach-Nick Markoff, 1962*
  A—63, Jim O'Toole-Joe Albano, 1968*

INTERCEPTIONS
  N—100, John Raster 1951
  A—63, Jerry Lodge, 1953*

SCORING
Most points scored
  N—20, Charles Emrich, 1890
  A—18, by 7 players (most recent, Charlie Jarvis, 1968)
Most touchdowns
  N—4, Charles Emrich, 1890
  A—3, by 7 players (most recent, Charlie Jarvis, 1968)
Most extra points kicked
  N—6, Steve Young, 1983
  N—6, Ned Snyder, 1951
  A—4, Dennis Michie, 1891; Whitey Grove, 1935
Most 2-points attempts scored
  N—2, George Bezek, 1951
  A—1, by 5 players (most recent, John Simar, 1971)
Most field goal attempts
  A—8, Ed Garbisch, 1924
  N—7, Jack Dalton, 1910
Most field goals made
  A—4, Ed Garbisch, 1924
  N—4, Steve Fehr, 1980

*Did not score.

Most points scored by kicking
  N—15, Steve Fehr, 1980 (4 FG, 3 PAT)
  A—12, Ed Garbisch, 1924 (4 FG)

PUNTS
  A—79, Joe Sartiano, 1981
  N—77, Bill Busik, 1941

PUNT RETURNS
  A—81, Paul Johnson, 1933
  N—44, Ned Oldham, 1957

KICKOFF RETURNS
  A—96, Charles Daly, 1901
  N—95, Eric Wallace, 1983

FIELD GOALS
  N—50, Steve Fehr, 1980
  A—45, Ed Garbisch, 1922

PUNTING
Most punts
  N—17, Earnest Von Heimburg, 1915
  A—14, Jack Buckler, 1933
Highest average per punt (min. 5 punts)
  A—57.6, Joe Sartiano, 1981
  N—44.8, Bill Clark, 1932

PUNT RETURNS
Most punt returns
  A—11, Elmer Oliphant, 1915
  N—8, Carlyle Craig, 1915; Sneed Schmidt, 1935
Most yards returned
  A—129, George Smythe, 1922
  N—87, Larry Becht, 1933
Highest average per return (min. 3 returns)
  N—20.25, Phil McConkey, 1976
  A—20.0, Paul Johnson, 1933

KICKOFF RETURNS
Most kickoff returns
  A—5, Travis Jackson, 1983
  A—5, Devon Maness, 1976
  N—4, by 4 players (most recent, Eric Wallace, 1984)

Most yards returned
A—105, Jeff Washington, 1975
A—100, Charlie Daly, 1901
N—95, Eric Wallace, 1963
N—95, Carlyle Craig, 1915

Highest average per return (min. 2 returns)
N—35.0, Sneed Schmidt, 1935
A—30.0, Clarence Jones, 1965

INDIVIDUAL RECORDS

Career

TOTAL OFFENSE
Most rushing and passing plays
N—128, John Cartwright, 1965-67
A—97, Leamon Hall, 1974-77
Most rushing and passing yards gained
N—547, Eddie Meyers, 1978-81
A—359, Glenn Davis, 1943-46

RUSHING
Most carries
N—105, Eddie Meyers, 1978-81
A—66, Pat Uebel, 1953-55; Greg King, 1975-77
Most yards gained
N—547, Eddie Meyers, 1978-81
A—295, Pat Uebel, 1953-55
Highest average gain, per carry (min. 30 rushes)
A—5.8, Glenn Davis, 1943-46
N—5.4, Gerry Goodwin, 1974-75

FORWARD PASSING
Most passes attempted
N—89, John Cartwright, 1965-67
A—70, Leamon Hall, 1974-77
Most passes completed
N—49, John Cartwright, 1965-67
A—26, Leamon Hall, 1974-77
Most yards gained
N—537, John Cartwright, 1965-67
A—338, Leamon Hall, 1974-77
Most touchdown passes
N—4, Bob Leszczynski, 1976-78
A—3, Vern Prichard, 1912-14
Most passes had intercepted
N—8, Tom Hamilton, 1924-26
A—7, Leamon Hall, 1974-77

PASS RECEIVING
Most passes caught
N—16, Rob Taylor, 1965-67
A—11, Joe Albano, 1968-70
Most yards gained
N—216, Rob Taylor, 1965-67
A—200, Joe Albano, 1968-70
Most touchdown passes
A—3, Lou Merillat, 1913-14
N—2, Earle Smith, 1954-56

PUNTING
Most punts
A—36, Bill Wood, 1921-24
N—33, Bill Clark, 1932-34
Highest average per punt (min. 15)
A—42.6, Joe Sartiano, 1980-83
N—38.6, Dave Church, 1965-66

SCORING
Most points scored
A—36, Doc Blanchard, 1944-46
N—32, Bob Jackson, 1973-75
Most touchdowns
A—6, Doc Blanchard, 1944-46
N—5, Joe Bellino, 1958-60; Bob Jackson, 1973-75
Most extra points made
N—11, Bob Tata, 1976-78
A—7, Arden Jensen, 1968-70
Most 2-point attempts scored
N—2, George Bezek, 1958-59
A—1, by 5 players (most recent: John Simar, 1971

PLACEKICKING
Most career points kicking
N—25, Steve Fehr, 1979-81 (7 PAT, 6 FG)
A—16, Ed Garbisch, 1921-24 (1 PAT, 5 FG)

Most career field goals attempted
    A—11, Ed Garbisch, 1921–24
    N—8, Jack Dalton, 1910–11
Most field goals made career
    A—6, Steve Fehr, 1979–81
    N—5, Ed Garbisch, 1921–24

INTERCEPTIONS
Most passes intercepted
    N—4, Mark Schickner, 1970
    A—3, Bill Wood, 1921–24; Charles Long,
    1936–38

KICKOFF RETURNS
Most yards returned
    A—199, Ken Waldrop, 1961–63
    N—146, Napoleon McCallum, 1981–85

Highest average per return (min. 4)
    A—26.0, Pat Uebel, 1953–56
    N—26.3, Joe Bellino, 1958–60

PUNT RETURNS
Most yards returned
    A—148, Elmer Oliphant, 1914–16; George
    Smythe, 1920–23
    N—134, Hal Hamberg, 1942–44
Highest average per return (min. 6)
    N—15.7, Phil McConkey, 1975–77
    A—12.3, George Smythe, 1920–23

TEAM RECORDS
★

Single Game

TOTAL OFFENSE
Most rushing and passing plays
    A—97 (1969)
    N—89 (1967, 1980)
Most rushing and passing yardage
    A—506 (1969)
    N—460 (1973)
Fewest rushing and passing plays
    A—18 (1919)
    N—43 (1930)
Fewest rushing and passing yards
    A—37 (1919)
    N—89 (1967, 1980)

RUSHING
Most carries
    A—84 (1932, 1984)
    N—74 (1952)
Most yards gained
    A—438 (1969)
    N—366 (1973)
Fewest yards gained
    N—15 (1932)
    A—21 (1940)

FUMBLES
Most fumbles
    A—8 (1956, 1961)
    N—8 (1952)
Most fumbles lost
    A—5 (1956)
    N—5 (1952, 1965)

FORWARD PASSING
Most passes attempted
    A—43 (1978)
    N—39 (1984)
Most passes completed
    N—22 (1984)
    A—17 (1983)
    A—17 (1978)
Most yards gained
    N—280 (1984)
    A—197 (1978)
Most touchdown passes
    N—3 (1954, 1962)
    A—2 (1913, 1935, 1966, 1971)
Most passes had intercepted
    N—7 (1924)
    A—5 (1939, 1950)

INTERCEPTION RETURNS

Most passes intercepted
   A—7 (1924)
   N—5 (1939)

PUNTING

Most punts
   N—18 (1915)
   A—16 (1937)
Highest average per punt (min. 5)
   A—57.6 (1961)
   N—45.2 (1941)

PUNT RETURNS

Most punt returns
   A—12 (1915)
   N—9 (1915)
Most yards returned
   A—129 (1922)
   N—115 (1942)

KICKOFF RETURNS

Most kickoff returns
   A—8 (1960)
   N—6 (1913)
Most yards returned
   N—140 (1913)
   A—135 (1975)

SCORING

Most points scored
   N—51 (1973)
   A—40 (1903)
Most touchdowns scored
   N—7 (1973)
   A—6 (3 times, last 1949)
Most extra points kicked
   N—6 (1951, 1983)
   A—5 (1903)
Most 2-points attempts made
   N—3 (1959)
   A—1 (5 times, last 1971)
Most field goals attempted
   A—8 (1924)
   N—7 (1910)
Most field goals made
   A—4 (1924)
   N—4 (1980)

FIRST DOWNS

Most first downs
   A—31 (1969)
   N—28 (1980, 1985)
Most first downs rushing
   A—26 (1969, 1984)
   N—22 (1985)
Most first downs passing
   N—14 (1966, 1967, 1984)
   A—11 (1963)

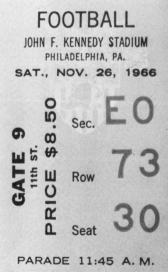

FOOTBALL
JOHN F. KENNEDY STADIUM
PHILADELPHIA, PA.
SAT., NOV. 26, 1966

GATE 9
11th ST.
PRICE $8.50

Sec. E O
73 Row
30 Seat

PARADE 11:45 A. M.

ARMY vs. NAVY

CLASSIC
ARMY vs. NAVY
SAT., NOV. 26, 1966

E O Sec.
73 Row
30 Seat

PRICE $8.50
11th ST.
GATE 9

GAME 1:15 P. M.

COACHES OF THE PAST

ARMY				
Year	*Coach*	*Won*	*Lost*	*Tied*
1890, 1892	Dennis Michie	3	2	1
1891	Harry Williams	4	1	1
1893	Laurie Bliss	4	5	0
1894–95	Harmon Graves	8	4	0
1896	George Dyer	3	2	1
1897–1900	Herman Koehler	20	11	3
1901	Leon Kromer	5	1	2
1902	Dennis Nolan	6	1	1
1903	Edward King	6	2	1
1904–5	Robert Boyers	11	6	1
1906–7	Henry Smither	7	2	1
1906, 1912	Ernest Graves	7	8	1
1908–10	Harry Nelly	15	5	2
1911	Joseph Beacham	6	1	1
1913–16, 1919–22	Charles Daly	58	13	3
1917	Geoffrey Keyes	7	1	0
1918	Hugh Mitchell	1	0	0
1923–25	John McEwan	18	5	3
1926–29	Biff Jones	30	8	2
1930–32	Ralph Sasse	25	5	2
1933–37	Gar Davidson	35	11	1
1938–40	William Wood	12	13	3
1941–58	Earl Blaik	121	33	10
1959–61	Dale Hall	16	11	2
1962–65	Paul Dietzel	21	18	1
1966–73	Tom Cahill	40	39	2
1974–78	Homer Smith	21	33	1
1979	Lou Saban	2	8	1
1980–82	Ed Cavanaugh	10	21	2
1983–	Jim Young	19	15	1
	Totals	541	285	50

NAVY				
Year	*Coach*	*Won*	*Lost*	*Tied*
1879–90	(Student coaches)	19	13	3
1891	E. A. Poe	5	2	0
1892	Ben Crosby	5	2	0
1893	Josh Hartwell	5	3	0
1894	Bill Wurtenburg	4	1	2
1895	Matt McClung	5	2	0
1896	Johnny Poe	5	3	0
1897–99	Bill Armstrong	19	5	1
1900	Garret Cochran	6	3	0
1901–2	Doc Hillebrand	8	11	2
1903	Burr Chamberlain	4	7	1
1904–6	Paul Dashiell	25	5	4
1907	Joe Reeves	9	2	1
1908–10	Frank Berrien	21	5	3
1911–14	Doug Howard	25	7	4
1915–16	Jonas Ingram	9	8	2
1917–19	Gil Dobie	17	3	0
1920–24	Bob Folwell	24	12	3
1925	Jack Owsley	5	2	1
1926–30	Bill Ingram	32	13	4
1931–33	Rip Miller	12	15	2
1934–36, 1946–47	Tom Hamilton	21	23	1
1937–38	Hank Hardwicke	8	7	3
1939–41	Swede Larson	16	8	3
1942–43	Billick Welchel	13	5	0
1944–45	Oscar Hagberg	13	4	1
1948–49	George Sauer	3	13	2
1950–58	Eddie Erdelatz	50	26	8
1959–64	Wayne Hardin	38	22	2
1965–68	Bill Elias	15	22	3
1969–72	Rick Forzano	10	33	0
1973–81	George Welsh	55	46	1
1982–85	Gary Tranquil	17	26	1
1987–	Elliot Uzelac			
	Totals	523	359	58

OUTSTANDING ARMY PLAYERS

ALL-AMERICANS

Player and Position	Year Selected	Player and Position	Year Selected
Charles Romeyn (B)	1898	Doc Blanchard (FB)	1944
Walter Smith (E)	1900	Glenn Davis (HB)	
Paul Bunker (T)	1901	Joe Stanowicz (G)	
Charles Daly (QB)		John Green (G)	
Paul Bunker (HB)	1902	Doug Kenna (QB)	
Robert Boyers (C)		Barney Poole (E)	
Arthur Tipton (C)	1904	Glenn Davis (HB)	1945
Henry Torney (B)		Dewitt Coulter (T)	
Henry Torney (B)	1905	Doc Blanchard (FB)	
William Erwin (G)	1907	John Green (G)	
Leland Devore (T)	1911	Henry Foldberg (E)	
Louis Merillat (E)	1913	Albert Nemetz (T)	
John McEwan (C)	1914	Doc Blanchard (FB)	1946
Elmer Oliphant (HB)	1916	Glenn Davis (HB)	
Elmer Oliphant (HB)	1917	Henry Foldberg (E)	
Edgar Garbisch (C)	1922	Arnold Tucker (QB)	
Edgar Garbisch (C)	1924	Joe Steffy (G)	1947
Gus Farwick (G)		Joe Henry (G)	1948
Charles Born (E)	1925	Bob Stuart (HB)	
Bud Sprague (T)	1926	Arnold Galiffa (QB)	1949
Harry Wilson (HB)		Dan Foldberg (E)	1950
Bud Sprague (T)	1927	Elmer Stout (C)	
Chris Cagle (HB)		Charles Shira (T)	
Chris Cagle (HB)	1928	J.D. Kimmel (T)	
Chris Cagle (HB)	1929	Don Holleder (E)	1954
Jack Price (T)	1930	Tom Bell (HB)	
Jack Price (T)	1931	Ralph Chesnauskas (G)	
Milt Summerfelt (G)	1932	Bob Anderson (HB)	1957
Jack Buckler (B)	1933	Bob Anderson (HB)	1958
Bill Shuler (E)	1935	Pete Dawkins (HB)	
Harry Stella (T)	1939	Bob Novogratz (G)	
Robin Olds (T)	1942	Bill Carpenter (E)	1959
Frank Merritt (T)		Townsend Clarke (LB)	1966
Casimir Myslinski (C)	1943	Ken Johnson (LB)	1968
Frank Merritt (T)		Don Smith (OG)	1985

HEISMAN TROPHY

Since its inception in 1935, three Army players have been awarded the Heisman Trophy, symbolic of the nation's outstanding college football player. Only three other schools have had more winners than has Army—Notre Dame (6), Ohio State (5), and Southern California (4).

Player and Position	Year Selected
Felix "Doc" Blanchard (FB)	1945
Glenn Davis (HB)	1946
Pete Dawkins (HB)	1958

NATIONAL FOOTBALL FOUNDATION HALL OF FAME

Player and Position	Year Selected	Player and Position	Year Selected
Earl "Red" Blaik (COACH)	1964	Harvey Jablonsky (G)	1978
Felix "Doc" Blanchard (B)	1969	Lawrence "Biff" Jones (C)	1954
Paul Bunker (LB)	1969	Doug Kenna (B)	1984
Christian Cagle (B)	1954	John McEwan (C)	1962
William Carpenter (E)	1982	Robin Olds (T)	1985
Charles Daly (B)	1951	Elmer Oliphant (B)	1955
Glenn Davis (B)	1961	George "Barney" Poole (E)	1974
Peter Dawkins (B)	1975	Mortimer Sprague (T)	1970
Arnold Galiffa (B)	1983	Joseph Steffy (G)	1987
Edgar Garbisch (C)	1954	Alexander Weyand (G)	1974
Donald Holleder (EB)	1985	Harry Wilson (B)	1973

OUTSTANDING NAVY PLAYERS

ALL-AMERICANS

Player and Position	Year Selected	Player and Position	Year Selected
Bill Dague (E)	1907	Buzz Borries (HB)	1934
Ed Lange (QB)	1908	Slade Cutter (T)	
Percy Northcroft (T)		George Brown (G)	1943
Jack Dalton (FB)	1911	Don Whitmire (T)	
John "Babe" Brown (G)	1913	Ben Chase (G)	1944
Ernest Von Hemberg (E)	1917	Bobby Jenkins (HB)	
Lyman "Pop" Perry (G)	1918	Don Whitmire (T)	
Wolcott Roberts (HB)		Dick Duden (E)	1945
Wendell Taylor (E)	1922	Dick Scott (C)	
Tom Hamilton (HB)	1926	Dick Scott (C)	1947
Frank Wickhorst (T)		Steve Eisenhauer (G)	1952
Eddie Burke (G)	1928	Steve Eisenhauer (G)	1953

Player and Position	*Year Selected*	*Player and Position*	*Year Selected*
Ronnie Beagle (E)	1954	Greg Mather (E)	1961
Ronnie Beagle (E)	1955	Roger Staubach (QB)	1963
Bob Reifsnyder (T)	1957	Chet Moeller (DB)	1975
Tom Forrestal (QB)		Napoleon McCallum (TB)	1983
Joe Bellino (HB)	1960	Napoleon McCallum (TB)	1985

HEISMAN TROPHY

The Heisman Trophy is awarded annually by the Downtown Athletic Club of New York City to the "outstanding college football player in the nation."

Player and Position	*Year Selected*
Joseph M. Bellino (HB)	1960
Roger T. Staubach (QB)	1963

MAXWELL TROPHY

The Maxwell Trophy, awarded annually to the "outstanding college football player in the nation," is presented by the Maxwell Club of Philadelphia.

Player and Position	*Year Selected*
Ronald G. Beagle (E)	1954
Robert H. Reifsnyder (T)	1957
Joseph M. Bellino (HB)	1960
Roger T. Staubach (QB)	1963

NATIONAL FOOTBALL FOUNDATION HALL OF FAME

Player and Position	*Year Selected*	*Player and Position*	*Year Selected*
Ronald Beagle (E)	1986	Bill Ingram (B)	1973
Joseph Bellino (B)	1977	Jonas Ingram (B)	1968
Fred "Buzz" Borries (HB)	1960	Anthony "Skip" Minisi (B)	1985
George Brown (G)	1985	Clyde "Smackover" Scott (B)	1971
John "Babe" Brown (G)	1953	Richard Scott (C)	1987
Slade Cutter (E)	1967	Roger Staubach (B)	1981
John Dalton (B)	1970	Donald Whitmire (T)	1956
Thomas Hamilton (B)	1965	Frank Wickhorst (T)	1970